Brendan Shanahan is a Sydney-based writer and columnist for the *Daily Telegraph*. He is the author of *The Secret Life of the Gold Coast* and has travelled widely.

www.brendanshanahan.net
www.inturkeyiambeautiful.com

In Turkey
I Am Beautiful

Between chaos and madness in a strange land

Brendan Shanahan

HarperCollins*Publishers*

HarperCollins_Publishers_

First published in Australia in 2008
by HarperCollins_Publishers_ Australia Pty Limited
ABN 36 009 913 517
www.harpercollins.com.au

HarperCollins_Publishers_
25 Ryde Road, Pymble, Sydney, NSW 2073, Australia
31 View Road, Glenfield, Auckland 10, New Zealand
1–A, Hamilton House, Connaught Place, New Delhi – 110 001, India
77–85 Fulham Palace Road, London, W6 8JB, United Kingdom
2 Bloor Street East, 20th floor, Toronto, Ontario M4W 1A8, Canada
10 East 53rd Street, New York NY 10022, USA

National Library of Australia Cataloguing-in-Publication data:

Shanahan, Brendan, 1976-
   In Turkey I am beautiful/Brendan Shanahan.
   Pymble, N.S.W.: HarperCollins, 2008.
   ISBN: 978 0 7322 8556 2 (pbk.)
   Shanahan, Brendan, 1976-
   Turkey – Description and travel.
   Turkey – Social life and customs.
914.961

Cover design by Jenny Grigg
Typeset in 11.5/16.5 Bembo by Kirby Jones
Printed and bound in Australia by Griffin Press
79gsm Bulky Paperback White used by HarperCollins_Publishers_ is a natural, recyclable product
made from wood grown in a combination of sustainable plantation and regrowth forests. It also
contains up to a 20% portion of recycled fibre. The manufacturing processes conform to the
environmental regulations in Tasmania, the place of manufacture.

5 4 3 2 1   08 09 10 11

For Tevfik.

Power be with you, baby.

Author's Note

In Turkish the letter 'c' is pronounced like 'j'. The 'ı' is like an 'uh' sound. The 'ş' character is 'sh' and the 'ç' is 'ch'. The 'ğ' is silent. Plurals are formed by adding a '-ler' or '-lar' suffix.

RUSSIAN FEDERATION
BLACK SEA
GEORGIA
ISTANBUL
SAMSUN
TRABZON
KARS
ARMENIA
TROY
ANKARA
AMASYA
IĞDIR
ERZURUM
DOĞUBAYAZIT
BERGAMA
TURKEY
IZMIR
GÖREME
KAYSERI
SOĞANLI
IRAN
VAN
KONYA
BATMAN
KHATA
DIYARBAKIR
HASANKEYF
BODRUM
ŞANLIURFA
MARDIN
ANTALYA
ADANA
HARRAN
FETHIYE
ANTAKYA
MEDITERRANEAN SEA
IRAQ
SYRIA
CYPRUS

Chapter 1

After two years Akil's English was much improved; a redundant qualification in some respects because he rarely used it, or any other language for that matter. Akil was the strong and silent type, a fact which made me — the weak and chatty type — feel self-conscious and rather shallow. Seeing me, he smiled in his familiar way, like a flower opening, but much else about him was unrecognisable. With his slicked back hair and bright Adidas trainers he had, I thought, more of an aura of the city about him, less of the boy from the village in Afghanistan who had arrived in Istanbul five years prior to do a computer course, but stayed to work in the carpet shop.

"Yes, I remember," he said, still smiling, and reached for my bags with hands so big they were like some film studio perspective trick. As his fingers wrapped around the handle of my briefcase they made it seem tiny and doll-like and I suddenly felt frail and unmanly. There was no one else in the shop.

Leaving me on a couch shielded from the street window by a row of shelves stacked with carpets, he disappeared upstairs to fix me a cup of tea.

The shop had changed. There was new furniture and new carpets on the wall, but the atmosphere was different in a more profound and elusive way, leaving me with a mild sensation of oppression where before I had felt only contentment and freedom. This I put down to the sentimentalising gloss of time. I had returned to Turkey two years after my last visit, when I had arrived for two weeks to write a magazine feature and stayed two months. Since then I had thought fondly and often of that happy winter in Istanbul that appeared in my memory as an extravagant mirage of minarets, carpets and hash smoke. Much of that indulgent, Oriental fantasy had been fuelled by the atmosphere in the shop, which was quite unlike any other I had encountered in Turkey or anywhere else. At the time, the owner, Hüseyin, had begged me to stay longer and help him sell carpets. Soon hordes of backpackers from Australia and New Zealand would arrive for the ANZAC Day services, signalling the start of the tourist season. Reluctantly I had refused. Back home, I had a book to release, a career to get on track. No more fooling around. As it happened, my book was a relative failure and my life soon atrophied into a humiliating round of hand-to-mouth freelance work, pub crawls and a punishing schedule of daytime television. There were other reasons I had for returning to Turkey, but even if I was motivated only by regret and boredom in an era where Kazakhstan and Tierra del Fuego were a box lunch and an inflatable pillow from anywhere, they seemed good enough motivations as any.

Akil returned with the tea on a silver tray and sat deferentially on the couch opposite. The silence grew, accented by the murmur of the Sunday crowds strolling by outside.

"Where is Hüseyin?" I asked.

"Hüseyin … gone to bunk."

The tinkling of my teaspoon against the glass of the tulip-shaped cup seemed awfully loud. "I see," I said, "and how is business?"

"Bizness," said Akil, considering the word for a moment, "slow."

"And where is Tevfik?" Akil produced a vaguely subcontinental rock of the head and a smile as if he were looking into strong wind. A grimace, in fact. "Tevfik," he said, considering the word for a moment, "he come sometimes." In silence I drank my tea while Akil sat on a

2

stool, cross-armed like some doleful temple guardian, punctuating his stillness only with crushing, millstone-like rolls of his neck.

A sudden blast of street commotion, a scratching of nails on a wooden floor and the slamming of a door broke the muted atmosphere. I peered around the carpets to see Hüseyin's dog, Zizou, bound into the room followed by her owner walking in his bent-backed way, as though he were continually crossing the line of a running race, head more ambitious than his feet. Seeing me, his arms flew outwards. "*Abi!*" he exclaimed using the Turkish term for "big brother", a rough approximation for "mate". "Where were you?"

I apologised. He had come to meet me at the airport that morning but I had given him the wrong time and he had spent several hours standing behind banks of wailing, headscarfed grandmas asking anyone if they'd seen a tall Australian man being dragged off by the drug squad.

"I know. I'm rubbish."

"Don't worry about it, bro, just come here and *hug* me!"

Hüseyin looked like the devil. Indeed, furnished with only this description a friend of mine who had recently travelled to Istanbul had recognised him immediately among a large crowd at the airport. His frame was stringy and slight, indelibly cast by the deprivations of the village. Although only in his mid-thirties he looked older, a legacy, in part, of his seemingly inhuman intake of alcohol and cigarettes and only emphasised by a brilliant white cowlick in his black hair which, when he grew it, ran like an elegant paint stroke from forehead to crown. His eyes were the sort that had sent Victorian ladies screaming back to their hotel rooms to write letters full of phrases like the "bestial appetites of the Orient". His eyebrows sat at a permanently upward angle, like an eagle swooping to catch a rabbit; between them was etched an indelible frown, an angry arrow of muscle pointing at the bridge of his large and broken nose — the legacy of a mysterious and obviously violent encounter with a baseball bat.

Unlike many Turks, who tended to be withdrawn, pessimistic and very solemn, Hüseyin was exuberant, optimistic and completely accepting. His energy was unflagging; parties and unlikely events erupted in his wake. This made him enormously popular with foreigners — especially colonials and Mediterraneans — who seemed to flock to him instinctively. His enthusiasm for life was infectious: he could dance on tables until five o'clock in the morning, have sex till eight, open the shop at ten and start again at nine that night. Meeting Hüseyin for the first time was a theatrical experience, remaking his acquaintance even more so.

"Man, I'm so *happy* to see you! I was *dying* at that airport, man." He gave a short burst of his familiar laugh: something between a mad scientist pulling a switch and the distant shriek of some jungle bird. "My old girlfriend is back from Spain — you remember Anna?"

I thought for a moment. "Anna's French, isn't she?"

"No, not that Anna. Anna from Bar-say-lona! Oh my God! She is *crazy* for me! Man, last night we went out dancing 'til three and then she fucks my brain out 'til six. It was totally *wild*!" Akil appeared with another tray of tea, distributing the glasses, stony-faced and indifferent, like a film technician on set. "Oh my God! These Spanish chicks, man. They are making me craay-zee."

Hüseyin was a man of his appetites, which were never less than of the all-you-can-eat variety. I had lost track of all the girls, coming and going or staying a while. They were from all nations: France, Italy, Spain, Denmark, Canada, the US, Australia, Brazil, Holland and Greenland for all I knew. Together they formed a kind of sexual UN, a highly charged version of the Small World ride at Disneyland. I decided to change the subject. "The shop looks good," I said.

"Yeah, but that wall is bringing us a lot of problems, man."

"Wall? What wall?"

Wearily, he began to tell the story, so typical of life in Istanbul. Hüseyin's shop was at an awkward angle on a corner, backing onto a serene Ottoman graveyard, one of hundreds that dotted the city. Between the graveyard and the shop was a tiny parcel of land onto which opened a large glass door, well positioned to scoop up customers. As it happens, this insignificant triangle of concrete, smaller than a car-parking space and of no practical use, was owned by one of the richest men in the city. How someone came to own such a piece of real estate is a story best left lost in the infinite maze of conspiracy that is inheritance and property law in Istanbul; suffice to say that he did. One afternoon, according to Hüseyin, the owner of the land called him and demanded an exorbitant rent, equal almost to that which he was currently paying on the entire building, for the privilege of the continued use of the land on to which the door opened. Hüseyin, on legal advice, refused. But the man with the power was keen to prove it, and the next day a team of builders arrived and bricked up the door to his shop.

"That wall," he said, pointing to a hanging carpet that failed to fully obscure the hasty stack of bricks, "is killing me, man." All at once, Hüseyin became sullen and withdrawn. Akil, sitting on his stool, began to slowly rock his head into his powerful shoulders.

The wall explained much about the changed atmosphere in the shop. It felt darker, less convivial. In the past, even when it had been empty, there had always been an infectious atmosphere of optimism, and as I looked about me I wondered whether it was just the wall that had changed. "So," I said, breaking the sudden reverie, "where is Tevfik?"

"Tevfik doesn't work here anymore."

"Why? Where is he?"

"Drugs."

"Oh," I said, momentarily taken aback. "What do you mean? What kind of drugs is he doing?"

"Coke, crystal. Whatever he can get his hands on."

"Oh," I said, feebly. "Have you heard from him at all?"

"No, not for a couple of months. He's disappeared." He shrugged and said, "He'll come back when he needs the money."

Tevfik had been Hüseyin's employee for more than two years, since he had first moved to Istanbul from the tourist town of Göreme in central Turkey. The pair had been friends for almost ten years before that. Since I had met them, both had become my friends but it was to Tevfik that I felt closest.

Slumped on the couch, arms folded, legs crossed, his eyes permanently shielded by dark glasses, there was a certain dissolute glamour to Tevfik. He exuded the aura of a reprobate aristocrat fallen on hard times or a jaded vampire, bored by immortality. Educated, well-read and unfailingly miserable, Tevfik was the polar opposite of Hüseyin with his village-boy-made-good *joie de vivre*. Fluent in Japanese and English, he came from a large and relatively well-off Istanbul family of recent fortune, his more privileged background evidenced as much by his appearance as his taste for literature and art. Tall and lanky by the standards of a generally short and stocky nation, he walked with his shoulders hunched and his arms crossed or jammed deep in his pockets, as if he were always cold, even in the height of summer. Pale and refined, his face was straight out of an Ottoman book illustration: a delicate, aquiline nose, high cheekbones and sleepy, vaguely Asiatic eyes. He looked a good ten years younger than forty-five, a fact all the more remarkable for his years of hard living.

Tevfik had been frank about his drug use. Sitting on the couch in the shop one day he had turned to me, quite without warning, and said, "I used to do crack." He paused and stared through his shades. "I did it about forty times. I was an addict. But I don't do it anymore." Slowly he turned, dropped his head on the back of the couch and appeared to fall asleep. It was not long after this exchange that I began to suspect Tevfik had a bad reputation. One night we had gone to meet some friends at a nightclub. After a brief, heated exchange between Tevfik and the door security we were refused entry. When I asked what had happened, he had casually replied, "Oh, that guy knows me. He said I couldn't come in because I'm a crackhead."

Tevfik's blunt manner (in part a Turkish national trait, but mostly all his) was only one of many qualities that endeared him to me. He did things we would all like to, but were too polite or too inhibited to act upon. If something was wrong with his meal he would send it back and scream at the chef from across the room. When a car tried to sneak through a red light while he was crossing, he'd walk up and kick the door. In the subway he yelled at hicks who stood on the wrong side of the escalator. Petty niceties meant little to him, a value he often extended to his salesmanship.

On one occasion during my last stay in Istanbul, Hüseyin had brought an American couple into the room where he kept his antiques. They were art teachers at some cut-rate international school in the Middle East. She was thoughtful and obviously long-suffering but her husband was an ignorant loudmouth who made the incalculable mistake of pointing to a carpet Hüseyin was holding — a rare shaggy-piled Kurdish piece that had been reserved by a big collector — to call it, several times, "ugly kitsch". The atmosphere became silent and tense. Hüseyin was offended but mute, the wife embarrassed. Tevfik, looking up from his customary spot in a distant corner, addressed the husband directly. "Excuse me, sir, but how did you end up as an art teacher?" The loudmouth laughed, uncomprehending. "I'm just wondering," said Tevfik, his tone growing to a roar, "because it seems that you know FUCKING NOTHING ABOUT ART!"

He was, needless to say, not a born salesman; but he did know much about art, and more besides. Tevfik could tell you which mosques in Istanbul used to be churches and whether they had been Florentine or Venetian. He knew the origin of Turkish words — French, Persian or Arabic — and how you could date a silver bridal helmet worn by Turkic nomads by the type of Russian buttons that ornamented them. He could tell you, immediately, which region almost any carpet had come from and he could impart an indelible enthusiasm for these objects which he loved more deeply and sincerely than anybody I had ever met.

Carpets seemed to be the only things that gave Tevfik any pleasure, and putting a price on them gave him nothing but pain. It hadn't always been this way. In the late-eighties he had run a highly successful hotel and carpet shop with a mostly Japanese clientele. With it he had made a lot of money and met his first wife, a Japanese woman he blamed for sending him broke. ("I gave her everything just to get rid of her, man.") Later, he was to remarry and have two children with another Japanese woman. Since that time he had worked an assortment of carpet jobs until, having exhausted many of his contacts and burnt almost all his bridges, he had wound up working for Hüseyin, one of the few people who could still tolerate him.

The term "work" is used loosely here, however, because only Jabba the Hut and citizens of certain remote Pacific regions have ever done less. As an official tour guide, a coveted qualification in Turkey, he would sometimes take people on private tours of the city, something he did too rarely for it to be a viable living. Other than that he relied on the commission earned selling carpets. Most days, however, he would simply show up at the shop in the morning, sit on the couch for ten hours and then leave that evening having sold and, often, said nothing. Turkey was full of characters like Tevfik: at any one time approximately half the workforce seemed to be sitting in shops doing little but drinking tea. But Tevfik's reluctance to sell was obviously rooted in a profound neurosis, more complicated than mere laziness or an aversion to putting a price on things he clearly regarded as above such mundanity. It was as if the very things that made him attractive and brilliant to others dragged him down like anaemia, every compliment a blow, every success the prelude to failure.

8

There was silence as Hüseyin stubbed out a cigarette and lit another. I asked him for more information but he couldn't tell me much. There were some slightly sordid stories. Tevfik, he said, had run off with a large sum of money lent to him for treatment at a rehab clinic by Hüseyin's number-one client and good friend, a Hollywood producer by the name of Linda.

"What about his wife and the kids?" I asked. He shook his head. "She's taken them to Tokyo." There seemed little I could add. Hüseyin said he still had a phone number for Tevfik; the one he had given me previously had stopped working months ago. The melancholy hush descended once more and my Anglo-Saxon anxiousness in the face of silence filled the room like gas.

"How are the pigeons?" I asked, brightly. Racing pigeons were Hüseyin's hobby. He kept a flock on the roof, handsome birds with feather flares covering their feet and ruffs like seventeenth-century Dutch aristocrats. During my last visit he had proudly announced that, after many years of breeding and swapping, he had completed what he considered the perfect set of nine.

"I had to kill them all because of the bird flu," he said.

Abandoning any attempts at cheering the mood I decided to go for a walk. Zizou sprang up excitedly and I struggled to push her disappointed nose back inside. Wishing Hüseyin farewell I promised to return in a few hours. Outside, the air was clear and the sun sharp. It was the end of summer, warm but full of the melancholy of a coming autumn, and as I walked towards the water, dodging trams full of people pressed against the glass doors, like jars of human pickles, I felt my jetlag fall away and my mood begin to lift. On I walked, by the walls of Gülhane Park, by the grounds of Topkapı Palace, where the trees were laden with crane nests and grass grew between the bricks. I rubbed my eyes in the glare and inhaled sharply. The smell of burnt fat, traffic fumes, cigarette smoke and sesame seeds hit me with a sudden Proustian rush and the world felt all at once joyful and full of promise.

Turkey was in some ways an odd place to be attached to. It had not been the site of any great revelations. I had not returned home and immediately enrolled in a language course or cookery class. I had not met a life partner or a guru. Most travel books I'd read seemed to skip over it entirely: a minor aristocrat in a tweed suit arrives in Istanbul, spends a week trying to secure a visa for an obscure area of Central Asia, then takes off to write about somewhere scarier and less hygienic. Part of me understood their reasoning. I had been to more exciting countries, both culturally and politically, as well as those that were wilder, more exotic and less tamed. In Turkey there are beach resorts and tourist information centres. Hardy German families go cycling on cliff tops and Irish backpackers bring home novelty hats and chlamydia. It was no longer the domain of frazzled hippies catching trains to Afghanistan with packets of grass down their Y-fronts. Now it was all Spaniards on package holidays and antipodean backpackers getting drunk on yachts. But Turkey had stayed with me; not because there was, probably, no other country in the world of comparable size with the same mind-boggling variety of historical and natural wonders, or the culture was especially seductive, or I really liked kebabs — although all these things had their charms — but because it was so difficult to pin down, so nebulous and ever-shifting.

Turkey appealed to my taste for the marginal, for things and places that were neither here nor there, the in-between worlds, a fascination that began as a child when I would sit and stare at the clock and wonder at what precise moment the second-hand ticked from one hour to the next, what sub-atomic distance separated one day from another. It was the boundary and margin that fascinated me because that was where I had always felt myself most at home. And Turkey was an entire country trapped in the margins, stuck in a no-man's land between Asia and Europe, Third World and First, past and present. These observations were a weary cliché — the compulsory blurb to every weekend liftout and in-flight magazine — but no less true or fascinating for their self-evidence. Turkey was a country with an identity crisis, one that, as a writer with my thirtieth birthday around the corner and a mounting sense of panic in the face of my own apparent lack of achievement, I could perhaps relate to.

At the end of the walls of Gülhane Park the road turns sharply to become a long street of cheap hotels and kebab shops, the pavements so narrow that pedestrians have to pinion themselves against walls as the tram passes. Dodging the lumbering juggernaut, the driver dinging his bell furiously, I descended a flight of stairs leading to Sirkeci train station, the terminus of the Orient Express. Slumped at the bottom was the same wailing Gypsy woman I had seen two years earlier. These days the child she cradled was much larger, his eyes framed by the white surgical mask shielding his nose and mouth and a rather comically unnecessary sticking plaster, complete with fake blood, taped to his forehead. He was doing his best to look sick but was managing nothing more than profound tedium. The woman wailed louder as I approached, gesturing to the boy. Ignoring these histrionics, I stepped over her outstretched hand, passed the train station and crossed the road to the waterfront.

Down by the ferry docks the crowd was heaving. Every Sunday tens of thousands of people make the journey from the suburbs of Istanbul to the downtown areas: the waterfront, the shopping district of Istiklal Caddesi and the historical attractions of Sultanahmet. All around me a controlled riot of pedestrians from every division of the city's social stratum crushed into the ferry terminals or down the causeway to the Galata Bridge, the arrival of every new boat pumping a fresh supply of citizens into the maelstrom. The air smelt of old fish, onions and diesel. Laid out on blankets were impromptu stalls selling watches, wallets and plastic toys. Men decked out in a Kebab Palace fantasy of black velvet and gold embroidery aurally assaulted passers-by with exaggerated claims for the freshness and value of their fish burgers. The crowd, apparently oblivious to the malodorous atmosphere, was young and in love. Everywhere were couples holding hands: rich kids in matching heavy metal T-shirts, spiked leather wristbands and black mascara; new immigrant boys in cheap jeans and square-toed shoes, looking uncertain but affecting a swagger as they scanned the crowd suspiciously for rivals to their girlfriends' affections; stocky, big-breasted girls with their pocket-sized boyfriends marching through the mob with studied determination.

The faces of Turkey are the features of many millennia, countless cultures. I can pick an Englishman at twenty paces and a German at fifty. Yet, try as I might, I could never spot a Turk with confidence. Their biology was too unkempt, a lucky dip of an incomprehensible number of miscegenations (a quality they had in common with the Spanish, of whom they sometimes reminded me). This was, after all, a country that had been at the crossroads of civilisation since the birth of the concept, and everyone had left their mark. In Istanbul you could feel the presence of innumerable cultures, living and dead, come and gone, preserved in the faces of its people. There were mono-browed Greeks and Slavic types with diaphanous blond hair; tanned, haunted-looking Kurds and stocky central Asians with Mongol eyes; fine-featured Persians and robust Arabs with strong noses. There were Caucasians, Eurasians, Gypsies, Jews and all the rest. And who knew where those redheads came from. Istanbul looked like a day-care centre at a border-town brothel, yet since the formation of the Turkish republic in 1923 the powers-that-be had been doing their best to convince Turks that they were a unified, mono-culture, a myth made patently absurd with only the evidence of your eyes. This was a city and a nation that had absorbed the world and would do it again, leaving only the question that held this country in the grip of something like a national neurosis: what did it mean to be a Turk?

Much had changed since my last visit and much had stayed the same. The streets were cleaner and a couple of grand buildings had been rescued and turned into posh hotels. But the colours of the crowd were still muted and sombre — black, grey and brown — and the men wore silly pointed shoes, like Ottoman pashas. One immediately obvious difference was that the number of women wearing the headscarf seemed to have grown considerably, a significant development with implications for more than fashion.

Contrary to the expectations of many outsiders, Turkey is not a country friendly to covered women. Although a majority wear some form of headscarf it is illegal for any public servant, school or university student to do so while on government property. (It is a common misconception that Atatürk, the founding father of modern Turkey, banned the headscarf. In fact, in the early years of their marriage, his own wife occasionally wore one. In his efforts to modernise Turkey he did, however, pass a "Hat Law", banning many items of clothing associated with the Ottoman Empire, including the fez, the loss of which was compensated by a national tour in which he handed out panamas and trilbies to an adoring public.) These restrictions have had major political implications. For instance, the wife of the prime minister, who wears the headscarf, has never been allowed to attend an official state function; and when a new member of parliament tried to take her oath while wearing one she was immediately ejected and had her Turkish citizenship stripped on a technicality. It is at the universities, however, where the headscarf issue has, if you'll forgive the term, come to a head. Since the late-nineties, when the ban was first enforced, campuses across the country have become sites of major protest, complete with rubber bullets and mass arrests. To get around the laws religious girls have employed a range of subversive tactics. Some have shaved their heads in protest, others simply jumped the fence and made a run for it. For a while it was popular to exploit a loophole by wearing a range of headgear not specifically prohibited by the law. The universities responded by banning what they referred to as the "ideological hat and wig", with a particular emphasis on that most cunning and insidious of all hats, the beret.

If the Turkish sense of humour seems occasionally unsophisticated, consider the fact that much of their reality reads like the most radical satire.

To outsiders these headscarf restrictions seem petty, paranoid and incompatible with the principles of a democratic society. In Turkey, however, where secularism is its own church and there is a constant fear of the country becoming a fundamentalist state, the headscarf is seen by many — especially the all-powerful military — as the Trojan Horse, the first step towards the stoning of adulterers, heads rolling through the town square and a fashion nuclear winter in which black is always the new black and hemlines are low every year.

The politicisation of the headscarf has spawned a complex semiotic language, a secret code of knots and fabrics, cut and colour, signifiers as much of class as anything else. The most politically charged of these styles is the *türban*, a silky double-layered affair stretched tight across the head, often teamed with a ghastly ankle-length raincoat in a wide spectrum of beiges and khakis. All over Turkey one sees packs of these *türban* girls, walking down the street in slow elbow chains, like dowdy cancan dancers, their poverty and homeliness so severe it is almost ostentatious, their earnestness intense and touching, in the way of all teenagers. Not all religious women, however, equate piety with dowdiness. Some of the wealthier *türban* girls — walking hand-in-hand by the water with their solemn, protective boyfriends — wore the new "Islamo-chic" fashion that had apparently gripped the city in my absence. It was a distinctive look, a flattering uniform of voluminous, calf-length skirts, knee boots, buttoned-up blouses with a hint of pirate ruffles and a colourful silk scarf pinned down like plastic wrap across the brow. This was a new style for a new breed of religious bourgeoisie, and as they walked past they shot me a look I was to come to see many times, a look that was slightly triumphant but spiced with disdain, as if to say, "You'll never get any of this, buddy."

* * *

Istanbul's waterfront, consisting of the Bosphorus, the channel where the Mediterranean and the Black Sea meet, and the Golden Horn, a branch stretching out to the northeast, is its heart and saving grace. To the west is the European shore, to the east Asia, or Anatolia, a name used by the ancient Greeks, meaning "The Land of the Rising Sun". The waterway that divides the two continents has been recorded and celebrated since the dawn of Western history. Through it the priestess Io waded after being turned into a cow by her lover Zeus, and Jason sailed on his search for the Golden Fleece. Recent archaeological evidence has even suggested that it may have been the origin of the Great Flood of the Bible when, seven thousand years ago, the Mediterranean broke through with cataclysmic force, creating the Bosphorus and filling the Black Sea.

Since its inception in the era of myth, the Bosphorus has been, arguably, the most fought-over, coveted and celebrated stretch of water in the world, a mantle of deep history it seems to wear lightly. Crossing the Galata Bridge on a fine day — with the bubbling lava domes of the mosques on the hilltops and the confetti of the painted houses landing on the dark hill of Pera, crowned by the elegant Galata Tower — is to feel your mood immediately lift. To look past the shoulders of the fishermen, and a handful of staunch-looking women, to see the silvery span of the suspension bridge linking Europe to Asia can make you smile involuntarily. It is a scene dazzling enough to make you forget about the hideous billboards, the fungal blooms of satellite dishes and the fact that the sad little fish seem to be swimming in something the colour of battery acid.

Istanbul is a Blanche DuBois city, best seen in low, artificial light. And much like the character in the Tennessee Williams play it has been the subject of some epic, and not entirely legal, fornications. Istanbul is the custodian of one of the most significant and beautiful waterways in the world, but it doesn't seem especially grateful for the privilege. Much of the shoreline has come to look like nothing more than a decaying monument to mismanagement and greed. The ferry terminal, for instance, is functional and lively but is quarantined from the shopping districts, and major monuments such as the Egyptian Bazaar, by a four-lane motorway traversed only by a dank tunnel — stalls selling flannel shirts and squealing electronic toys — and a hideous pedestrian overpass hung with a billboard proclaiming, with incongruous cheerfulness, "Welcome to Istanbul".

The situation is perhaps even more dismal on the other side of the bridge. Pera is one of the most historically significant districts of any city. Yet future archaeologists will surely scratch their heads in puzzlement when digging through two-and-a-half millennia of civilisation only to stumble on a layer beginning in the 1960s that seems to consist only of auto shops, hardware stores and dingy pedestrian tunnels selling handguns. (The guns fire only pellets, but, according to Hüseyin, it was an open secret that they could be easily bored out and converted to the real thing. Turkey has one of the highest rates of gun ownership in the world, a fact I was to learn first hand in spectacular style later in my travels.) Further to the west, all the way to the Dolmabahçe Palace, the banks of the Bosphorus are blocked, almost entirely, by crumbling shipping terminals and rows of disused warehouses. In the middle of the decrepitude sits the new art museum, Istanbul Modern, like a gleaming sports car parked in the driveway of a burnt-out house.

The outrages stretch across the city: from the dishevelled civic parody that is Taksim Square, to the boulevards of the Asian shore, where a handful of the grand nineteenth-century wooden mansions (called *köskler*) survive, like the last lonely specimens of some near-extinct creature, a reminder of the thousands that were burnt down across the city night-after-night for decades so that concrete tower blocks might be built in their place. It is difficult to credit some of the things that have been done to Istanbul, and in my time there I often found myself wandering the streets muttering exasperated questions under my breath: how did this grand marble bank become a grand marble doss house for homeless glue-sniffers? Who was it that thought building a reflective glass trucking depot, trimmed in bright green aluminium, on the edge of a cliff with one of the most spectacular views in the city might be a good idea? Why this car park and why here? Sometimes in Istanbul it felt as if someone had handed a blank cheque to ugliness and said, "Go for it."

Yet, try as they might, the combined forces of ineptitude, corruption and sheer barbarism could never completely kill the beauty of Istanbul. The poetry of the city is ancient and resilient; it comes from deep within the foundations and bubbles up to assert itself in the most unexpected ways. It was there in the arched back of a ginger cat picking its way through the accretions of filth in the alleys of Beyoglu; or the flashes of blue tile beneath the advertising hoardings stuck thoughtlessly across an Art Nouveau shopfront; or a corner of Byzantine foundation crowned by an abandoned wooden shack so rotten it seemed as if it had grown there, like a shell over a mollusc. It was a melancholy beauty, Istanbul being, fundamentally, a city of melancholy. And there were times when the deep sadness of the ruins, the alleys and the old advertising, peeling from the walls in rotten sheets of technicolour filo was almost overwhelming. I can think of no other big city in the world that makes me as pleasingly sad as Istanbul, sadness being to this city what health food and self-delusion are to LA. It was difficult to tell where this sensation came from, but it was there: in the faces of the people, sullen, doe-eyed and so reserved that if you laughed on the tram they would frown and press a chastising finger to their lips. It was in the torpor of the fat stray dogs lounging in the evening on the stone steps of the Galata Tower, their coats turned silver by the street lamp. Perhaps it came from the knowledge that almost all of that which came before had been swept away, strongly suggesting that all this, and you, too, would one day be gone.

Walking by the waterfront along the Golden Horn you pass the neighbourhood of Fener, once the centre of Istanbul's Greek community. It is here that the Orthodox Patriarchate, the Vatican of the Greek Orthodox world, still clings to life against all odds, the last vestiges of the citizens of Byzantium. Now the handful of churches are virtually empty or abandoned and the beautiful stone and wood houses with their latticed windows and carved lintels are falling apart. Other structures in the area have been reclaimed as blacksmiths or auto workshops.

In spite of or, perhaps, because of its ghosts and its decrepitude, Fener is one of my favourite districts of Istanbul. Much of it is on a high hill, offering views over the water, and the houses, although shabby, are among the most beautiful and untouched in the city. Most of the Greeks who once lived in these homes, who built the churches and the spectacular high school clinging to a precipitous hill, were driven from Istanbul in 1955 after a series of vicious riots when they were forced to "return" to a country where many were regarded as Turks and treated as outcasts. (Much of the violence committed during the riots — including forced circumcisions — was performed by paid gangs who had been shipped in by the members of the ruling Democratic Party with the apparent sanction of the then Prime Minister, Adnan Menderes. He was later deposed after one of Turkey's seasonal military coups, exiled to an island off the coast of Istanbul and, eventually, hanged. Even in living memory Istanbul's history reads like a Biblical epic.) Over the next twenty years, these expulsions were periodically repeated until the Greeks of Istanbul had been reduced to a fragile, aging population of only a few thousand, outnumbered even at their own church services by curious onlookers and superstitious Muslims keen to absorb the benefits of an older magic.

Today much of Fener is a fundamentalist neighbourhood, full of women shrouded in their *çarşaf*, some bold enough to ignore the law prohibiting full-face covering to walk the streets draped from head to toe, like black spectres with plastic shopping bags. Scenes like these have made indigenous *Istanbullular* sentimental for a time when the city was a multi-ethnic stew in which almost half the population was of non-Turkish ethnicity. In those days, along with the Greeks, Istanbul had large Armenian, Arab, Italian and Jewish populations, many of the latter the descendants of refugees from the Spanish pogroms of the fifteenth century who still speak a medieval Spanish dialect. (Next to Fener is Balat, a major Jewish area where some synagogues still survive. Istanbul's Jewish community is no longer as big as it was, although much larger than the Greek, and many are wealthy and influential.)

This dimly remembered era of multiculturalism, when you could get a beer on the streets and bacon was on the menu, has become sentimentalised and romanticised by those who feel they no longer recognise the city they once owned. Poor rural immigrants have changed the face of Istanbul, a fact frequently repeated to me by the native citizens of the city in tones of barely repressed despair. When I suggested to a friend of mine who was looking to buy a flat that Fener seemed a good and relatively cheap area, she laughed in my face. "I could never live there! The women would hit me for not wearing a headscarf. If I have a party they call the police straight away. They would make my life a misery because I don't pray. Fuck them!" Even in Istanbul in the twenty-first century the laws of God still trumped those of economics.

Istanbul is now one of the twenty biggest cities in the world. Since the 1980s its population has quadrupled to an official figure of over eleven million, but with estimates of the unofficial population ranging between twelve and sixteen million. Whatever the real number it is, essentially, worthless because every day there are at least five hundred new arrivals, the labour force of the booming Turkish economy. A large proportion of Istanbul's new immigrants live to the west beyond the old city walls, the boundary of old Constantinople, in vast, unknowable suburbs which, pictured in a satellite photo, look like a burst mutant cell. The lucky ones may have a room in one of the endless, numbing rows of concrete tower blocks that seem to cover at least half the country. Many, however, live in the jerry-built slums known as *gecekondular*.

Turkish is a marvellous, not to mention deceptively literal language (more on that later), and *gecekondu* is one of my favourite words in it. "Gece" means night and "kondu" means, roughly, "to put". Thus a *gecekondu* is "that which has been put up at night", so-called because those who build them are exploiting a legal loophole allowing any structure built at night and still standing in the morning, undetected by the powers-that-be, to remain. And so, every night in Istanbul, much to the horror of many of its ancestral residents, more and more *gecekondular* are created and the city grows bigger and bigger, in secret and under the cover of darkness.

Wealthy, urban Turks often spoke to me of the *gecekondu* as Dantean visions of urban despair and chaos: badlands to be avoided at all costs and irrefutable evidence of the inevitable decline of their city at the hands of rural rednecks. One girl who had researched the structures for her university course was to tell me in whispered horror that she had actually seen houses where the kitchen and bathroom *were joined together*. The *gecekondular* were, in fact, well kept, occasionally well built and often, as urban slums went, and compared to those I had seen in places such as Southeast Asia, rather pleasant. The streets were generally clean and only the newest structures conformed to the slum prototype: rough wooden frame, plastic sheeting or plywood for walls, a tin roof weighed down with old tyres. Most, however, were made of bricks, stolen from building or demolition sites, tiled roofs were not uncommon and a large number were completely indistinguishable from legitimate apartment blocks. Many had a little patch of garden, well-stocked with peppers, melons and tomatoes, and walking through the winding streets, past the chicken coops and wailing portable tape players blasting out *arabesk*, the music of the slums, I was frequently delighted by details that made these districts much more charming than their equivalents in many parts of the world: blooms of red geraniums in old white-painted vegetable tins sitting by the doorway; a rusted chimney poking from the side of a house, bent like an "s", as in a children's drawing of a witch's house; doors and window frames painted in bright blue and pink; one house all in rainbow stripes. I rarely felt threatened.

It would, of course, be absurd to claim that the *gecekondular* were some sort of proletarian utopia. A large number of these buildings have no services — water, electricity or sewage — and almost all are overcrowded. In addition, they remain prone to flood, fire, collapse due to poor construction and, deadliest of all, earthquakes. (When a massive earthquake hit the satellite city of Izmit in 1999, most of the official fifteen thousand who died there and in Istanbul were living in *gecekondular*, especially the apartment buildings which crumbled like sandcastles.) Tensions run high in these conditions. Many rely on illegal power, hijacked from the grid, but, over the years, in a pattern of slum politics repeating itself throughout the world, swathes of *gecekondular* have become official or, at least, semi-official and attract most of the basic services common to any city. The politics of the *gecekondu* are complicated; during election times the ruling party used to hand out title deeds to the occupants of the land on which they were built, guaranteeing votes. Furthermore, most are still controlled by various branches of the all-powerful Istanbul mafia who "sell" the land to the new arrivals, control many of the utilities and, of course, the heroin refineries that process the estimated 80 per cent of the drug that ends up on the streets of Europe.

Reading the statistics and the gloomy newspaper reports, it was tempting to get bogged down in a vision of Istanbul as a crumbling dystopia: a fading, moth-eaten duchess, forced to sell off her estate, piece-by-piece, to an encroaching suburban ugliness. In fact, contrary to the persistent complaints of seemingly all its citizens, the city has handled its massive population growth comparatively well and is one of the most pleasant and sophisticated metropolises in any developing nation. Istanbul was a city of melancholy but also one of unexpected poetry and tenderness. I felt it whenever I encountered one of the gloomy but friendly street dogs that roamed the dark alleys of the old city, their ear tags signifying they had been immunised against rabies, the locals not having the heart to shoot them. Or the time I was sitting in a café in a corner of a fashionable inner-city area full of antique stores selling late-modern furniture, only to look up from my table to see a man carefully tending a patch of high, shaggy corn that he grew on a traffic island. Istanbul was sad but never grim: in the windows of the dire hardware stores on the waterfront, the nuts and bolts were displayed in neat rows of short fluted glasses, like a robot's dessert. And I remember how excited I had felt while driving on a drab stretch of road to an unremarkable shopping district to pass under a Roman aqueduct straddling the highway, the road fitting perfectly the width of the archways, as if it had been foreseen fifteen hundred years earlier.

I crossed back across the Galata Bridge, oblivious to the advertising hoardings, the car parks and the traffic. Descending into the concrete tunnel which would take me back in the direction of the shop, I passed the men screaming the prices of shoes and rows of crazed bellydancer dolls, their stocky plastic arms issuing frantic karate chops to unfamiliar music, then emerged into the fading daylight. There was a slight chill in the air. I began to head past the Yeni Mosque, a huge structure opposite the ferry terminal, where men sat by a row of taps, washing their feet before prayers. In the square in front, old women and little boys were feeding stale bread to pigeons. The birds gathered to eat until they became a single shimmering grey mass, like wet stone, a child's sudden ambush sending them scattering skyward to give the illusion of evaporating masonry. Istanbul: I said the name out loud. Is-tan-bul: I just liked the sound. Oh, Istanbul — it was good to be back.

★ ★ ★

The shop had sprung to life. Hüseyin was entertaining. Inside, three women were seated on small stools, drinking coffee, reserved for celebratory occasions. The girls were introduced as Adella, Sabina and Anna. "From Barcelona, right?" I asked, shaking hands.

"Yeth," said Anna, a little taken aback.

Before our conversation could progress, the door opened. With Zizou snapping at his heels, a good-looking young man entered and, with comically exaggerated chivalry, genuflected in front of each of the women. "I love *you* and I love *you* and I love *you*," he said, kissing their hands in turn. The women giggled and smacked the top of his head. Having finished his performance he sat on one of the stools, cross-legged, and regarded me with an ironic eye. Hüseyin looked up. "Wait a minute — have you never met my brother?" As it was, I hadn't but had heard much of him.

In his early twenties with a Tintin mound of hair and soft brown eyes, Mehmet was the baby of the family and, although he shared his brother's monstrous ego, was, in many other respects, completely different. Where his brother was hawkish and wiry, Mehmet was cute and puppy-like, his physique turning slack from too many beers and sleeping bouts that could last days. His manner was as exuberant as Hüseyin's but completely untempered by his brother's sense of responsibility. As a result he was shiftless, cheeky, lacking in discipline of any sort and completely and utterly adorable. Everybody loved Mehmet. He was like sesame snacks or chocolate-covered peanuts; you couldn't help yourself. It was this irresistible charm that had helped him sell carpets for his brother while on his summer break from university in Cyprus and enabled him to get away with damn near anything.

Hüseyin barked something in Turkish. His little brother fetched up his stool and assumed his position outside the door on the pavement, scanning for customers.

For the next half an hour we sat, sipping thick, grainy coffee, while Hüseyin regaled the girls with stories in their native tongue which, although incomprehensible to me, I was certain featured the narrator at their centre, more than likely performing amazing feats in the fields of business and late-night table dancing. Like most carpet dealers, Hüseyin was a decent linguist, speaking English and Spanish fluently, albeit with some minor and wholly endearing idiosyncrasies, and had enough Italian, German, French and Japanese to sell a carpet with. People bought carpets from him not because his were necessarily the best or the cheapest but because they got to take home a good holiday story, a fact which perhaps went some way to explaining the galaxy of female admirers who orbited about him. All his stories were told in a style of manic pantomime, peppered with wild gesticulations and marionette jerks of the head. His speech was full of dramatic modulations and his tone would often grow higher as he neared the end of a sentence, as if he were too excited to breathe, which he often was.

"Oh my GOD!" he squealed in English, concluding one anecdote. "It was cray-zee." The girls laughed appreciatively even though it was obvious that only one of them was really listening.

Hüseyin leaned forward in his stool and began to tell a new story, in English and Spanish alternately. I had heard it before, but I still enjoyed hearing it again. It concerned a time he had been at a nightclub in London, dancing with some mutual friends from New Zealand, only to realise that it was now the early hours of the morning and that his plane to Istanbul was due to leave in less than an hour. By some miracle he had managed to make it across the city, high as a kite, and board his plane with five seconds to spare. Feeling rather smug, but with a come-down of immense proportions waiting in the wings, he staggered through customs in Istanbul and fell into a cab. When he came to pay the driver he put his hand in his coat pocket only to retrieve, in horrified astonishment, the half-dozen ecstasy tablets he had been minding for his friends at the club. "Shit, man!" he exclaimed, staring into his empty hand in an exaggerated posture of astonishment. "I thought I was fucking *dead*. I almost *wet my pants*."

Now the girls were laughing hard. So was I. It was difficult to tell how exaggerated many of these stories were, but it didn't matter: Hüseyin encouraged the suspension of disbelief. Then, as quickly as he had assumed it, Hüseyin broke out of character and called for tea. The girls protested. They had to be going. He begged and cajoled but they insisted: they'd been in Istanbul three days and seen nothing but a carpet shop. To choruses of "adioth'" they made out the door, pausing to allow Anna a goodbye kiss with her carpet dealer. A time for dinner that night was agreed upon.

As the women disappeared down the street Hüseyin moved to the back of the shop, slumped into the couch and lit a cigarette, one of an unbroken chain since the age of twelve. "Oh my GOD! Anna is bee-u-ti-ful!" he exclaimed, inhaling, before adding, "and horny — shit, man!" He gave his tropical bird laugh and reclined on his elbow in a cloud of Mephistophelian smoke.

"What's the deal with Anna?" I asked.

"What do you mean?"

"Well … when a girl comes all the way from Spain for a week to visit an ex-boyfriend she's been calling for a year …"

"Ha!" he squawked. "Nah, she's not like that, man. She even said to me, 'It's just for fun.' She knows, man. She knows."

Deciding to add nothing more, I sat nursing my tea, the scent and taste inducing an immediate *déjà vu*. Tea is a cornerstone of Turkish culture, a fact every visitor is quick to notice — no travel blog about the country is complete without some implausibly wide-eyed American blathering on about the sense of belonging and kinship they felt after being offered a cup. I regarded this constant tea drinking, however, as an imposition more often than not, a mechanical ritual that often left me feeling nothing more than ill and jittery. This is because Turkish tea is not only plentiful but virulent; it is to a mug of English Breakfast what bootleg Russian vodka is to diet cola. Like many tourists I was to spend countless hours trapped in various homes and shops drinking it from a seemingly bottomless glass until, either, I left or my kidneys failed. To make matters worse one small glass is sweetened by as many as four lumps of sugar, a habit which has not only raised the country's obesity levels but wrought havoc with its dentistry.

The horrors of Turkish tea are as nothing, however, compared to those of so-called "apple tea". A brew of synthetic fruit so sweet it hurts your teeth, apple tea is often described as a "traditional Turkish beverage", a lie on all three counts, having been made in factories within the last decade by Kurds for the purpose, I suspect, of reviving people from diabetic comas. Apple tea tastes like something that was invented during the war to combat rationing, yet for some inexplicable reason it has become the preferred beverage of the Turkish tourist trade. Subsequently, at any one time in Turkey there are approximately half a million people sitting in carpet shops sipping this vile concoction, doing their best to appear appreciative and culturally sensitive while fighting the urge to either gag or tip it into the nearest pot plant.

"What are you going to do, man?" asked Hüseyin, lighting another cigarette.

"Do?" I replied, with the dawning of a realisation that I had no idea. Indeed, I had few concrete plans for my time in Turkey, no real goals other than to see as much of the country as possible. I had envisaged spending at least some of my free time eavesdropping on the carpet trade, but with the news about Tevfik and the more muted atmosphere in the shop I was starting to wonder if it wouldn't be better to spend more time elsewhere in the country.

"I don't know," I said. "I suppose I'm going to travel." I paused, before adding, "To the east."

"The east," said Hüseyin, as though I had just announced I wanted to be an astronaut. "Where do you want to go?"

Like most travellers to Turkey I had seen many of the major sites in the west of the country: the ruins, the mosques and the rock formations. Western Turkey was easy to love. The east, however, was a big blank. I knew nothing about it and neither did anybody else I'd met, especially Turks in Istanbul who regarded it as one might a nuclear wasteland.

"I don't know," I said. "What is there to see?"

Chapter 2

Dinner with Anna sounds like a 1930s Broadway comedy, and was not unlike one, minus the martinis and the happy resolutions. Ever since the return of the Spanish girls to the shop in the evening, the altercation that I sensed had been brewing began to acquire a horrible inevitability. Dinner was a slightly awkward affair. In addition to the three girls and myself was Hüseyin's brother-in-law and business partner, Hazım, his English limited to a few stock phrases — "Hello Brayn-dan" and "I like you" — meaning that everything required two separate translations, delivering most anecdotes stillborn.

Abdicating any role in the conversation, I allowed Hüseyin to dominate the table. After a while he began to talk about the time he had spent in Spain, where he had lived after studying English in London. "I met a girl there I could have married," he said. Anna's smile grew fixed. "But," he announced with something more like naïvety than thoughtlessness, "I've decided that I could never marry a foreign girl. And that is why I have decided to allow my mother to arrange a marriage for me." There was uncomfortable laughter as the announcement was translated into two other languages.

"Are you serious?" I asked. Arranged marriages were not uncommon in Turkey but Hüseyin had not struck me as a likely candidate.

"Yes," he said brightly. "I have promised Mama that I will marry before she dies. I have been meeting with many girls. But my mother always says, 'You don't like anything I show you!'" He laughed and thumped the table. There was a pause and a sudden drop in the social temperature. Next to him Anna stared fixedly into the distance, her arms crossed, very quiet. When she finally spoke she did so in English, signalling that it was for the benefit of everybody. "OK, I understand now," she said, making a gesture of finality with her hands. "Con-cloo-thee-on." The sparkle of tears began to film her eyes while one of her friends rubbed her back. Dinner became a purgatory of social embarrassment as we attempted to ignore the unfolding drama.

From across the table Hazım smiled fixedly. "Hello Brayn-dan," he said.

Later, at a bar, the feuding lovers sat in a conspiratorial corner, he trying to charm her back to happiness, she slamming her glass of gin down on a wooden table and giving high hoots of disdainful laughter. Hüseyin went home soon after, the evening ending at a rickety nightclub across town where a lounge singer belted out Turkish hits for the benefit of an audience as rigid and unresponsive as crash-test dummies. The singer ignored the girls, preferring instead to sit in my lap and tousle my hair while serenading me with Turko-pop. Hazım, an infrequent drinker, quickly reached a state of complete stupefaction. By the time he tipped a bowl of pickled carrot down the front of Anna's dress, it was time to go home.

If dinner with Anna had been a light farce, then dinner with Tevfik was like the final act of some terrible Scandinavian modernist play — one where they've all gone mad from booze and it turns out the son has been sleeping with his mother. After several days of trying, I had finally gotten in touch with Tevfik and he had sounded extremely pleased to hear from me. I arranged to meet him on Taksim Square, at the top of Istiklal Caddesi, where the antique tram turned to make its trip back down the hill. For a while I waited at a bus stop among the crowds that filled the traffic-choked square every night until late. When Tevfik walked past I almost didn't recognise him. In his shabby fleece, his hair at odd angles poking under the sunglasses on his head, he looked even paler, thinner and more unkempt than usual. "Brendan!" he cried, embracing me. He was very loud and it made me a little self-conscious. "Brendan! Brendan! Brendan!" he called, ecstatically. "Oh, Brendan, I'm so happy to see you!" Clutching me by the shoulders he stared intently into my eyes. "It — is — so — good — to — see — you — man."

"Good … good, I'm glad," I said, wondering if this had been an enormous mistake. Violently he pulled me towards him, wrapped his arms about me and said, "I love you, man."

"Ah, have you eaten?" I asked.

"Come!" he announced grandly, pushing me away. "I will take you to a restaurant that will blow your fucking mind!" Together we went walking down the human river of Istiklal Caddesi.

Tevfik started talking. His thoughts were rambling and disconnected. "Man, I am not good. I see these things on the news. I'm too sensitive. I can't take it."

"What things?"

"Everything, man. War, starvation. I don't know what to think anymore, I really don't. This bullshit in Lebanon, it's depressing me."

Only a few weeks before, Israel had stopped bombing southern Lebanon. The war had started in mid-July of 2006 and, after only a little over a month, was already over. Despite its relatively brief duration, its impact on the region had been profound. In Turkey, a nation which has always had a tenuous pro-Israel stance, almost unique in the Muslim world, there had been public outrage by what was perceived as the disproportionate Israeli response to Hezbollah attacks and the war had been the subject of some major protests. Recently, all across the country, a billboard funded by Islamist political parties had appeared featuring a picture of a baby being held up from the rubble under the slogan "While they die we do nothing." Earlier in the day the Turkish government had announced it would send troops to help the UN peace-keeping effort in the country, a not entirely popular move for various, and not always obvious, reasons.

Tevfik continued. "Now we help these Arabs! These Arab *motherfuckers* who sold us out to the British and shot us in the back. You've read *Lawrence of Arabia*, right? You know how these Arab bastards made a deal with the British? Well, now they're putting arms factories over pre-schools. Sick, man. Sick!"

I had only a vague idea of what he was talking about. I knew that the Ottoman Turks had once ruled over much of the Middle East — a fact their neighbours still resented — and that, in an attempt to secure independence from their colonial masters, many Arabs had collaborated with the British at the end of the First World War. But the details of the so-called Arab Revolt were hazy to me. Furthermore, I hated TE Lawrence. None of this concerned Tevfik, however, who was obviously going to continue regardless.

"We got our own war, man. We can't be fighting a war for these arseholes, bringing home more bodies from Lebanon! What the fuck is this shit!" As he spoke we walked against the thick crowds and people stared from the corners of their eyes at his wild gesticulations. "It's a civil war we are fighting in the east. No one wants to call it a civil war, but that's what it is. Shit is going down, man. Borders are gonna change." He stopped and turned towards me, staring very intensely. "Mark my words — borders are gonna change and thousands of people are going to die." He held his finger aloft then sliced it across the air. "Thousands of people are going to die!"

It was at this point that I began to suspect Tevfik was completely losing his mind. His disjointed rants about the state of his nation and the world may have been because he was high, having a manic episode, or both. But there was something else; a kind of terror seemed to be overwhelming him. He was like a person being slowly crushed. Fear, fatalism, disaster: these things were crushing him.

"Come on, let's eat," I said.

The restaurant was just off Istiklal Caddesi, down one of an endless dark labyrinth of backstreets. Inside, we waited to be seated. Tevfik was agitated, crossing his arms and rocking exaggeratedly side-to-side. We had obviously made an impression on the management and I could feel some disapproving looks. Together we stood for some minutes. "Are they ignoring us?" I asked.

Tevfik turned and raised a declamatory finger. "They're not ignoring us," he said, getting louder. "Because if they ignored us I would kill them." I gave a nervous laugh. "I'm not joking," he said, almost shouting. "I would kill them!" Before he could start throwing cutlery, I grabbed Tevfik and bundled him out the door.

"Those mother*fuckers!*" he cried as we entered the neighbouring, far less choosy restaurant.

As we ate he began to grow a little more subdued, his thoughts switching to the carpet shop and Hüseyin. The wall that had been bricked up over the door obsessed him. "That wall ... that *wall*, man. It has killed that shop. Absolutely killed it!" A waiter came to take his plate, but Tevfik hadn't finished. He turned and barked rebukes at him. Like a humbled courtier the waiter retreated, walking backwards and slightly bowed. "That shop used to be so lively! I mean, come on. You know why he did it?" he asked, referring to the landlord. "Just 'cause he could. Just because he was rich enough and wanted everyone to know that he had the power. What an ... arsehole!" he screamed through clenched teeth.

Suddenly, he reached into his fleece and produced a large gold medal. "My father gave me this," he said, pulling a thick blue cord from around his neck. "Here, look."

Gold coins are a common gift in Turkey. This one was very fine, covered in elaborate script, shiny and weighty.

"It's worth about eight hundred bucks," he continued, dropping it back into his shirt. "My father said, 'Sell it if you ever need to.' But I never will, no way."

"How's it going with your dad these days?" I asked.

Tevfik had a fractious relationship with his father. They argued constantly and he had told me he had been a strict disciplinarian who had beaten him as a child.

"Better, man. Better. We are all forgiven now. It's great. I love my dad." He thumped himself in the chest with a fist to emphasise his feelings. I said this was good to hear. As Tevfik started, once again, on the wall, I called for the cheque.

Outside the crowds had not thinned. Istiklal was bustling; one of the few places in Istanbul that always felt alive and joyful.

"So," I said, "how long have you not been at the shop?"

Tevfik exhaled, irritably. "About two months."

"Why did you leave?"

"I can't ever work in the shop again. Hüseyin and I, we're too different."

"I see," I said, bracing myself. "And I heard that you were having some … problems."

"What problems?"

"Oh, like, you know … drugs."

Tevfik paused, silent with fury. "Hüseyin told you that?"

"Yes."

His arms went stiff by his sides and fists bunched. He trembled with rage. "He doesn't know shit!" he spat. Our pace had slowed as we walked towards the end of Istiklal. "What else did he tell you?" he asked.

"Well … he mentioned a problem with Linda."

"That's none of his fucking business!" he cried. "That's my personal, private business. He had no right to tell you that."

"Well, is it true?"

"It wasn't like that."

The silence descended as we shuffled along, past the nineteenth-century embassies and the Art Nouveau shopfronts, Tevfik smoking furiously.

"My problem," he said, eventually, "is not drugs ..." He drifted off.

"Depression?" I suggested.

"Yes. Deep, deep depression."

By now we were in the long, steep alley that connects Istiklal with the waterfront. The steps leading down past the Galata Tower were wet and slippery with grime. Together we sat on a window ledge under the portico of a boarded-up shop. The street was empty. A big grey dog looked up from its trough of garbage, its cataractous eyes shining like silver marbles in the dark. Tevfik said that he had been seeing a psychiatrist and was on a powerful medication. I didn't have the heart to ask about the circumstances of his wife's departure but he told me he was planning to visit his children after the airfares came down in the New Year.

"I'm missing them, man," he said, clenching his teeth. "I'm missing them so bad." With some violence he punched himself in the side of his head. The dog, startled, turned and padded off.

Chapter 3

It had been two weeks since my arrival in Istanbul and I was now preparing to leave. Most of my time had been spent sitting in the shop watching Hüseyin sell, chatting with an incongruent parade of customers: a jazz-singing knife salesman from France; an Argentine fashion designer who claimed her father had stolen Pinochet's sword after the revolution; a Dutch psychiatric nurse who was cycling to Iran with her karate black-belt boyfriend; a Swiss–Italian real estate agent based in Miami and his ferociously tanned Cuban wife, who when excited or amused would grin and silently hold up her craggy, red-nailed hands to shake dozens of gold bracelets like maracas. I didn't know whether the customers at Hüseyin's shop were any more eccentric than at any other in Istanbul but he did seem to attract a disproportionately large number of them.

After the shop closed Hüseyin would take customers out on the town. He was unfailingly generous, insisting on paying for everything when you were in his company, and every evening of the last fortnight had stretched into an early-morning blur of nargile smoke and belly-dancing on restaurant tables. The rift with Anna had been healed and she and her friends had gone home on good terms. Later they sent me photos and one of them slept with Mehmet. Tevfik was still around but he and Hüseyin refused to acknowledge one another; one of my favourite amusements was to watch the charade of mutual obliviousness every time the pair came into proximity, Hüseyin skulking up the back of the shop, reading the newspaper, while his former employee hovered out the front, drinking tea and making inept attempts to entice customers. Perhaps out of some subconscious desire to force a reconciliation, I began to discuss Tevfik with Hüseyin. I told him about his plan to visit his children in January and of the new medication he was on. Hüseyin would not be swayed. "Don't believe anything he tells you," he said, shaking his head, wearily. "He'll never change."

Part of me believed this. A much larger, stronger part wanted it not to be true.

The days were blissful and lazy. Together with Tevfik and Mehmet, the three of us would sit on stools on the pavement, basking in the autumn sun, hustling for business and watching the passing parade, tourists and locals alike.

"Hey there," Mehmet called to a pair of strolling American geriatrics. "How's the honeymoon?"

Mehmet and I had formed an almost immediate friendship — like a big spoilt baby or a neighbourhood cat, he was sluttish for affection and I was more than happy to give it to him. Like his brother he was a dreamer and full of energy. Unlike him he was emotionally unguarded, well-read and very intellectually ambitious. Yet, despite his broad general knowledge — or perhaps because of it — Mehmet's mind was often as confused and purposeless as the Google search engine to which he was addicted. In the morning he would conjure a plan to import T-shirts to Cyprus. By afternoon there were ambitions to start a local newspaper in Istanbul. In a bar that same evening he was inventing a radical new advertising agency that would sell products only between developing nations.

"Tevfik," he announced one day, "don't you think this is a great idea — hot Coke!"

Tevfik exhaled his cigarette smoke. "Shut up, Mehmet," he said. "You are an idiot."

Since our first meeting Tevfik had cheered up immeasurably. He was still miserable, but no more so than normal, and his conversation had not returned to the manic heights of our reunion. Yet, despite the apparent restoration of near normality, there had been some tense moments, and he could still be enormously difficult. He never paid for a meal or a beer, was occasionally mocking in a more than good natured way and at the end of one lunch had turned to me and demanded, quite sharply, three hundred dollars. The fact he wanted money did not, in itself, concern me — I refused and he settled for fifty — but the question of what he wanted it for did. There were other things, too: signs that he was slowly casting off the vestiges of a former life and retreating from the world. Recently he had moved into a one-room apartment around the corner from the shop. It was above a bar and, even though I had not seen the interior, looked like the kind of place they found dead pensioners being eaten by their cat. The hot water didn't work and he was using his sister's house to take showers. His only remaining assets, from what I could see, were the gold medal that hung about his neck and his beloved carpets.

Yet, despite his complete lack of work, Tevfik's mysterious, osmotic ability to support himself continued. During the day we would sometimes meet with his friends, gathering at a tea garden well known as a haven for reprobates and weirdos. Friends like the interior designer with fang teeth who wore mittens with cut-off fingers all year round, the glum architect who hated post-modernism so much he claimed to have once been physically sick in front of Philip Johnson's AT&T building in New York, or the slightly condescending exiled Iraqi academic who now sold washing machines. Together they formed a kind of oddball intellectual salon that would meet almost daily on the pavement to discuss their employment woes, decry the state of the nation and wonder aloud whether it wouldn't be better if they just packed up and left. By night we prowled the city's backstreets, working our way through jazz dens, odorous heavy metal bars and a dirty alley where transvestite prostitutes called from high windows, cooing and waggling their tongues to the passing street trade.

For all the fun I was having in Istanbul hanging out at the shop, I was now itching to leave. I had frittered away enough time; winter was coming and the east would be ferociously cold. But weather was, in many respects, the least of my problems. Ramadan was approaching and I had been warned that it would make travel more difficult, if only because it would be impossible to find food during daylight hours. I had only travelled in one other Islamic country during the month of fasting — Indonesia, a nation where concessions to Ramadan often extended to nothing more than hanging lacy curtains in restaurant windows to save blasphemous diners the social embarrassment of being spotted by their neighbours tucking into a big bowl of deep-fried beef skin. But I had been warned by Tevfik, who had travelled extensively in remote parts of the country, that east Turkey was a far different proposition and that my godless, Western presence alone might be enough to inspire a certain antipathy. The perils of lunchlessness paled in comparison, however, to the very real dangers posed by the most recent outbreaks of violence in the southeast, where I intended to spend much of my time. At the centre of the storm was the government's seemingly endless guerrilla war with the Kurdistan Workers Party, better known as the PKK.

The so-called "Kurdish issue" is far too complicated, not to mention depressing, to be done much justice in these pages. Yet not even a weekend beach holiday in Turkey can expect to be completely free of its pernicious influence. So it is less in the interests of political elucidation than personal safety that I impart the briefest possible summary of a problem that, in many ways, holds modern Turkey hostage.

The Kurds are a distinct ethnic identity in Turkey and constitute approximately 20 per cent of the population, most concentrated in the southeast and big urban centres in the west where they have arrived in their millions, either displaced by war or looking for work. As well as a large presence in Turkey, Kurds are spread across Iran, Iraq and Syria, with a smattering of smaller populations in other areas of the Middle East. They are, however, a minority in all their lands and for a hundred years they have been suppressed and ethnically cleansed by almost everyone — I still remember the horror I felt as a child in the late-eighties on seeing unspeakable images of Kurdish villages gassed wholesale by Saddam Hussein.

Turkey has a long history of trying to repress Kurdish dissent. For a long time speaking Kurdish languages (there are a few, but the dominant one in Turkey is Kurmanji) was banned; and while that prohibition has been lifted, and there have been some recent concessions to broadcasting, it still remains effectively illegal to teach Kurdish or even give your child a Kurdish name. Until 1991 Kurds weren't even recognised as a separate ethnicity, classified instead as "mountain Turks" who had "forgotten" Turkish, a nonsense numerous Turks will still repeat with a straight face.

Since the end of the Ottoman Empire, after the First World War, Kurdish uprisings have been a regular feature of life in Turkey. The most recent incarnation is the PKK, an illegal political party and terrorist organisation, with numerous offshoots, based, for the most part, in southeast Turkey. As their name suggests the PKK claim to represent the Kurds in Turkey, and their alleged aim is to create a separate country for the Kurdish people, who, as the cliché goes, are the largest stateless ethnicity in the world. Like all good Marxist terrorists, the PKK are not shy of committing murder in the name of "the people", and it would probably be impossible, and definitely boring, to catalogue all the attacks that had happened across the country in the previous year. Suffice to say that they were doing their best to make good on their promise, issued a week before my arrival, to "turn Turkey into hell".

Istanbul was tense. Two weeks prior a series of bombs had detonated across the city targeting police and military forces, killing two. Although most of their targets were still governmental, the PKK were becoming bolder in their strikes on tourists and civilians. In the six months before my arrival a number of explosions had rocked the beach resorts of Kuşadası and Antalya, killing a total of five tourists and six locals. One bomb had been planted under a mini-bus and another in a portable tape player. In a country where tourists were petted and coddled like prize merino rams, this was as provocative as you could get.

Despite the military's ominous warnings of revenge it was a tactic that seemed to be working, at least in upsetting the government if not in advancing the cause of the Kurdish population. Tourist numbers had plummeted and people like Hüseyin were starting to make contingency plans for the possibility it might never recover. (The government, keen to protect the industry, had gone so far as to cover up the Antalya bombing by claiming it had been an accident caused by a faulty gas canister. The rather clumsy fraud was soon debunked by a newspaper, prompting the government to warn the media, rather sternly, to "stop exaggerating" the terrorism problem in Turkey.)

Of course, not all terrorist attacks in Turkey were directly related to the PKK. In 2003 two huge truck bombs destroyed a bank and two synagogues, killing twenty-seven people, including the British Consul General. An Islamic extremist organisation (thus the synagogues), funded by Al-Qaeda, with the catchy moniker of the Islamic Great Eastern Raiders' Front, claimed responsibility and the plotters were later jailed. But violent religious fundamentalism is comparatively rare in Turkey. Almost all the deaths, on every side, had been due to the coyly euphemistic "Kurdish problem". And now, with the war in Iraq raging just over the border, there was a real possibility that, for the first time in modern history, Kurds would be able to claim a territory for themselves, perhaps even a nation if Iraq continued to fracture along ethnic and religious lines. The possibility of a Kurdish homeland on their doorstep made Turks very nervous, especially considering the fact that Iraqi Kurds had already taken control of that region's oil supplies. With a new source of funding, Iraqi Kurds sympathetic to the cause of their cousins in Turkey were now supplying the PKK with money and guns, fuelling the conflict and creating a new dimension of danger and uncertainty. In the high school yearbook of political unrest, southeast Turkey was being voted most likely to descend into bloody chaos.

★ ★ ★

As I left the shop in the morning Tevfik looked at me through his sunglasses. "The east has some power, man," he said in his biblical jazz-singer manner, before hugging me very tightly and delivering a stinging high-five. Hüseyin, meanwhile, issued me with a mobile phone and a solemn instruction. "Car accident, terrorist, bar fight, nuclear-fucking-war, bro, I don't *care*. You call *me* first, understand?" I promised and we kissed each other's cheeks in farewell. To say that I had no aim to my journey was mostly true. I had promised only to return before the delightfully named Şeker Bayramı, or "Sugar Holiday", the festival marking the end of Ramadan. Until then I had only my whims and a handful of recommendations to guide me. The east was an unknown quantity and I liked it that way.

Turkey's bus system is probably the best in the world and one of the country's infrastructural wonders. The buses themselves are brand new Mercedes, manufactured in Turkey (as you can be sure you will be informed on at least a dozen separate occasions during any given week in the country), which can be seen at all times of the day and night moving in humming convoys, like gleaming valkyries down the highway. There is nothing I don't love about these buses: from the seats that hold you like a giant hand to the satisfying sound, ripe with German mathematics, made by the tray table when it hits the seat in front.

Patrolling the wide aisles are serious young porters, dressed in coloured uniforms like members of a barbershop quartet but worn with all the dignity of Imperial Cossacks. Always on call, they roam from seat to seat distributing a variety of drinks, cakes and sesame snacks from a little aeroplane cart that stows away with space-shuttle precision in a hollow by the back stairs. Undoubtedly their favourite duty is the distribution of *kolonya*, a perfumed-alcohol-based, hand-and-face wash found everywhere in Turkey, from restaurants to *hamamlar*. The merest whiff of *kolonya* had the power to make me immediately nauseous (the smell transporting me instantly to family holiday vomit-fests mopped up with perfumed "moist towelettes") but it clearly appealed to the Islamic mania for ritualised ablutions and its distribution was performed with all the solemnity of a priest granting Holy Communion to a condemned man.

If the buses are a testament to the entrepreneurial spirit of the Turkish people, then the bus stations are a convenient symbol for the indifference and lack of imagination that has characterised the country's leadership. Called *otogarlar*, Turkey's bus stations are among the largest and most soul-crushing structures not specifically designed to incarcerate or torture ever constructed. The Istanbul *otogar* is the biggest and definitely the most depressing. A vast concrete monolith, like something MC Escher designed for Kim Jong Il, it's not a pleasant place at any time, still less on a warm day with a big bag, staggering from ticket office to ticket office, slapping at pickpockets while trying to find an empty seat on the final day of university holidays. Depending on the size of the city it services, the *otogar* is divided into dozens, sometimes hundreds of shopfronts, each representing a different bus company, each with their specialist destination. In normal circumstances, catching a bus in Turkey is simple and my vague plan to travel with no booking to Konya, a large city in the centre of the country and an ancient religious capital, would have been no problem. I had, however, not counted on the end of holidays and was now involved in a complex combination of mime show and dictionary consultation with the man who represented my last chance of getting to my destination any time within the next week. "So," I began, in a needlessly procedural tone, "are there any seats on any bus to Konya leaving earlier than midnight tonight?"

"*Yok*," said the man behind the counter, invoking the greatest and most powerful of all Turkish words, a "no" of such harshness and finality only the Russian *nyet* comes close. I looked about the concrete wastes of the *otogar*. at the incongruously jovial signage, the shifty porter waiting hungrily at the door and the weary passengers, blurry in the heat haze. Without further delay I turned, walked back to the subway entrance, took the train to the airport and boarded the first flight to the beach.

Chapter 4

As an Australian the appeal of European beach resorts has always eluded me. Sitting in a deckchair among rows of scarlet Scandinavians, listening to a tide of Evian bottles clatter on the pebbles, is not my idea of a day at the ocean — if I am justified in feeling smugly nationalistic in any respect then it is in matters coastal. For this reason I have tended to avoid beach destinations in most areas of the world, even in Turkey which has, by common consensus, some of the best in the Mediterranean. Antalya did little to annul my prejudices. A large, hot city in the centre of Turkey's southern coastline, Antalya looks like it was rebuilt after an earthquake some time in the early seventies. The beach is the colour of concrete and there are hotels lining it built to look like the Titanic and the Kremlin, the banality of it all only emphasised by shifty-looking Russians in tracksuits striking musclemen poses for photographs taken by their girlfriends who wear high heels on the sand.

I am, of course, being somewhat unfair. Antalya is, in fact, a pleasant city with moments of magnificent beauty. It is neat and well tended, a novelty in a country which often seems to have only the dimmest notions of civic pride. There are free concerts, pedestrianised shopping malls and a gay bar. The pavements are even, the streets palm-lined and traversed by an adorable little tram with an old-fashioned bell. The park on a cliff by the ocean, where boys breakdance on a skateboard ramp, is watered, cool and impeccably landscaped. The Roman harbour is a charming keyhole of blue water where swaying yachts neatly dock. The old town is endearingly dishevelled, thick with Ottoman houses and studded with more than the usual share of ancient wonders; Roman, Byzantine, Seljuk and Ottoman. To stand on a cliff top looking out across the water to the soaring Taurus Mountains, a Chinese ink in the mist, as the first shards of the setting sun pierce the clouds, is to stray into hyperbole.

Yet, after only a day in Antalya, I was already plotting my departure. There was a nagging aloofness to the city, a sense of being corralled and quarantined: imagine the mental "happy place" of a fifty-year-old German real estate agent and you might come close to the atmosphere. Nuisances one took for granted in almost every part of Turkey were here glaringly absent. The call to prayer appeared to have been banished from areas near accommodation; the beggars and shoeshine touts were moved along before they could sit down; and the stall holders flogging waterpipes and fake handbags could only stare sullenly as crowds of Frenchmen in Hawaiian shirts walked by unmolested, orders not to harass the tourists having clearly been sternly issued. Despite the mood of studied gentility, Antalya was not untouched by the turmoil that had swept Turkey in the last few decades. A short journey inland from the coast revealed a city fraying at the edges, the suburbs a sprawling mass of slummy tenements, *gecekondular* and weary family regiments making perilous dashes across the squalling freeway. There was little logic to my dislike of this attractive, civilised, liberal city other than the vague sense of being lied to.

My urgency to move east had redoubled. But with my eagerness came a renewed caution. On the front page of every newspaper was the news that a massive bomb had gone off the night before in the eastern city of Diyarbakır, killing seven little boys who had been playing in the park opposite. According to some reports it was believed that the device had exploded accidentally en route to a police station. TV footage of the scene showed images of a man bending down to pick up a little leg off the street, school sock still attached. Before I had left, Hüseyin had unfolded a map of Turkey on the floor and circled places I should see and those I should avoid. Diyarbakır had been the subject of some especially adamant warnings. And with this latest news — the expectation of more violence and counter-violence — the little red rings on my map began to look increasingly ominous.

To make matters worse, Pope Benedict XVI had, a few days before, created an uproar across the Muslim world after delivering a speech in which he quoted a fourteenth-century Byzantine emperor who had, apparently, accused Islam of being a "wicked and inhuman" religion. The response had been somewhat hysterical, invoking memories of the still-warm Danish cartoon scandal, and protestors had embarked on the usual round of effigy and American flag burning (although what the United States had to do with this latest incident was beyond me). I wouldn't have said that I was nervous heading to the east but it had become a darker, more alien place for me, a source of dim foreboding that only grew sharper as I gathered my things and made my way, once more and not for the final time, to the *otogar*.

★ ★ ★

Adana is the fourth-largest city in Turkey, and it shows. After a bus ride of ten hours, much of it spent passing a procession of beach resorts of varying tattiness, I had found myself in the early hours of the morning in a hotel room downtown, in bed, under blue rayon sheets and a mirrored chandelier that tinkled like icicles in the breeze of the air conditioner. Adana is a completely unremarkable industrial centre at almost the furthest extreme of the Eastern Mediterranean, notable only for having the biggest mosque outside of Istanbul and a large American military base. It was not exactly the exotic east but buses to the city were frequent and swift and after the coy fussiness of Antalya it was, at least, unself-conscious. Walking the streets, however, it struck me that there might be no other city in the world that reeked as much of the spirit of fourth. The archaeology museum was the standard school hall affair, dank and creaky with yellowing labels written on a typewriter. The anthropology museum was marginally better, housed in a handsome Crusader church. Unfortunately the carpets and other objects were literally rotting and the nomad tent with the mannequin family inside had dry cat shit on the roof. But if anything came closest to embodying the spirit of Adana, it was the Sabancı Mosque.

The largest modern mosque in Turkey, the Sabancı Mosque is named in honour of the family who paid for it. The Sabancıs count themselves among Turkey's mega-rich, a tiny elite of about a half-dozen families who, between them, like tribal chieftains, control seemingly every industry in the country. The Sabancı name is, almost literally, on every building and public work in the city.

But if Florence got the De' Medicis then Adana wasn't to be so lucky. A brick-by-brick copy of Istanbul's fifteenth-century Blue Mosque, the Sabancı Mosque is a soulless pile of marble and stained glass, the illusion of antiquity somewhat compromised by the state-of-the-art speaker system and the men lounging in corners chatting on mobile phones. Cooling and peaceful, the mosque was not unpleasant; and as a gesture of corporate philanthropy struck me as admirable in a country where the rich seemed to make their millions and then flee to Switzerland or spend the rest of their lives arranging staged meetings with minor actresses for the benefit of hidden TV cameras. But if it is the task of a religious building to inspire wonder then the Sabancı Mosque succeeded only because it was difficult to believe that someone would spend as much as they undoubtedly did to create something as banal as it undoubtedly was.

Collecting my shoes from the cheerful man at the door ("I wish you good health in Australia!") I left the mosque and wandered out into the hot, confused streets of Adana. For a while I walked among the crowded shopping areas before turning to walk aimlessly north where I stumbled across an upmarket residential district. Among the Irish theme pubs and shops selling Tommy Hilfiger was a park of exceptional beauty. Symmetrical and lush with water features spouting thin sprays like the comb of some exotic seashell, it was an oasis of first-rate in the city of fourth. The day was now very hot and as I sat in the shade watching the perfect arc of the water jets from the fountains, mentally thanking the Sabancı family for their munificence, I was approached by a young man in a singlet and jeans. Sitting down beside me on the bench, he offered his hand. I shook it, rather half-heartedly. "Where are you from?" he demanded in English. I told him. "Oh!" he exclaimed enthusiastically. "I am from Adana!"

"Really?" I said.

"Yes!" he replied, as though I were a quiz contestant. "Come, let me show you my town."

Encounters like these in Turkey are fairly common but can be ambiguous. Turks are among the most welcoming people in the world and their sense of personal space is decidedly non-Western. It is not uncommon for complete strangers to offer their services as tour guides, even if only to practise their English. There are, however, a small number of shady characters who exploit this natural gregariousness and experience had taught me to be on guard.

Grabbing me by the hand my new best friend lifted me from my seat and locked his arm with mine as we went strolling through the park. "What is your name?" I asked, conscious of the fact I was walking arm-in-arm with a complete stranger.

"Mehmet," he replied.

"Everyone in Turkey is called Mehmet," I said.

"Ha, ha. Yes!" he cried, and released me momentarily to turn and make expansive hand gestures. "We have all the same names! Mehmet, Hüseyin, Murat, Muhammed, Erhan. In Turkey, everyone is same! But not me. I am *different*." He took my arm again. "Come. I show you Adana."

Mehmet dragged me back down to the shopping areas I had just come from, offering a detailed tour of his favourite internet cafés and jeans stores. "Do you need to buy clothings?" he asked. I said I did not. "Would you like to drink alcohol? I do not drink — I am Muslim, but in Adana alcohol is OK. Adana is good city. Not like the east. I *love* Adana!"

I said I did not need to drink and then politely implied that I was getting rather bored and hot.

"Come, we will eat."

In a cheap restaurant I ate pide and drank Sprite while Mehmet conducted a monologue about his deep and abiding love for his home town. "Adana is fourth-biggest city in Turkey." He held up four fingers for emphasis. "Good city. Big city. Everything is here. Many Americans in Adana. Can get anything you want. Anything …" He trailed off and stared at me. Leaning over the table slightly he lowered his voice and said, "Brendan, do you like make sex?"

I paused. "With you?"

Mehmet threw his head back and hooted with laughter. "No! With women." He leaned in once more. "You like women? I can get for you. Russian women. Turkish women. Many women."

"No thanks, Mehmet," I said.

"You sure?"

"Yes, thank you, Mehmet."

Mehmet went silent and looked so dejected I felt genuinely sorry for him, as if he were a vacuum-cleaner salesman who had just failed to meet his monthly quota. As I finished eating he spoke again. "It's OK, man. Come," he said, rising from his chair, "I still have to show you Adana." He stood back from the table and spread his arms wide. "I fucking *love* Adana!"

I was growing to like Mehmet. He seemed genuinely unconcerned that I didn't want his services and his sincere enthusiasm for his town, especially one so difficult to love, endeared him to me. It was a testament to Turkey that even the pimps were full of home-town pride.

We walked back in the direction of the park, Mehmet pointing out various features ("Here is a bank") until we arrived in front of a warehouse-like building. Mehmet gestured towards it. "Here is American Bazaar," he said with notable pride. "Here is all American products." Inside was a nondescript Turkish covered market, stalls piled high with products featuring names like "Mondo Jeans" and "Desperado Shoes". One shop stocked only Gillette razors, packets of American cake mix and children's party masks. Another sold shoes but with a supplementary line in American breakfast cereal. Lucky Charms and Chex sat in a big stack in one corner, the boxes crushed and covered in filth. I had a strong suspicion it had all been stolen or illegally traded from the military base. We were the only customers.

Twice we walked purposelessly in a circle, inspecting razor blades and soap, Mehmet trailing behind, anxiously asking if there was anything I would like to buy.

"No, thank you, Mehmet, there's nothing I need."

We walked outside into a dusty car park. Mehmet had become withdrawn and quiet. At a slower pace we walked back towards the park until he suddenly stopped, turned and gestured behind him. "It say 'American Bazaar'," he said with amused exasperation. "But is not American. Is shit!"

Chapter 5

The next day I left Adana, the east on the horizon. Mehmet had proposed that I meet him and some friends the previous night at a bar, but he stood me up and I never heard from him again. The last I saw of him he was standing in the park, arms spread wide, yelling, "I fucking love Adana!" Originally I had planned to go straight to Urfa (its official name is Şanlıurfa, or "Glorious Urfa", a flourish added in 1984 to compete with their neighbours Gaziantep — "Heroic Antep" — but I preferred the earlier, simpler version), a famous city near the Syrian border, the home of the prophet Abraham and much recommended by Tevfik. But first I would make a detour to Antakya, more widely known by its Biblical name, Antioch, a small city on a neck of land between the Mediterranean and the Syrian border which, on maps, looked like a stump of umbilical cord in the belly of the country.

Like Xanadu or Timbuktu, Antioch is one of those places with magical associations. Established by the Greeks in 300BC it later became an important Roman city, renowned for its liberality. It was this quality that attracted many Christians to the city where they were to have great success in winning converts. Antioch was the site of many crucial developments in the Christian church. It was here that the first cathedral was established by St Peter himself, and the issue of whether Christians ought to be circumcised or recognise other Jewish practices was debated. Perhaps most significantly it was in Antioch that the term "Christian" was first used, an appellation probably invented by Roman administrators to distinguish this new cult from the hundreds of others in the region and separating them officially from the Jews — a reminder that the early Christians were, in many ways, not attempting to establish a new religion but only to improve upon an old one. Since that time, Antioch has been contested and fought over as much as any other city in Turkey and modern Antakya retains a strong Arab identity, with many of its citizens still speaking Arabic. None of this is anything that hasn't been noted before, but my reasons for visiting Antioch were less out of historical curiosity than a desire to see the city that has been part of my imagination since I first heard it mentioned in so many half-understood and quickly forgotten readings from the church lectern.

The road to Antakya passed a large grey mountain range, shrouded in mist and upholstered on the lower reaches in a thick velvet of pines. The land in this far-eastern corner of the Mediterranean was unexpectedly lush, the trees reaching all the way to the ocean, threatening to engulf the small concrete houses which drowned under the weight of vines and sagging banana trees. The first petrol refinery to mar this Eden came as a shock; the half-dozen others, half-submerged in water and belching cones of grey smoke into the cloudless sky, merely depressed me. Soon we turned inland and climbed higher, the land growing drier and deforested. Finally, after a complex series of utterly inexplicable transfers between mini-buses, we arrived.

My first impressions of Antakya constituted a useful lesson in the gap between imagination and reality. Where I had half-expected some exotic outpost of the ancient world, peopled by camels and men in turbans, I found instead a ramshackle semi-industrial dump which, even by the competitive standards of Turkish urban ugliness, was fairly dire. Making my way along the concrete banks of the river — petrol-green water choked with plastic bags — I found a hotel, checked in, and then headed to the mosaics museum. Turkish regional museums are usually a sad affair. They all seem to have been built by the same architect — almost certainly the guy who did the Istanbul Otogar — and are invariably manned by scowling security guards who are in a good mood if they turn the lights on for you. The Antakya museum, however, was a superior effort and I spent some time contemplating the eerie mosaics, which stared like startled acquaintances, too vivid, it seemed, not to be the work of some Hollywood set designer.

Conspicuous for its arresting crudity was a sinister, enigmatic image of a wide, staring eye being attacked by (or were they radiating from it?), among others, a crow, scorpion, centipede and a little degenerate priapus, a massive penis bent back through his legs, the tip pointing at the pupil. This was an ancient Roman take on an image that is central to Turkish culture — the evil eye. The origins of the evil eye are lost in time but its influence is widespread and profound. The modern evil eye, the one familiar in Turkey and parts of the Middle East and North Africa, is a disc or orb with radiating bands of blue and white and a dark "pupil" in the centre. The evil eye is on literally everything in Turkey. It is nailed to the lintels of houses, shop shelves and restaurant walls. It hangs as air freshener from the rear-vision mirrors of cabs, as bracelets from the wrists of university students and from the keyrings of almost every driver in the country. It can be bought in the form of bath mats, furniture upholstery, vases, incense burners, mudflaps and tiny ceramic clogs. The fact it is totally ugly is, apparently, of no concern. The evil eye is taken very seriously and I cannot think of a home I saw that did not have one, in at least some form.

Many times I was to ask Turkish people to explain the evil eye, only to find myself peering across an incomprehensible cultural gulf. Hüseyin said it "broke the energy", but I could never get him to be more specific. The best explanation was as a talisman to ward off jealousy. There is a strong tradition in many Mediterranean countries (and far beyond) that to give a compliment is to secretly covet that which has been complimented and wish its destruction. To say someone has a nice car, for instance, is to hope that it crashes. (Due to the strong associations of the evil eye with infertility, babies are considered especially vulnerable to this sort of envy and so the poor things are invariably found fighting for breath under the weight of ropes of evil-eye beads, earrings and brooches — even evil-eye nappies.)

I did not think I understood the concept of the evil eye and the Turkish obsession with it bemused me. After all, how much evil could one person be warding off; who were your neighbours: Fred and Rosemary West? And unless you were a sixteen-year-old girl who had recently lost her virginity to the captain of the football team, what did you care if someone was jealous of you or bitching behind your back? More importantly, what did it say about a society in which the unifying cultural value was the assumption that everyone was out to get everybody else?

My contemplations were interrupted by the arrival of a party of Spaniards who walked about the room, wildly gesticulating and jarring my nerves with their pushy manners and a relentless barrage of sibilant conversation. I turned to leave but not before I was struck by the realisation of how strange they looked, how radically different from the Turks. Dressed in their lemon yellow pants, pink blouses and lime green polo shirts, incessantly gabbling, they might as well have been a gang of clowns that had gate-crashed a funeral. All at once I realised that in only a few weeks I had become accustomed to the grave, earnest Turks with their dark clothes, few words and sweet, endearing melancholy.

* * *

Outside, the streets of Antakya were looking a little better for the softening sun. I crossed a bridge and headed to what appeared to be the centre of town. Following nothing but instinct, I pressed past a row of modern shops and found myself in the knot of narrow alleys of the old town. Here was a labyrinth of high-walled houses, whitewashed or tinted with thin coats of blue, peach and parchment yellow. Inner courtyards were guarded by heavy iron doors studded with bolts, some ajar to reveal tranquil domestic tableaus, women sweeping or laying on couches in small groups, eating oranges and figs. The details were marvellous: metal doors, painted and repainted in coats of slick dark green or blue; iron talismans in the form of hands gripping spheres; stone lintels carved in Arabic script; crescent moons and Koranic passages painted in green on either side of the doorframes; a ginger cat sitting in a precariously rotten window. Children ruled the streets; everywhere they ran about my feet, chasing one another, hiding from their friends, smacking them, skipping over drains and calling from high windows. It was like a toy town they had built themselves, and as I walked past, some shyly stared while others ran up to laugh wildly at nothing before running to hide.

For some time I lost myself in the streets, peering through windows thickly latticed in wood or iron, spying on women in hammocks or blaring televisions watched by nobody. Following a trail of signs to a Catholic church I came to a door, bigger and heavier than most. Heaving it open revealed a serene courtyard ringed in vines and overshadowed by the twisting minaret of a neighbouring mosque. A small group of churchy-looking teenagers sat chatting in a corner. As I entered they looked up, momentarily suspicious, then returned to their conversation. Rising from their group, a very small, rather hairy boy approached me. He told me he worked at the church and was a member of one of the last ten Catholic families in Antakya; that the area where we were now had been the Jewish neighbourhood at the time of Christ and so was probably where St Peter and his followers had lived. He was terribly earnest but so might I have been had I been on the verge of extinction. I asked about the church but he said that a group of Spaniards were at Mass now, so I would have to come back later. From a far corner behind closed doors came a familiar lisping chorus. I bought a book from him about the history of the area and asked if the Christians in Antakya had experienced any problems since the uproar over the Pope's comments. He pointed to a photograph on the back of the book and said, with more than a hint of rehearsal, "See, the symbol of Antioch: a church and a mosque, side-by-side. Together in peace."

As I emerged from the alleys it was almost dark. The day had been hot and humid and I was slippery with grime. Turning a corner, propelled by the forces of kismet, I stumbled across a *hamam*.

The bathhouse is, in my estimation, Turkey's greatest contribution to world civilisation. Inherited from the Romans but perfected by their ultimate successors, the Ottomans, I can think of no other form of institutionalised laziness that even comes close to the pleasure it provides. Ranging from Baroque marble masterpieces to dank cesspits held together only by mould, the public *hamam* was originally built as a communal washhouse for those with no bathrooms. Almost every town in Turkey still has several *hamamlar*, often found next to a mosque where they double for ritual ablutions. Modern plumbing has, however, rendered the institution almost completely redundant and driven *hamamlar* to the verge of extinction, their continued existence owed almost purely to nostalgia and the tourist trade. These days, the *hamam* offers little more than permission to do nothing but lounge naked in a hot room all day, washing yourself as you watch the sun fade through glass portholes in the domed ceiling. If I could somehow combine the experience with red wine and an episode of *Antiques Roadshow*, I would never leave.

For foreigners the *hamam* can be an intimidating experience: a number of people I met refused to go, paralysed by the dread of making a cultural gaffe. There was some legitimacy to their fears; Turkish culture is full of obscure hygiene regulations and the frequently baffling etiquette of shoe removal, washing procedure and towel usage (I was never to come to grips with the complex hierarchy of waist, feet and head towels) contrives only to make a very pleasant experience less so.

A number of male travellers I met were turned off by the reputation of the *hamam* as a den of sodomy. This is, mostly, a myth. Like any place where men take their clothes off, *hamamlar* have a distinctly homoerotic element but sexual activity is rarely tolerated by the management and they are nothing like the gay bathhouses in the West. In most of the major cities there are, however, *hamamlar* that cater to a specifically gay clientele ("gay" in Turkey being an especially malleable term). My only experience of one proved to be a tepid affair of blown kisses and some covert heavy petting which ceased the moment an attendant entered the room, scolding everyone and telling them to put their towels back on. My session ended soon after a bearded religious zealot claimed a seat next to me and began waggling his tongue from side to side in my direction. Disheartened by my puzzling indifference to what I initially took for a mild epileptic seizure, he quickly reached out and, in a gesture with all the erotic appeal of an oil massage by Margaret Thatcher, snatched at my penis hard enough to cause me to cry out in pain and spend the rest of the day walking like Charlie Chaplin. I left immediately, clutching my groin and pitying the poor unfortunate who counted him her husband.

At the door of the *hamam* was a sign, in English, proclaiming the building to be five hundred years old, and it was immediately obvious it had not been cleaned since the late Renaissance. After being handed a towel and room key I was shown to my shabby cubicle, the floor a Pompeii of cigarette ash. I changed and headed to the steam room where I soaped myself alone among the echoes of running water. The bath was, if anything, worse than the vestibule. The old marble had been chipped off and plastered over with large red-and-white check tiles, giving it the appearance of a seedy ice-cream parlour. The mould was inches deep. I did my best to ignore the décor, staring instead at the domed ceiling, watching the light change from pink to purple through the star-shaped windows. Soon I was joined by a young man, powerfully built. After some effort it was made clear that his name was Hüseyin, that he was a shoemaker with a wife and two children, one a week old, and wanted to know where I was from. I tried as best I could to communicate and when I told him that my next stop was Urfa he reared back in horror. "Urfa no good!" he exclaimed. "Diyarbakır no good!" He waved his hand to indicate the east. "No good!"

It was soon made understood that his prejudice against the east was rooted in the fact that he had done his military service there. "Urfa no good," he repeated, and displayed the deep scars on his arms and neck. They were from combat, he claimed. He indicated that he had killed eight men. "Pe-ka-ka," he said and mimed firing a machine-gun. I didn't disbelieve him but my awe was tempered by the fact that half the men I'd met in Turkey had claimed to kill eight PKK during military service.

Military service is compulsory for all Turkish men and can last for anything between six months and a year-and-a-half. It is almost universally dreaded and is an enormous source of stress. This is because, unlike many European countries where you can expect to cycle around mountains eating chocolate for six months or, if you're a peacenik, delivering meals to old ladies, military service in Turkey can potentially get you killed. Inventing ways to get out of it is one of the favourite preoccupations of Turkish teenagers. University students may complete their service after their degree, but there's only so long they will let you put it off. Rich kids used to be able to buy a shortened sentence of three months, but a stop was put to that. Being gay is a good excuse but, to prove it, you must submit yourself to a medically specious "anal exam" and present photos of yourself having sex with another man; whereupon your parents are called and informed of your proclivities, which, in a country like Turkey, can be a fate worse than death.

Not even émigrés are exempt, and if you refuse to return to Turkey to complete military service your citizenship will be stripped. (I know a very successful Turkish–Australian businessman who, at the age of forty, was forced to return and pay ten grand for the privilege of running around a field for three months.) There was only one person I had ever met who had successfully escaped military service — a carpet dealer who, armed with a kilo of weed and exceptional dramatic skills, made himself so sick he was sent home after five weeks in hospital.

Hüseyin leaned forward and doused himself with water. An old man walked in and crouched in a corner to do the same. I disappeared into the sauna. Soon the door opened and a tall young man walked in and sat opposite. We began to converse in fractured high-school German. His name was Halil and he was a German–Turk from Regensburg, his foreign origin conspicuous in his pale skin, unusual height and full-faced look of one raised on a high-protein diet. On his wrists he wore fashionable rubber bracelets. His parents, or so he explained, had been *Gastarbeiters* who had left Antakya in the seventies. These were men and women who had migrated from Turkey to Germany in their hundreds of thousands, from the sixties until the eighties, to work as cheap labour but now formed a population of considerable size in their adopted country. Returnees from Germany also constituted a sizable community in Turkey, which is why second-hand record markets in Istanbul are full of Bavarian beer hall albums with pictures of men in lederhosen and beermaids sandwiching their breasts with steins of frothy ale.

Halil sold VWs for a living but now he was back, he thought, for good. He didn't regard himself as Turkish, and didn't even speak the language very well, but he felt more at home here than he did in the country of his birth. It was a familiar conundrum. In Turkey these people are referred to as *Almanca*, a word which means the German language but which has acquired the additional meaning of an ethnic Turk who grew up in Germany. The *Almanca* are in the classic bind of many immigrants: they are foreigners wherever they go, especially in Germany which doesn't even recognise the children of *Gastarbeiters* as citizens, forcing them to apply for citizenship even though many speak only German and have never been to Turkey.

I wanted to hear more about what it was like to be a stranger in your own land, but before I could ask another question, the door flung open and a man who looked like he wouldn't take no for an answer announced it was time for me to be washed.

Pot-bellied and pale, with an optional complement of various deformities and growths, *hamam* attendants are all ugly, but always in the same way. This must be partly because almost all of them are from the same town — Tokat in central Turkey. (Why they all came from the same city was a mystery no one seemed able to explain. Scrubbing people was just an industry there, like farming or a canning factory.) Mostly, I suspect, it's because rubbing someone until coils of dirt and old skin like fat black worms drop to the floor is a job beautiful people would simply never do. Despite the aesthetic impediments, being washed and massaged in the *hamam* by an attendant is one of the joys of the Turkish bath experience. The sensual pleasures are as nothing, however, when compared with the opportunity the process offers to be completely infantilised. Having a very large man stand over you and clean out your ears with a cloth, for instance, is to be suddenly transported to a happier, simpler time, to negate yourself even of the responsibility of basic sanitation. Having my hair washed and then feeling a big hand wipe the suds from my eyes is a forgotten pleasure that could only be bettered if I had been lifted from the spot, placed in a bed and had a story read to me.

An hour later, after being swaddled in towels and sent off for a nap in my grotty cubicle, I was back on the street with Halil, Hüseyin and the old man, who, as it turns out, was Halil's father. With his clothes on, Hüseyin's tough-guy demeanour had dissolved, replaced by a slightly effete dandy in a bright red, open-necked shirt, turquoise necklace and a pair of blinding white loafers he had clearly made himself. In one finger he held a leather jacket hooked over his shoulder. For a while he and Halil conducted a mumbled conversation while the old man barked incomprehensible monologues in German at me. Halil announced that Hüseyin would take me to dinner. Hüseyin withdrew his mobile and began to send a text. Halil leaned in and asked, somewhat portentously, "Do you understand him?"

"Not really," I said.

"You must be careful," he replied.

"Of him?"

"In Turkey."

Hüseyin and I ate dinner in a restaurant around the corner. The food was delicious but the meal marred somewhat by my companion's unending monologue on the evils of the east: "Diyarbakır — terrorist! Urfa — terrorist!" Drawing back the collar of his shirt he showed me the scars on his neck. "No good!" he said. As if to underline the spirit of foreboding, a man walked from table to table with a box of chewing gum balanced on the stumps of his dismembered arms. After dinner we walked, arm-in-arm, across the bridge to a beautiful tea garden in a park by the river. Here, to my surprise, was an old black-and-white Turkish movie playing on a big screen watched by a group of intellectual types — easily identified by their beatnik beards and poor posture — led by a Trotsky-faced man in wire glasses who would rise intermittently to pause the film and deliver a brief speech from a lectern. The film, a domestic comedy, caused much amusement among the aficionados, both for its slapstick and dated manners. I laughed too; and, as I watched the flickering image, sipping tea and inhaling the scent of pines, feeling clean and pleasantly tired, I thought to myself that Antakya was a beautiful and civilised place and that I would one day return.

Hüseyin, once again, was the only jarring note of the evening. Completely ignoring the film, he spoke loudly into his mobile phone, bringing disapproving stares from some of the bearded film buffs. Noting their censure he grabbed me by the arm and dragged me to the periphery of the garden where he began to engage in a conspiratorial conversation with one of the tea waiters. The waiter turned and began to "translate", pointing at the mobile phone and babbling in Turkish. When it became clear that I had no idea what he was talking about, Hüseyin took my hand and walked me into the dark park. It was at this point questions began to present themselves. Questions such as: what was I doing holding hands with a trained killer in a park at night in a country where people sold handguns in subway tunnels? Nervously I walked through the unlit paths, eyeing the other couples — boys and girls, boys and boys — strolling past in the half-light. In the distance the figure of a stocky man leaned, arms crossed, against a parked car. As we approached, Hüseyin hailed the fat man as a dear friend and his hand gripped mine tightly. The man responded, reaching into his back pocket to retrieve a wallet which unfolded to reveal an identity card and a shining badge. "*Polis,*" he said, giggling in a manner that seemed at odds with the authority of his position.

For a moment I began to panic. Neon signs in my mind began to blink the words "scam", "Turkish jail" and "violent anal rape". I braced myself to make a run for it.

"*Bist du Deutscher?*" asked the policeman, in a manner warm and jovial. Hüseyin wrapped his arms around his friend's neck, draping himself across his chest. The policeman laughed and slapped his head.

I answered his question, cautiously, in German.

"Ah, Sydney!" he cried, in English, throwing Hüseyin to one side. "I have been."

"Really?" It was most unusual to encounter someone on a cop's wage who had travelled outside of Turkey.

"Yes! I was at Sydney Olympics."

"What?"

"In karate." He aimed a punch at Hüseyin's head. Our friend ducked and began to slap the policeman's belly. "I am Turkish national champion!"

"Oh … I see," I said. "Well, congratulations." I shook his hand and he began, once more, to giggle.

Hüseyin conversed with the cop in Turkish. "Where did you meet him?" asked the policeman. I told him and he laughed, hard. "Do you know what he wants?"

I was starting to get some idea, but little in Turkey was ever certain.

"I cannot explain," he said, " … my English." He laughed and laughed.

The conversation soon degenerated into an endless round of mistranslations, awkward silences and giggling fits. I announced my intention to go home to bed. "Where is your hotel?" asked the policeman. I indicated over the river. "Wait!" he cried, diving into his car. "I have a map."

"Really it's not necessary," I said. "I can see it from here." But no one was listening: no matter where I went in Turkey everyone would always be convinced that I was either lost, hungry or German.

"He will show you the way," said the policeman, ignoring my protestations and turning his attentions to his crackling CB radio. Once again, Hüseyin took my hand.

Back at the hotel I lingered in front, hoping my new friend would leave. Pushing past he headed into the foyer and leaned over the desk to kiss the receptionist on each cheek. They were obviously familiar. The conversation proceeded and soon I watched in astonishment as the receptionist handed my key to Hüseyin who began to walk upstairs, dangling it in front of him between two fingers.

For a while I sat in the foyer, watching TV, hoping he would take the hint. After a minute or so he ducked his head back down and beckoned me impatiently. Upstairs, he had already shown himself into the room and switched on the television. Standing by the bed, he flicked through the hundreds of cable channels, pausing occasionally to consult me in a half-hearted way, before settling on a music station of his choosing. "Madonna," he said, throwing the remote aside before lifting the phone to order two cups of Nescafe. Lighting a cigarette he sat on my bed and pulled out his wallet. From within he began to withdraw various pieces of ephemera — photographs, identity cards, bus tickets. He presented me with a small passport photo of his newborn daughter. "*Bebek*," he said, meaning "baby", my favourite Turkish word.

The receptionist appeared with the coffee and we sat drinking on the bed with the door open while Madonna's version of *American Pie* came to an end. He gave me a business card, one of a thick pile, featuring a gauzy photo of himself in a stilted glamour pose, arms crossed over one knee, leaning into the camera. From what I could make out by the writing on the card he was a member of a talent agency in Adana. "TV?" I asked. "In Adana?" He nodded and held the business card up to his face. "TV," he said. His hands folded over his heart and his eyes rolled into his head in sainted ecstasy. "Love TV." I laughed, but he remained impassive. Solemnly, he placed the card back into his wallet. My anxiousness and annoyance had gone now, replaced by an amused affection for this unlikely killer with his demonstrative manner, dreams of TV stardom and the aura of sadness that hung over him like a veil. He reached over me to take the ashtray from the side table and I saw down the collar of his wide-necked shirt. His scars were deep, deeper than I had realised: slashes that went right into his shoulders, purple but flat. They had been well stitched, probably by good army medics.

For a while I sat in silence watching the TV, while he went through my wallet. Then, one-by-one, he began to return my driver's licence and library membership cards to their pockets, downed the rest of his coffee and announced he wanted to sleep. I was worried he would try to take the spare bed in my room but he made it clear he wanted to leave. Stubbing out his cigarette, he stood up to say goodbye at the door. With gentle gestures he embraced me, kissing me on each cheek, Turkish style, before, most unexpectedly, leaning in to kiss me lightly on the lips. Releasing me as if nothing had happened, he nodded goodbye, slung his leather jacket over one shoulder and walked into the dark corridor, his shoes like neon tubes in the night.

Chapter 6

I arrived in Urfa just before dawn. The receptionist at the hotel was a man of few words. Pointing to himself he said "Kurd", then to the sleeping porter, "Arab," before raising his eyebrows ironically and kicking his colleague's chair, which rolled on its castors gently into a wall, with predictable results. Through my window, dawn was breaking, unmasking a yellow ruin in an empty, dusty street. I fell gratefully into bed, ignoring the calligraphy of hair in the sheets.

The bus journey to Urfa had been a nail-whitening, bowel-loosening, headlong assault into the abyss. Driven at demonic speeds, we made our way through a Grand Theft Auto of nocturnal carnage; all of it presided over by a calm young porter in a natty yellow tie and red velvet shirt who deftly poured cups of hot coffee while carrying a crying baby through the aisle, patting it gently on the bottom. Unable to sleep for fear, I could only sit and marvel at the chaos around. To each side of the road lay wrecks: cars and upturned trucks, like dead elephants, their payloads of lumber and fruit spread across the highway and into ditches. In total I was to count eleven accidents that evening, most with people still milling around, indicating that many had happened quite recently. With the threat of death so immediate it came as a particular affront, therefore, when the porter kneeled before me and, by means of pinching his nose with one hand and fanning his face with the other, indicated I should put my shoes back on. Much amusement was had at my expense.

My sleep didn't last long. After only a few hours, curiosity roused and frogmarched me out the door. On the streets the sun was weak although the day would be hot. The dense wood smoke made even the mobile phone shops, with their strands of blinking lights rimming the windows, seem otherworldly. At a bus stop, two women draped in full *çarşaf*, their faces illegally covered, like black ghosts in the mist, drew towards one another and had a whispered conversation. I imagined pulling at the cloth to reveal nothing beneath. As I neared the bazaar the crowds thickened. Men walked, bandy-legged, in enormous *şalvar*, baggy pants gathered at the ankle and drooping from the crotch to the knee in an unflattering saddle of material. On their heads they wore *keffiyeh*, long scarves in purple or white braced by bands of braided hair. But it was the women who demanded the most attention, their garish spectrum of outfits a sudden bloom in the desert. Maroon, gold-embroidered kaftans were teamed with diaphanous green headscarves, studded with sequins. Electric blue velvet robes shimmered under brown coats, striped in white. Headscarves were a candy feast of raspberry, lime, lilac and lemon. One woman, held at the elbow by her husband and trailed by an assortment of ill-disciplined children, wore a pavement-scraping robe so heavily embroidered in bronze sequins it swayed and rattled like chainmail. As I stared she stared back from under her purple scarf with an unnerving ferocity, cocking her head haughtily, like a queen glanced through the curtains of a litter.

These people were Arabs. Before arriving in Urfa I had not even realised they existed in Turkey, let alone in such apparent numbers. Partially this was due to the policy of successive Turkish governments — enthusiastically embraced by a relatively small, albeit vocal, section of the population — to impose upon the people of Turkey an unvarying monoculture, a mythic notion of "Turkishness" unchanged since the first tribes rode out of Central Asia and onto the plains of Anatolia.

For about seven hundred years, until the beginning of the twentieth century, the Ottoman Empire ruled over an enormous territory. At the height of its power, from the mid-1500s until the early-1700s, it controlled huge areas of North Africa, Eastern Europe and the Middle East, including modern Hungary, Egypt, Greece, Iraq and the Persian Gulf states. It was, for a period, more wealthy and influential than many contemporary European powers and people from all over the empire lived, travelled and traded within its borders. With the decline of the Ottomans, and the eventual establishment of modern Turkey by Atatürk, there arose a problem: how to create a nation-state with a cohesive, nationalistic identity out of the ashes of a fractured, multi-ethnic empire? The solution was not entirely ineffective though brutal in its simplicity: declare that everyone was a Turk, ban other languages, restrict all religions and treat dissenters as enemy agents, intent on destroying Turkey and the Turkish people.

Since the country's foundation Turkey has nursed a fear of ethnic or religious separatism. Legitimate though some of these anxieties are, as the Kurdish situation can attest, they are too often nothing more than a kind of nationalistic paranoia and an excuse for some fairly unapologetic racism. On numerous occasions during my stay in Turkey I was to hear even educated Turks speak of Kurds in the lowest possible terms and Arabs described as "liars", "thieves" and, most commonly and often with a disturbing vehemence, "dirty". (These prejudices were often happily reciprocated throughout the Arab world, only reinforcing paranoid Turkish notions of being surrounded by enemies.) The fact that many foreigners thought Turks were an ethnically Arab people filled many Turks with something bordering on despair. By the end of my stay I was to lose count of the number of times I had been bailed up and asked in imploring, earnest tones,

"In your country, do they think we are Arabs?" Looking into their pleading eyes, I often didn't have the heart to tell them the truth.

Outside the bazaar, dozens of motorcycles were parked, their fuel tanks upholstered in flower prints, thick wool stripes and velvets of green and red. One was covered completely in a thick red shag. Across the back of the bikes were slung rough-woven saddle bags, the same that had once been draped over horses or donkeys. Inside the bazaar, the streets shrank in places to an arm-span. The shops and services were a medieval mirage, the illusion punctured only by the occasional, incongruous invasion from the modern world: a sheikh in a purple *keffiyeh* talking on a mobile phone; a stall selling clock radios. In a hide tannery, sheep skins hung from the rafters, motioned by the activity of the tanner behind. A tiny butcher shop, spilling entrails onto the pavement, sat between a hobbit cobbler's and a barbershop so small that mothers waiting for their boys to be shorn were forced to stand huddled in the back, heads bowed beneath the ceiling. Every spare inch of space was occupied by a shop of some sort. Below street level, viewed through windows that stretched from my knee to the pavement, men made flatbreads in broad ovens. Haberdashery shops the width of a doorway were vulgar jewel boxes of sequins and rhinestones. Sacks of spices and dyes sat like stumpy crayons on the pavement. The air smelt of coffee and oregano.

The women here seemed especially untamed. A pair passed me, powerfully built with broad shoulders and tanned, creased faces like cigar-store Indians. One wore a hot pink satin gown trimmed in gold and rhinestones. She was draped from neck to ankle in jewellery. Her companion wore a pale blue outfit covered in a delicate web of gold filigree, her thumbs hooked, cowboy-style, in a glittering belt studded with orbs of lapis lazuli.

Many of the older folk, men and women — but the women more conspicuous for it — had their foreheads, chins and hands scrawled in blue tattoos: tridents, stars, hatched designs, numbers and thin lines drawn down either side of their mouths to give the appearance of a ventriloquist's dummy. The talismans were only more wonderful for the cell-block roughness of their execution, giving their owners a radiant authority as they cut a swathe through the market. Even their headscarves seemed less like a religious observance than a form of team colours. Unlike in the west of the country, where the headscarf was often worn self-consciously tight, full of political implications, the Arabs and Kurds wound theirs in careless loops about their faces, allowing scraggly tendrils of hair to whip in the wind. It seemed to suggest they wore their scarves because they enjoyed them, because they were part of their life and culture, rather than to make a point.

Through these narrow alleys children ran with impunity, although they didn't play here in the same way I had seen in other parts of the country. There were no new bikes or Michael Jordan T-shirts in Urfa. Here, the boys were like little men. They cleaned the windows of their fathers' shops with newspaper and strutted their way through the streets delivering trays of tea or bags of onions balanced on their heads. A pair pushing a trolley as tall as themselves knocked a portly old lady to the ground, sending her shopping flying. As she sat spread-legged on the ground, abusing the boys, they giggled uncontrollably and made a vain effort to lift her. Much comedy ensued.

Emerging from the market, I climbed the hill to a residential district. The streets were steep and the houses plain, poorer-looking than those of Antakya, the palette of whitewashed stone cheered only by bright blue doors and window frames. The children were thin and dirty, their eyes and ears prominent with hunger. They emerged from everywhere to practise their "hellos" and "goodbyes". Some became confused: "Sorry, goodbye." Older children were bolder. "Mahnee, mahnee!" they demanded. "No money," I replied. "*Yes*, mahnee," they insisted, dogging my heels, rather aware of their own cheekiness. I collared one, a fat redhead, and grabbed a fistful of his stomach to demonstrate that he'd had quite enough to eat. "No money," I said.

The joke was an enormous hit. In these streets I didn't have to go far to feel like an alien. Old men stared in astonishment. Smouldering piles of garbage sat in stepped alleys, sour smoke rising from them. The call to prayer came from miniature minarets attached to tiny mosques. A ruffian stabbed his playmate with the silver bayonet of a plastic machine-gun, the victim rising only to chase me with an outstretched hand, crying, "Mahnee, mahnee!"

Urfa was a revelation. I could not credit the existence of this biblical vision in the same country where, only a week before, I had been dancing in bars and getting propositioned by transvestite prostitutes. There were no bars in Urfa, nor any obvious transvestites. Neither were there many cars, uncovered women or displays of wealth, other than the tatty jewellery the women wore, but even that was less like decoration than a fetish. The atmosphere of the city was unrefined but not uncivilised. At the Gölbaşı, where it was believed King Nimrod of Assyria had tried to burn the prophet Abraham alive but failed after God turned the pyre into pools of water, "sacred" carp broke the surface and snapped their horrid yellow mouths while squealing girls dropped pellets into them. The gardens were well tended and the new buildings showed a degree of planning and sympathy with the old structures that was especially surprising given how many cities in the west had made no effort in this respect. My apprehensions about the east, stoked by the prejudices of others, appeared to be foolish.

Up on the cliff above the pools I stood among the ruins of a fort, built and rebuilt by every civilisation to have crossed the land. Two huge columns, dirt orange against the blue sky, cast long shadows to the east. Resting in the shade were a couple: broad of thigh and straight of teeth, conspicuously, almost comically, American. The Americans, as it happened they were, were the only other foreign tourists I had seen and, even then, were only tourists of a sort as both were living in Adana, he being in the army. We spoke for a while.

Initially, they seemed an utterly unremarkable pair: the sort of people you'd meet in a queue for a roller coaster at a theme park. As conversation progressed, however, it quickly became apparent that he, in defiance of his crew cut and football jersey, was a little smarter than the average soldier. This combined with references to time spent in West Africa piqued my curiosity. "So, what do you do?" I asked.

"I'm in the army," he said.

"Yes, but doing what *exactly*?"

"I work in administration."

Growing up in Canberra we had neighbours who worked for the American embassy: their home had reinforced steel on the doors, motion-sensitive floodlights and when I once babysat their children they gave me the number of the restaurant they would be at *and* a direct line to the marines. When I asked them what it was they did they had also said "administration".

I asked for his thoughts on the latest wave of violence in the east, about the Kurds and his predictions for the future. He said he had a feeling things were going to get worse, that it might open a new front in the Iraq war and that the Americans were completely unprepared for the consequences of such a development. "Down there," he said, pointing in the direction of the Iraqi border, "the Kurds are standing with guns ready to go." At that moment, a group of four teenage boys came scrabbling over the rocks towards us. As they came near they stopped, drew themselves up and began to stare. "Where are you from?" asked one, in Turkish. This was not a question, but a demand. There was a pause. The Americans remained silent. "We're Australian," I said. They considered us for a moment, their eyes full of suspicion and barely concealed antagonism. "Australia," he said, looking me up and down for a moment before turning to his friends and leading them on their way over the rocks.

★ ★ ★

It was not until I strolled out the next morning to find there was no breakfast, indeed food, did I realise I had miscalculated the start of Ramadan. As we drove in the mini-van the streets were almost empty, mirroring the state of my stomach. I had booked a trip to the town of Harran the day before and was now heading south on my way to one of the world's oldest cities. Our driver and so-called guide was enthusiastic but without much English. What he lacked in language skills, however, he made up for in joviality: as he drove he would point to things out the window, shouting incomprehensible dictums over the noise of the bus before bursting into private laughter.

My companions were a mysterious pair — she Dutch, he Belgian — who although separated by at least thirty years and two rows of seats were, apparently, travelling together. Pieter was, I guessed, in his mid-thirties and the younger of the two. Bespectacled, bald and very pink, his comic appearance was emphasised by hooting Flemish pronunciation and wildly camp mannerisms that turned every sentence into a fast-forward kabuki of swishy hand gestures and dancing eyebrows. I assumed he was gay but it was difficult to tell where his campness ended and his Belgianness began. His companion, Madelon, was in her mid-sixties. Birdlike and dressed in a flimsy black silk blouse, raw cotton pants and a stylish necklace of pierced crystal discs, laid flat across her chest. There was a suggestion about her of modern pottery and museum fund-raising dinners. Most distinctive was her laugh which was very high and piercing but came at a slightly disconcerting delay, as in a dubbed Italian movie, often leaving you a little uncertain as to what it was she had found amusing.

As we drove, the city quickly gave way to green fields of cotton. Pieter produced a plastic bag of cheese rolls. "Are you not going to make an effort to fast?" I asked. While I had absolutely no intention of going without food during the day, the etiquette of fasting made me anxious and I had already found myself formulating elaborate plans for covert meals.

"No," he said, tearing a piece of roll with his middle fingers and raising his pointer skyward for emphasis. "In the Koo-ran it says traffalers may eat."

"Yes," I said, as he popped the piece of bread into his mouth, "but I'm not sure they'd meant on mini-buses."

There was a silence of at least five seconds broken suddenly by the sound of a hammer banging on copper pipe. "Ohh, ho ho ho," chortled Madelon. "You are *fanny.*"

As we drove towards the Syrian border I ate one of Pieter's cheese rolls and watched the chessboard of cotton stretch flat in all directions. Only a couple of years earlier, it had all been desert. Women worked the fields, bent double in the sun, their headscarves punctuations of colour in the endless plains of green and white. The massive growth of the cotton industry perhaps explained why every time I turned on the television in Turkey there was an American movie about the Deep South playing. In these films slaves always had bleeding hands, ruined backs and went mad under the sun. I doubted much had changed since then and, as I watched the women, felt a brief pang of guilt at being allowed the luxury of regarding their labour, if only for a moment, as picturesque.

First stop was an ancient gate, apparently Arab in construction, but of which our guide could tell us nothing.

"Arab?" I asked.

"*Evet, evet!* Arap!" said the guide, shaping a gate with his hands.

"I do not think he knoos," said Pieter suspiciously. "And, what is more, I think this has been *re*-boolt." Pieter turned to the guide. "Mongol?" he asked.

The guide nodded, cautiously. "*Evet, evet.* Mongol."

"I think if I said it were Martian he'd agree with me," I said. There was a pause, then, from atop an ancient wall on which she stood, Madelon hooted with laughter.

Harran is one of the oldest continually inhabited communities on earth. It is mentioned in the Book of Genesis as the place where Abraham heard God call him to Canaan and where Rachel drew water for Jacob. Later it was home to the Temple of Sin, the Moon God of the Assyrians, and planetary worship stretched into the Christian and then Islamic eras, existing parallel with the age of monotheism. To the north is the birthplace of Job. The history of Harran — encompassing as it does everyone from Nebuchadnezzar II to Alexander — makes Europe, with its churches, art galleries and film stars on scooters poodling round tizzy little fountains, look rather feeble.

Harran was one of the crossroads of the ancient world, for dozens of civilisations, until 1264 when it was completely destroyed by the Mongols. Eight hundred years later, it was little improved. Modern Harran appeared to be nothing more than a grim border town drowning in dust, the sense of having arrived at the end of the world given eerie veracity by colonies of domed houses, like upturned egg cartons made of stone and mud.

As we arrived a small regiment of children ran to the bus, greeting our exit with the usual chorus of "Mahnee, mahnee", although tainted with an aggression and a hint of mockery I had not encountered before in Turkey. We fought our way through the Lilliputian skirmish and stood on the hill overlooking the Syrian border. The fields stretching to the horizon were green with cotton; the brown eggs of the desert houses contrasted with the standard whitewashed boxes that covered Turkey like concrete hail. We walked down the ridge to the houses, Madelon making voluble exclamations of astonishment. "Ohhh, isn't it eear-ee!" From one of the egg houses a woman appeared brandishing a broom, screaming and pointing at Madelon's camera as if it were Pandora's Box. "Madelon, I think we shoot leaf," said Pieter.

Back up on the hill, we joined our guide in the courtyard of one of the beehive houses. Nobody lived in them anymore, most having been relegated to stables and storage. Inside, however, they were surprisingly cool (preferable surely to the modern concrete huts) and this one had been preserved as a sort of museum. Seated in a horseshoe in a corner shaded by the courtyard wall were a group of half a dozen young people, mixed boys and girls. They were easily picked as outsiders, not merely for their smarter clothes and the lack of headscarves, but because they were sitting together at all. Off to one side sat a battered sheikh in a lilac *keffiyeh*, a face like polished red granite. Next to him were two women — a mother and daughter, perhaps — neither of whom said anything nor made any eye contact from under the awning of their veils. Immediately the boys rose and offered us seats in the shade, a generosity which, despite our hollow protestations, we immediately accepted. Pleasantries followed; the magic word "Australia" inspiring the usual chorus of awed exclamations followed by a barrage of familiar questions. "Tell me," said one of the girls, "in Australia, do people think we are Arabs?"

Their English was good, which was to be expected as they had all been English teachers who had studied together in Diyarbakır. As is the Turkish way, they immediately began to apologise for a variety of imagined inconveniences they thought we might have experienced in their country. A blond, green-eyed boy who sat forward tensely on his stool took the job of spokesman. "We are sorry," he said, very gravely, "for the woman who screamed at you."

"I don't care," said Madelon. "I would scream too if people came to take photographs of my house."

"But it's not good for Turkey," he said, very forcefully. "This is very bad and I am very embarrassed." Apologies in Turkey never sounded like anything less than the prologue to ritual suicide.

They said they had come to Harran to pay a surprise birthday visit to their friend who was here to do his teacher training. In Turkey, they told me, all new teachers had to do a compulsory two years' work in a location assigned to them by the government, invariably somewhere poor, often in the east. "I wouldn't have chosen Harran otherwise," said the unfortunate trainee who sat off to one side staring forlornly at the thin sails of dust that rose outside the gates of the compound in the harsh afternoon sun. Perhaps some of his despondency was due to more than the lack of an obvious nightlife in Harran. During the 1990s the PKK had abducted and executed more than a hundred teachers in the eastern part of the country, their excuse being that the school curriculum was allowed to be taught only in Turkish, making the teachers agents of the state and, therefore, legitimate targets. The practice had, apparently, stopped but pockets of the kind of hatred that inspired such atrocities remained.

The backwardness of the east embarrassed them. The semi-chaos of Istanbul made the blond spokesman quite apologetic, as though he were personally responsible for the traffic conditions there. Only one girl, very beautiful, with Chinese eyes like black sunflower seeds (her ancestors had probably destroyed Harran), was from the east, a village on the Iraqi border. All the rest were from the west — Izmir, Antalya and Eskişehir. The geography of their births had assured that the boys had been sent to do their military service in the east: as in the teaching profession it was common for army conscripts to be sent as far from home as possible. Between them they had served in some of the most notorious places in Turkey. Their descriptions of their experiences were light on detail and peppered with long, uncomfortable silences. "I was in Mush," said one boy, his striking blue eyes beneath a heavy black fringe. "It was very hard ..." He trailed off. "Much suffering." His head dropped slowly. Someone changed the topic and, in defiance of Ramadan, drinks were brought to us by the stony sheikh, his hands scrawled in talismanic tattoos.

I asked them about Diyarbakır. Their ears pricked up. "Diyarbakır is a good place, *normal* place," said the spokesman. There were nods and affirmations. After their bemoaning the horrors of the primitive east, it came as a surprise to hear them so defensive of a city widely regarded as the poorest and most backward of them all.

"Will you go to Diyarbakır?" asked the black-eyed girl. I paused. That I should not go to Diyarbakır was the one thing every person I had met in Turkey seemed completely united on.

"I don't know," I said. "Is it dangerous?"

"What do you do?" she asked.

"I'm a writer."

"Then you must go to Diyarbakır," she said, and, all at once, there was a feeling in me: the same when at the age of five I pressed the hot metal coil of a cigarette lighter into the flesh of my hand simply because I'd been told not to.

★ ★ ★

After bidding the teachers goodbye, Madelon, Pieter and I walked the perimeter of the ruins of the oldest mosque in Turkey. "I want to get through this fence!" demanded Madelon.

"It doesn't bother me," I said.

"Well it bothers me," she announced, attempting to wriggle on her belly beneath some wire, loose in the red dirt. Half-heartedly a local tough approached and demanded five lira each from us for the privilege of looking. "I do not think that he is ee-fan working hair," said Pieter, dismissing the boy with a flutter of his hands. The mosque, 1250 years old and one of Harran's more recent structures, sat in ruins, its geometry laid out in burnt bricks, a de Chirico under the blue sky. There was little left, but from what remained of the square minaret you could see the elegance of its proportions and marvel at the creation of, what was then, a relatively new civilisation and religion. It was still beautiful but only in the way of all ruins: as if you had seen this before in a dream.

Back on the bus we drove from the town, the weakening sun turning the dirt to sulphur. As the sheikh waved goodbye his purple scarf lifted gently in the breeze, making a snake on the ground.

Through the cotton fields we returned to Urfa. In the distance, little boys in blue-and-white school uniforms, like tiny sailors, no older than six or seven, were wading through the green, laden down with bulging hessian sacks as big as themselves. I asked Pieter what he did for a living. "I work in airport seck-you-rity," he said, adjusting his glasses. "But I was, in a previous life, an archay-olo-joost."

"Did you ever work in Turkey?"

"Ah, well … nooo. I only ever did my training. I was never profesh-onal."

There was a little whinny from Madelon in the back. Pieter twisted in his seat. "You laugh, Mard-e-loon! But it has trained my eye. You know, I have spotted a doz-oon fake passports!" He twisted back to the front and plucked a cheese roll from the bag; Madelon's laughter was high and musical.

Madelon was a professional tour guide and part-time jeweller, facts that distanced her somewhat from the society matron with bohemian pretensions I had taken her for. The striking necklace she wore was one of her creations. "It's made of plastic," she said, tapping the beads with a nail. "If I lose it or get robbed, I just make another." Her childhood had been spent on the Indonesian island of Sumatra and she spoke fluent Bahasa Indonesia. There was, I suspected, a slightly calculated quality to her daftness but it was outweighed by her sense of humour, as well as a certain amount of genuine daftness that had a habit, as I was to learn, of emerging at unpredictable intervals. I was about to ask her about the nature of her relationship with Pieter, but she suddenly turned from me and stared out the window and I felt that conversation had come to an end.

Pieter, Madelon and I ate dinner overlooking the pool of Abraham. In the dark, the town had come to life. As the first day of Ramadan the streets were covered in food stalls and a large tent for distributing meals to the poor had been established near the water. On one side of the pool families sat on a stepped outdoor theatre to watch a free concert; on the other, couples walked through the park illuminated by fairy lights.

As we ate we discussed our travel plans and proposed going further east together. Our itineraries were similarly vague but, curiously, we were all keen to visit the relatively obscure northeastern city of Kars, a coincidence explained by the fact we had all been reading the same novel. The book was called *Snow* and it had been a big hit that year for its author, Orhan Pamuk, Turkey's only writer of international renown.

The plot of *Snow* centres on a spate of suicides in Kars, mostly among young women, many of them religious. A journalist is sent to investigate the phenomenon, only to witness a murder of an education official by an Islamic fundamentalist and stumble onto a mini-revolution staged by a radical theatre group. If this plot sounds slightly cracked then that's because it is. In fact, in many ways, *Snow* is really quite ridiculous — a post-modern melodrama full of "yearning" breasts, "flashing" eyes and various mouthpieces and archetypes wandering around town alternating long-winded proclamations on God and national identity with endless whining about how poor and miserable they all are (I can't vouch for the rest of it, but in this respect *Snow* is an extremely accurate depiction of the Turkish national character). For all its flaws, *Snow* remains weirdly compelling — partly because it clarifies much of Turkey's political complexity better than most non-fiction, but mostly because of its descriptions of Kars, a city that Pamuk maps with all the loving detail of Isherwood's Berlin or Chandler's LA.

Pamuk is a contentious figure in Turkey. Born into the ruling elite, he was seen by many I'd spoken to as a snobby dilettante intent on sucking up to the West by peddling derogatory clichés about Turkey designed only to appeal to the prejudices of foreigners and win him prizes and fat sales. For all I knew there may have been some truth to this charge, but if Pamuk had "aligned" himself with the West then this must surely have been out of necessity after the treatment he had received in Turkey. In 2005, in an interview with a Swiss newspaper, Pamuk was quoted as saying, "Thirty thousand Kurds and a million Armenians were killed in these lands and nobody but me dares to talk about it." The Armenian genocide (always prefaced by "so-called" in Turkey), during which Armenians were deported and massacred at the end of the First World War by the dying Ottoman Empire, is the greatest taboo in Turkey, less open to question than even the "Kurdish problem". Pamuk's quote was enough to have him arrested and charged under the notorious Article 301, which makes it a crime to "insult Turkishness". In most any other country Article 301 would be nothing more than a source of comedy, "insulting Turkishness" evoking in my mind an image of a man in a fez with a handlebar moustache, saying, "Stop laughing! This is not funny!" But Turkish nationalism has little room for irony and, after a brief and highly publicised trial, Pamuk was found not guilty on a technicality. These days he lived in America, the constant death threats in Turkey proving too much.

"It's a rather odd book," said Madelon, speaking for us both, "but it makes you want to go to Kars, doesn't it?"

After dinner we made our way through the market stalls. There were stands selling scarves, electronic gadgets and creepy little toy soldiers with Kewpie Doll faces and machine-guns. By far the strangest items you could buy in the east were the postcards and envelopes brightly illustrated with cartoonish battle scenes: images of grimacing soldiers firing rounds into psychedelic mountains or parachuting out of planes, a starburst of artillery in their wake. My favourite featured on its front a platoon of machine-gunning soldiers locked in mortal combat with a terrorist gang, and on the reverse a montage of nearby historical attractions. At first I had thought these cards were for little boys but, when I saw a pair of uniformed soldiers writing on them, realised they were aimed at enlisted soldiers doing their military service. Reassuring your mother you were still alive by sending her a postcard printed with images of extreme violence struck me as, to say the least, terribly odd. Were there, I wondered, similar postcards for nuclear technicians, featuring images of little men in lab coats running screaming from distant atomic blasts; or miners trapped in a collapsed tunnel staring gravely at a dead canary? You could accuse Turks of a lot of things — of being paranoid and pessimistic, of taking themselves way too seriously — but you could never say they were afraid of death's grim certainty.

At the mosque by the pools was a market in a big tent, cordoned off from the crowds on the street. Here you could buy tapes of the Koran, sermons by imams and various books appealing to the insatiable Turkish appetite for conspiracy. Conspiracy theories are as Turkish as sweet tea or the evil eye and in my time in the country I was to find myself repulsed and fascinated by them in equal measure. Impossibly complex and assuming an almost superhuman intelligence on the part of various world leaders, Turkish conspiracy theorists make Grassy Knoll advocates and UFO internet cranks look like editorial writers for *The New York Times*. (Indeed, in Turkey they often *are* editorial writers.) Conspiracies encompass every aspect of Turkish life and are shared willingly and without embarrassment: from the standard lectures about the Jewish robots that flew the planes into the World Trade Center, to more imaginative efforts, like the rumours that US soldiers were harvesting the organs of dead Iraqis for sale on the black market, an insanity that was reported as fact by at least one major newspaper and later became a plotline in one of the most successful Turkish films of all time.

As crazy as Turkish political fantasies undoubtedly are, much can be blamed on the fact that they are modelled, in part, on Turkish political reality. Take the case of possibly the most cherished of all Turkish conspiracies — the "Deep State", a shadowy alliance of politicians, mafia and senior public servants who between them (supposedly) control the Turkish economy through a system of blackmail, standover tactics and political assassinations. The Deep State sounds like something they teach you in a UFO cult: "When the aliens came fifty billion years ago they became the 'Deep State' and they look just like you and me." But then in 1996, near the small town of Susurluk on the west coast, there was a car accident. In it three people were killed including the heroin trafficker, wanted murderer and fugitive ultra-right nationalist, Abdullah Çatlı, the former Deputy Chief of Police of Istanbul (a famous leftist) and Çatlı's mistress, a beauty queen turned mafia assassin. The only survivor was a powerful Kurdish MP and tribal leader from Urfa. Found in the car were diplomatic credentials given to Çatlı as well as numerous officially-issued fake passports and ID cards, a stash of US currency and a large collection of guns and silencers belonging to the Interior Ministry. Suddenly the Deep State didn't seem so crazy and the "Susurluk Scandal", as it came to be known, seemed to confirm the worst fears of many Turks: that their government was using the mafia as a private intelligence agency and hit squad. The only problem was no one seemed able to say which part of the government and to what end. Islamists, leftists, nationalists and everyone in between all accuse one another of being in control of the Deep State, which only makes everything more complicated and tends to reinforce the notion that conspiracy theories, like star signs, can mean whatever you want them to.

I inspected some of the books, many of which I had already seen in Istanbul, their titles translated for me by Mehmet. There was one that had been banned for questioning Atatürk's Turkishness — much favoured by fundamentalists who despised the man for crushing religious opposition to the secular state. Another had an amateurish but rather sinister cover featuring an image of Jesus crucified on an Egyptian ankh, the only word I recognised being "Illuminati". Next to those was a small stack by an author who needed no introduction, his distinctive features gracing the cover just below the title of his best-loved work, *Mein Kampf*.

The three of us walked back to our hotel, fate and limited accommodation options seeing to it that we were all staying at the same place. In the foyer were a row of plastic peach trees in pots, plastic peaches sitting in the plastic dirt to give the illusion of ripeness. The television was playing a film of the life of Abraham that I recognised. It had been made by a fundamentalist American Christian organisation and was sold in Australia via television advertisements and a toll-free phone number. Dubbed into Turkish it became here, in distant Urfa, a suitably pious Ramadan entertainment for good Muslims. I was struck by the fact that even as the world grew smaller it didn't grow any less strange.

While Madelon and Pieter tried to engage the humourless receptionist in conversation I sat in a couch printed with daisies and watched bubbles rise through an empty fish tank. Urfa was a puzzling and lonely place: cities this old always were. Thinking about all the countless layers beneath my feet, of people and their forgotten voices, made me a little panicked, like hearing how far the stars are from the earth and suddenly feeling small, useless and a little futile.

I decided to call Tevfik. When he answered it sounded as if he had just woken, though it wasn't late. "Hey, baby," he said, in his dated beatnik patois. For a while we talked about the east. He warned me to be careful about looking at women ("The men will just kill you, man") and answered all my obscure questions. Once again I was impressed by the scope of his knowledge, and wondered why he had never made more of his gifts and his learning.

"I saw my father recently," he said.

"How did it go?"

He sighed. "OK, not too bad, but my father is a very strange man, Brendan. Did I ever tell you that he has an obsession with Adolf Hitler?"

"Ah, no."

"When I was a child he had his portrait on the wall and he used to make me salute it every morning. When he wanted to discipline me he would make me head-butt the wall underneath it."

I laughed in spite of myself.

"I know," he said, resignedly. "It's crazy. My father is a crazy man, but I still love him. What can you do?"

There was an awkward silence as I considered an appropriate response. Tevfik spoke first. "You like Urfa?" he asked.

I told him it was one of the most beautiful places I had ever seen, but that it was also slightly melancholy.

"You can feel it, man, can't you? Urfa is so beautiful but so sad it can kill you. I mean, *kill you*, man. What is the saying in English? Devastatingly beautiful? Well that's what the east is, man — devastating."

Chapter 7

Madelon proved herself to be deceptively spry. Leaping over the freeway barrier with her backpack attached, she joined Pieter and me to make a bolt down the dusty highway to the bus, already revving its engines in threat of departure. On board, dawn faces stared at us, pleading and indignant, a fog of instant coffee, feet and *kolonya* testament to the privations of an overnight journey. From up the back Madelon's Fellini laugh suddenly filled the cabin. A dozen pairs of puffy, resentful eyes followed her passage down the corridor in the company of the porter. "I have been told," she said, affecting an aristocratic accent, "that I arm naught to sit up the back in the event that I arm … *molested.*" She lost control, her laughter spilling forth like the payout on a poker machine.

We were on the bus to Mardin, a small city east of Urfa, famed for its beauty and the vestiges of an ancient Christian culture, now all but gone. Mardin had been recommended to me by Margaret, an old American hippy artist living in Istanbul and friend of Hüseyin's, who I had met the day before I had left for the east; and to her I am grateful because of Mardin I shall say, in advance, I have nothing bad to report, other than the fact that, after four days, I had to leave.

Mardin is not large: hardly a city at all. It clings to the side of a yellow, bell-shaped mountain that rises out of the cotton plains, the streets a bewitching knot of steep alleys, almost every building carved from the same chalky, biscuit-coloured limestone. Mardin was a city of exquisite details; you could see the care that had gone into its construction and the pride in its preservation. Almost every door and window frame was enlivened by sinuous vine-like carvings and interiors shielded from the street by elaborate wrought-iron grills. Garbage men collected rubbish using grumpy donkeys that clopped up the streets laden with steel bins, their necks and bridles decorated with ropes of rainbow-coloured beads, like reluctant Mardi-Gras revellers. There was something sensual, almost decadent, about Mardin. Every second shop seemed to be selling either candy or gold. Strings of walnuts dipped in grape syrup hung like fragrant stalactites from shop awnings. In jewellery store windows, necklaces of gold filigree strung with turquoise beads lay stretched out in long strings. Together we bought tins of cherry juice and drank them in the shade of a stepped alley, looking at the chequerboard of plains below.

"Ohh," said Pieter, speaking for us all, "I think it is fairy beewt-a-full."

After finding a hotel we walked together through the bazaar which, in contrast to Urfa, was sedate and relatively empty. On each side of the alley, the stalls faced one another, many unmanned, the proprietors apparently unconcerned about theft. There was a stall for repairing donkey saddles (made of stiffened carpet) as well as a felt maker and a man hammering copper coffee pots, finished vessels stacked in shining pagodas behind him. Between piles of fruit and vegetables a blacksmith's workshop was a black hole in the colour. Smiling shyly, children approached us, taking our hands to walk a few steps before running, giggling, back to their friends. At one stall, evil-eye bras were stacked into a big cone. Madelon lifted one to her chest, wiggling indecently while I mimed trying to grasp her breasts. The shopkeeper, unsure how he should react, stared gravely at the ground.

"Hoo hoo hoo!" Madelon's laugh echoed through the narrow alley.

In the shaded courtyard of the Great Mosque, boys with wet feet shuffled on high wooden sandals from the ablutions fountain to the prayer hall, like Japanese geishas, the cuffs of their jeans rolled up. The Seljuk minaret was exceptional: salmon pink, carved with mazes of abstract, Kufic script and leaf-shaped calligraphy.

Pieter pointed skyward. "Look at the doom."

"The what?"

"The doom," he said exasperatedly, pointing at the dome topping the minaret, "I am lorfing thees doom."

For some time we sat in the courtyard watching the boys in their sandals, the girls talking shyly in the corner. A caretaker approached, offering us tea and coffee. We were taken aback. "But Ramadan?" This, he assured us, was of no concern. We were guests. Out of some misguided sense of courtesy, we refused. The caretaker gave us a tour. The mosque, he explained, had once been a church, and the courtyard fountain the baptismal font.

"I do not think he is cow-rekt," said Pieter, adjusting his glasses. "I think this was something else."

"Perhaps," said Madelon, "it was a bidet."

"Noo," said Pieter, peering closely at the structure. "I do not think so."

Madelon bit her lip in deference to the worshippers inside.

Losing ourselves in the alleys we came to a school. In the central courtyard children ran in demented circles around a pair of smoking teachers seemingly oblivious to the chaos. Gesturing with their cigarettes they signalled for us to enter. Upstairs, off a magnificently carved colonnade, the pandemonium of the classrooms was no improvement on that in the courtyard. Running through their rows of desks in giddy currents, the children entertained themselves as they saw fit.

"Where are all the teachers?" asked Madelon.

"Downstairs, smoo-king, I think," said Pieter.

As we tentatively entered one of the rooms the children erupted as if we were the Beatles. There were none of the bedraggled urchins of Urfa here: all were well fed and strikingly good looking, their blue-and-white uniforms neat and clean, their fancy lace collars hand-embroidered with flowers, crescent moons and the alphabet. Each girl had her hair pulled back in a pair of shining plaits. We called for quiet and they responded with an obedience unheard of in their Western counterparts. Some of the cheekier boys stood to give a soldier's salute.

Our impromptu English lesson soon dissolved into a frenzied call-and-response: "YES please!" "NO thank you!" "My name IS!" "Kan-ga-roo!" The classroom was small but not overcrowded and more beautiful than any school had a right to be. The cornices, doors and window frames were all intricately carved. Small panels of stained glass dappled the room in colour and an ornate niche containing a small cupboard was chiselled into the back wall, crowned by a decorative tiara of stone. Eventually, a vaguely senior-looking teacher appeared and quietened the class. As we left, the mob returned to their original anarchy, hanging between the bars of the windows to wave goodbye and call to us: *Yes! No! Kangaroo!*

Mardin is home to some of the world's oldest churches: the dates on the bronze plaques by the doors listed years in the four and five hundreds. Very few Christians, however, had survived the upheavals of Mardin's recent history. Most had been killed during the First World War or left for Syria, Lebanon, America and everywhere else. There were probably no more than a dozen Christian families remaining. At the Forty Martyrs Church the caretaker opened the ancient door to the fortified complex to reveal a little Garden of Eden: his wife in one corner spinning wool from a big pile of fleece, his children chasing each other through the citrus trees. The church was still distinguished but all its treasures had disappeared. The only remaining notes of colour were the carpets and bright, naïve icons hanging from the walls on loose cloth, embroidered with sequins and fake jewels. "Kitsch," sniffed Pieter.

"But very sad kitsch," said Madelon.

The day passed quickly. In the old manner, a cannon was fired into the cotton plains, announcing the end of the fast. Our meal was exceptionally good and the restaurant served wine which, although dreadful, we drank simply because it was available. On the terrace, the black plains of Syria in the distance, we discussed many things. The bombing in Diyarbakır was still big news. "Why would they do these things to their own people?" said Madelon. "It makes me so terribly distressed."

"Will you go to Diyarbakır?" I asked.

"Noo," said Pieter. "I think it is a little bit dan-jeroos. And I am not sure there is really so much to see." He paused. "Will you?"

I said I hadn't made up my mind.

Slowly, the conversation grew more personal.

"I have never been to Australia," said Pieter, "but I did once have a girlfriend from New Zealand."

For a moment I wondered whether he meant "girlfriend" as in, "Some girlfriends and I are going to spend all Saturday night eating ice cream and watching Meg Ryan movies."

He continued, "Yes, she was a fairy nice girl, but we broke up. I met a Greek girl instead."

The revelation that Pieter was not gay had been unexpected, but was in some ways the least curious thing about him. Ever since I had met them, Pieter and Madelon had intrigued me and I had spent the last few days concocting elaborate scenarios to explain their unlikely pairing: she was his biological mother who had given him up at birth and had now reluctantly agreed to go to Turkey to rekindle their relationship; he was her nurse who had agreed to accompany her on one final journey before she died of an inoperable brain cancer; they were a con-artist team preying on gullible tourists in remote parts of the world, befriending them before drugging their meals, robbing them and running off to buy jewellery and cheese rolls on their credit cards. One possibility that refused to die, a possibility that defied all logic but still woke me at 3am, feeling distraught and violated, was that they might be ... though surely they weren't ... lovers? The truth was less scandalous but, perhaps, just as odd.

"I was on a plane to Syria," said Madelon in her high, fluted voice. "Then, suddenly, I began to panic. 'What am I doing,' I thought, 'going to Syria on my own? I must be crazy!' Well, the flight went via Brussels. So we arrive and this big bald man sits down across the aisle from me and we started talking."

"I in-fighted her to ah-cum-pony me for deen-er," said Pieter.

"So, I said, 'Thank you very much,' because I hate eating alone. And we have been travelling together now for many years."

Over the next decade, Pieter and Madelon had escorted one another on journeys through India, China, the Middle East and, now, Turkey. Despite this, however, and regardless of the fact they lived within only a few hours' drive of one another, neither had been to the other's home.

"Why do you not visit one another at home?" I asked.

"I have my own friends," said Madelon. "I never feel that I have to entertain him and Belgium is, well, so *Belgian*."

"Besides," said Pieter, "her friends are fairy *old*."

This time it was Madelon's turn to stare while Pieter laughed. With that we drank our wine and I thought how content I felt and how glad I was to have met Pieter and Madelon. When they disappeared without warning in the early morning two days later, leaving a farewell note written in green ink under my door, I was genuinely saddened by the prospect that I should never see them again.

Chapter 8

The four days I spent in Mardin stay with me as a sensation of overwhelming happiness. Everything in that city seemed calculated to delight. I felt no pressure here; no need to play the tourist, or worse, journalist. My days were occupied by nothing more than purposeless wandering, every turn bringing some new and unexpected detail. I am willing to accept that the overwhelming sense of peace and welcome I felt in Mardin may have been an illusion — this region had suffered as badly as any other in the southeast and only five years prior was considered too dangerous to visit. But fantasy or not, nothing could upset the sense of well being I felt in these streets, making my decision to go to Diyarbakır all the more difficult.

Normally, I'm not easily frightened off visiting supposedly dangerous destinations. From my experience their reputations are often exaggerated and spring from a particular kind of Western arrogance that assumes tourists are the unique targets of violence, that out there somewhere are thousands of headbanded Omars and Abdullahs plotting the best way to blow up a bus or poison the punch at the luau. In reality, tourists, specifically Western tourists, are comparatively rarely the victims of crime or terrorism. In far greater danger are the people who serve them, people for whom travelling to dangerous places is not a risqué amusement but an unfortunate necessity of poverty. Why then did Diyarbakır make me so nervous? It wasn't as if I hadn't had close calls in the past: the year before in India I had narrowly avoided being blown up in the holy city of Varansai and then again, a couple of months later, in Mumbai. But a bomb in India seemed like little more than local colour, part of an indivisible fabric of sub-continental insanity as simultaneously confronting and unremarkable as the snake charmers, lepers and the three-year-old beggar girl with a leg growing out of her forehead. Turkey was far more earnest and solemn; a bomb here seemed an altogether more serious affair, and as I stepped onto the *dolmuş* to Diyarbakır the various warnings I had received ("Diyarbakır no good!") rang in my ears. Just as loud, however, were the words of the girl in Harran, and I knew I would be an idiot to have come this far and not see what was undoubtedly the most infamous city in the country.

The prelude to my entry to Diyarbakır did little to ease my sense of foreboding. After less than an hour of driving we arrived at the first army checkpoint. From behind rows of sandbags and stone walls, cut with peep holes, soldiers aimed machine-guns at the mini-bus. Seeing this I was suddenly struck by the seriousness of the situation — the only person who didn't have to be here was me. One soldier in a bullet-proof vest, gripping the butt of his weapon, put his hand through the window and demanded our ID cards. As is my practice in such situations, I reverted immediately to a childhood state. With great earnestness, as though being graded on my efficiency and deportment, I handed my passport to the front where, to my disappointment, the soldier barely glanced at it before handing it back to the hand relay which returned it to me. The second checkpoint was far less lax. Dutifully, everyone presented their ID cards and the soldier disappeared to register each one. No exception was made for me and slightly paranoid fears concerning the validity of my visa began to take hold. Here the defences were even more menacing. Armoured personnel carriers formed a wall on either side of the bus and the road was laid with rows of long metal spikes, the scene lent some levity by the appearance in the field behind of an enormous bush of olive branches supported on four spindly legs by an otherwise invisible donkey. Eventually the guard returned. Our identification was handed back through the window and we were allowed to continue on our way.

The decrepit Diyarbakır *otogar* was the first hint that this was not a city many came to for sightseeing. All the facilities one usually associated with the Spartan yet functional bus station were here either notable by their absence or in an appalling state of repair. In defiance of the stares of the other passengers I caught a bus into the centre of the city, marked by the appearance of the famous black basalt walls that had once barricaded the old town and a sign translating as something along the lines of "Diyarbakır City Council wishes you a Happy Ramadan". The sign was crowned by a black papier-mâché turret supporting a large watermelon, the fruit being, or so I was to later learn, Diyarbakır's number one crop. I was starting to get the feeling this was not a town working overtime to sell itself.

The man at the tourist office was uncommonly helpful. Insisting that he carry my bag, he walked me to a hotel where, or so he assured me, he had placed a German who had arrived from Mardin a week prior. Excitedly he asked whether I had met him. "He was from Berlin," he said.

I shook my head.

"Tall, with an earring?"

"No." He looked crestfallen. "It's quiet after the bombs," I said, consolingly.

"Quiet before the bombs," he replied.

After checking in I went for a walk. The centre of Diyarbakır seemed bustling, relatively prosperous and in almost every respect, to quote the green-eyed boy in Harran, normal. There were the usual array of mobile phone shops, internet cafés and racks of fake sportswear. There were electronics stores and market stalls selling backpacks featuring ill-defined cartoon characters with names like "Bulky Mean", "Beauty Lady" and "Double Grill". There were even one or two open kebab shops, meat twirling brazenly in their windows. So far, Diyarbakır looked very much like every other city in the country; which meant either it was an inadequate symbol of all that was wrong with modern Turkey, or the whole country was screwed.

At the Great Mosque, very old and quite unlike anything else in Turkey, I stood in the busy courtyard and stared at the carvings. The stone was ripe with vegetation, the columns a crazy tea party of zig-zags, checks and interlocking patterns, no two the same. The stone was dirty, the carvings as rotten as old wood. As I took a photo I was immediately surrounded by a dozen thin young children shouting their familiar chorus. "Mahnee, mahnee."

"No money."

"*Yes*, mahnee."

It was like a Marx Brothers routine now.

A child, his face a mess of scabby red blisters, took my arm and, with surprising force, pulled me away. Like one half of a wrestling tag team, he released his grip just as the carpet vendor secured his. The dealer began to speak in German. I attempted to disabuse him. "Ah, Austria!" he cried, forcing me towards his shop by the entrance to the courtyard. Fighting off the old man with hollow promises of return, I made my escape into the alleys behind the mosque. Here was a bazaar, but with none of the charm of Urfa or Mardin. Stalls were plastic tarpaulins, the goods on offer cheap and relentlessly utilitarian. There was little colour and I looked in vain for something special, something that I could point to and say *that* came from Diyarbakır. Only the pyramids of watermelons suggested that anything at all was produced in this city.

The deeper I walked into the centre of the old town the more chaotic the street life became: the gutters filled with garbage; the paving fell apart beneath my feet; many of the children were shockingly thin and bedraggled. As I passed they stopped pushing their wheelbarrows full of bricks, put down their buckets of car parts, and stared.

At the walls, family groups sat in the shade of an ancient iron gate, selling bits of salvaged metal lain out on a blanket. On the grass a miniature battle was unfolding: a group of little boys argued with one who stood alone, slashing a blue-handled kitchen knife menacingly in their direction. I climbed the steps and walked along the walls. They were thick and very black, especially against the warm blue day. At first they seemed ominous: the turrets were full of garbage and human shit, the paths patrolled by packs of teenage boys darting conspiratorially behind fallen battlements. But after a while the sense of menace lifted. Around every corner couples canoodled; friends sat in intimate conspiracies. As I climbed one parapet, arriving in a bottle-strewn wasteland, a girl in a headscarf drew back from her boyfriend, as terrified at my sudden appearance as she was grateful for my rapid retreat.

Within the boundaries of the old city the streets were disorderly but not chaotic. New parks lined the walls, smart light fittings and benches punctuated the trimmed grass. On the other side, however, beyond the confines of the old city, the *gecekondular* spread out: huts of concrete bricks, their roofs weighed down with tyres and stones, small yards with chicken coops and piles of oil cans. Brightened with coats of blue and aquamarine, their roofs laden with neat bundles of firewood and fleece, ready for spinning, the houses seemed homely and not unpleasant. Yet taken as a whole they became a sea bed of dereliction and disorder rising to engulf the city, making the designer lamps and the new park benches look incongruous and futile. Symbols of all the problems and divisions of modern Turkey didn't come more convenient than this.

For some time I walked, before climbing down to continue my wanderings along the main road, hugging the inside of the walls.

Overhead, black military helicopters criss-crossed the skies, flying low, as though looking for something. I could see it would be easy to become paranoid in this city. Following a sign to a church, I arrived in a shambolic residential area. The alleys were narrow; the buildings appeared on the verge of collapse. In a wasteland, some barefoot children ran, throwing stones while others jumped on the wire frame of a stripped mattress. As I walked, a stone clipped my ear. I turned and glared but the children stood their ground. In Diyarbakır you made your fun where you found it.

The church, one of the last still functioning in the city, was enclosed by high walls. I banged on the huge wooden door, shiny with age, and was ushered inside by an elderly caretaker. The courtyard was peaceful and clean. Small fruit trees grew against the walls and a little girl rode in circles on a tricycle in the centre. On a seat by the gate the old man was fast asleep, returned now to the position from which he had been roused. The church was locked. I waited for some time, watching the girl on the tricycle, unwilling to wake the old man. Finally a young man appeared clutching a rubber hose. Without acknowledging me he washed the courtyard. I began to have the strange sensation of being invisible. Eventually he stopped and, without a word, unlocked the church. I was surprised to find the interior was round, its roof a high, perfectly proportioned dome. There were naïve paintings on the wall, the same as in Mardin, but older. Finally the man spoke.

"Where are you from?" he asked, in Turkish.

I told him.

"Ah, Austria."

As I walked through the backstreets people stared, some stopping in their tracks to follow my progress with a twist of the head, as if I were nine feet tall and wearing a hooped petticoat. I am accustomed to being gawked at: I am a large and obvious target for the curiosity of people from cultures free of the Anglo prohibition on public staring.

But this wasn't the kind of curious staring people did in places like India, as though they would have stared had you been there or not. This was purposeful staring, resentful and suspicious, and I soon retreated to the comforting bustle of a main road.

For some time I walked without aim, past the rainbow bundles of plastic shoes and stacks of silver cookware, their shine dulled by the dust settled on them. A photo development shop displayed personalised versions of the postcards you could buy on the street: portraits of serious young policemen and soldiers — some clutching bouquets of roses, others firing machine-guns — superimposed against sangria sunsets and rows of snapping Turkish flags. Some portraits had been superimposed over local attractions, causing eyes to hover eerily in the streams of waterfalls or the lintels of Roman temples. Others, more dramatically, posed next to lions and snarling wolves, the symbol of Turkey and of Turkish nationalism. There were, as I have already noted, many things that struck me as odd about these postcards. Yet surely the oddest was the fact that in a city where people were sending vans full of explosives to police stations, you could buy on any street corner these strange, sentimental pictures of the same boy-soldiers you were doing your best to kill. Conflict and terror had, it seemed, become just another commodity here, a dull economic fact as banal and unremarkable as the stacks of plastic shoes.

Kurds were in the majority in Diyarbakır and it showed. Faces here were ruddier, features sharper and hungrier. Their outfits were modest but distinctive. The men wore flat caps and tailored vests, like thirties tap-dancers; the women white lacy veils tied in front to hang in a loose bib of material that spread across their shoulders and down their chests, like fencing undergarments. Most didn't bother to cover their face but some, in the manner of surgeons or bandits, pulled the scarf over their noses. Others let it rest just above the top lip, leaving a dramatic diamond of bare skin. Embroidered on the rims of the scarves were clumps of little beads, like electric blue mulberries, or sprinkles of orange caviar. Under flowered skirts they wore baggy pants in matching material or flannel pyjama bottoms. They were much less colourful than the Arabs in Urfa but wilder than the Turkish women: as they shopped they screamed at stall holders and sat in the gutters or squatted against walls to take their breath and count their change.

I walked on. In a pastry shop a man wearing silly yellow goggles fried oversized doughnuts, the mixture dropped from a big hose held by a small boy who stood precariously on the bench over a vat of oil. When I went to take a photo, the baker lifted one of the metal rods he used for removing the pastries and slashed it in my direction, making it clear I should get out. Shocked into submission, I almost bolted down the street to an area where a clutch of metal workshops stood by a small rococo mosque. Inside, a solitary man kneeled under the chandelier, facing the wall, praying. For a while I sat up the back, savouring the quiet. His prayers finished, the man stood up and walked to the door to gather his shoes. Seeing me he turned, shoes in hand. "Christian?" he asked.

"Yes."

Hearing this he began to deliver a clearly well-rehearsed lecture. "Torah," he said, counting on his fingers, "Bible, Koran." Upon reaching "Koran" he folded the first two fingers down and gestured throwing them away. It was a lecture I had been subjected to by fundamentalists in other countries, the notion being that the relatively recent appearance of the Koran was inarguable proof for its infallibility, an argument that suggested the Book of Mormon had made redundant the combined wisdom of Moses, Jesus and Mohammed, and the works of L. Ron Hubbard were the final word in spiritual enlightenment. In my hurry to get away, I tripped on a steel grate being welded by a child on the pavement. Without expression he stared at me; annoyed or grateful, perhaps, for the unexpected pause in his labour.

Deeper I walked into the black basalt lanes of the old city. Here it was quiet and clean, the cobblestone pavement sloping into the centre to form a gutter. The doors and many of the walls were painted in a bright turquoise blue, strikingly beautiful against the dark stone. The door of the old Armenian church was locked. At the time of its building it had been one of the largest cathedrals in the world. Now it sat in ruins behind tall walls, its portal topped by two stylised lions, pressing their cheeks together like cute children. A passer-by, noting my attempts to find an entry, banged on a neighbouring door. A woman emerged and the two had a long discussion concerning my plight. It was all to no avail. I thanked them and the pair made gestures of apology as I walked away.

Dusk was approaching and everywhere people ran grabbing last-minute provisions for the Ramadan meal. Metal carts along the street balanced round trays of hot meat sprinkled in sprigs of broad-leaf parsley. On closer inspection the meat proved to be sheep's heads, a Ramadan speciality. The heads lay on the trays with their little teeth on the end of their long snouts meeting in the centre to form a macabre grinning circle, their black eyes staring hideously. The stall holder motioned that I should buy one. For a moment I considered the possibility: the image of myself sitting alone in a hotel room eating a head seeming a fitting end to a day in Diyarbakır. I settled for a photograph.

Seeing me, a man emerged from behind a neighbouring pastry stall and began babbling wildly in what I think was Kurdish. He smiled broadly and excitedly in the way of the mentally deficient. Out of some misguided civility I smiled back. All at once, he grabbed my arm very hard, laughing, grinning and babbling in my face. The only words I understood were "Israel", "Sharon" and "George Boosh". It was all I could do to say "*tamam*", the Turkish word for "OK", over and over again while trying to unclamp his hands from my arm. Noticing my dilemma another man approached. He was old and wore a brown three-piece suit. In one hand he fiddled with wooden beads.

"Can I help you?" he asked in English. "No, thank you," I lied, tugging at my arm while the cretin continued his rant. I smiled at the old man as one in a mutual conspiracy of social embarrassment. He gestured at me with his worry beads. "Who are you?" he asked, suspiciously. "Where are you from?" In my idiotic way I tried to give him answers to his questions, all the while attempting to free myself from the cretin who had not paused for a moment his incomprehensible political rant: "George Boosh ... no good!"

"What do you want? What are you doing here?" demanded the old man.

"I'm from Australia," I said feebly, and, with a final violent gesture, secured my freedom. As I ran across the road, it occurred to me that I looked every inch the police informant or whatever it was the old man had taken me for.

That evening, with every television and radio in the city echoing the news that the time to eat had come, I ventured out to find a meal. Steaming heads sat in restaurant windows. Next to those, piles of skulls picked clean by previous diners were stacked in decorative pyramids like trophies. On a big square near the hotel I ate something more familiar under the pitying gaze of the other diners. Looking about at the emptying restaurant I was suddenly overwhelmed by a sense of alienation, an acute awareness of my aloneness in this place and an attendant desire to either fly home immediately or get more drunk than I had ever been.

Earlier, not far from the square, I had noticed a promising doorway lit with an advertisement for Efes, Turkey's only indigenous brand of beer. Against all likelihood it appeared to be open, the entrance leading down a flight of stairs to a long corridor lit in ultraviolet light, the walls lined with suggestive pictures of broad-thighed girls clutching microphones. At the end of the corridor was a set of plastic doors, like those at an abattoir. From within, music played and coloured lights strobed across the opaque plastic. I pushed open the door. A fat man sat on a stool near the entrance; he stared impassively as I entered. Sitting in a tight clump at one of the tables were a group of four girls. On the other side of the room three men sat at separate tables staring at a stage furnished with a Casio keyboard and a microphone, the coloured lights rolling across the empty stage.

It was a scene of indescribable despair.

From behind an empty refrigerator cabinet a bow-tied waiter appeared; the notepad in his hand and crisp linen napkin slung over his wrist seemed calculated only to emphasise the absolute decrepitude of the surrounds. For some time I persevered, drinking beer and writing notes under the disco lights, watching as one of the girls disappeared into an unlit back corner where another man, unnoticed until now, was waiting in the dark.

I wouldn't say I was shocked to discover a fully operational brothel in a town like Diyarbakır in the middle of Ramadan, so much as I was disappointed and slightly confused. In my imagination brothels were red velvet affairs with a battered chaise longue in the corner and a fat woman called Mabel behind a desk, filing her nails over an antique telephone. This place couldn't manage a bead curtain or a few nervous sailors. The girls were not even especially tarty: one wore jeans and a flowing hippy blouse, another a pink tracksuit and velvet high heels. They looked like cruise ship divorcees on shore leave. Where they came from was anybody's guess.

Many of the prostitutes in Turkey were Russian or Ukrainian, their nickname "Natashas". On my first arrival in Istanbul the visa queue at the airport had been a scrum of skinny girls in leather pants and hooker fur coats, dyed blue and pink. Since then, however, the government had cracked down and Natashas were in short supply. These girls had a vaguely Central Asian look, Georgian or Azeri, perhaps, but they could just as easily have been poor rural immigrants like so many others in this city. It was hard to imagine anyone with a choice coming to Diyarbakır.

Another beer and I could stand no more. As I walked out the door one of the girls rose from the table and strolled into the darkened corner, eyeing me suspiciously. In the flood-lit square, thin, dirty boys played soccer by the huge basalt gate. Nearby, an Adidas boutique, a precarious outpost of international capitalism, glowed in the dark: its air-conditioned whiteness, the precision and order of its window display, looked utterly incongruous in these surroundings, as if it had been left by mistake. In a liquor store I tried to buy some beer but none was cold. The shopkeeper smiled apologetically and explained he could sell beer during Ramadan but only if it was not refrigerated. In my room I switched on the television and found a horrifically violent Syrian soap opera: little volcanoes of red gore exploding from the chests of women in full chador as they were machine-gunned by savage militia. I settled down to watch, intrigued by the gruesomeness of it all, only to discover, for reasons which will always remain a mystery, that my bed was sopping wet.

Chapter 9

It is quite possible that had I stayed longer in Diyarbakır I would have discovered a different side to the city: a cheerful and friendly side, a hopeful and welcoming side, perhaps a small but thriving Latin Quarter or struggling alternative music scene. As it was, Diyarbakır had made me feel very unwelcome, and I was more than happy to make everyone comfortable by leaving town. As I waited for the mini-bus that would take me from the city I watched the fighter jets from the nearby airforce base pass over an enormous fibreglass watermelon. Every city in Turkey, it seems, has one of these sculptures. Like giant mini-golf props they sit on traffic islands or at the entrance to the *otogar*, a view of the world from the perspective of the Incredible Shrinking Man: oranges the size of compact cars; tea urns like oil rigs; evil, dinosaurian birds. As the jets moved overhead they made the watermelon pulse and rattle, like an alien pod about to hatch.

In a large walled paddock by the *otogar* a livestock auction was in progress. With every sonic boom the sheep — their tails as fat as their black, conical heads — ran in panicked currents down the street, beaten back into submission by shepherds in flat caps or loose purple scarves, rolled at their foreheads like women fresh from the shower. On the wall of the paddock a handsome, bare-foot teenage boy sat in a classical pose, a huge knife by his side tucked, pirate style, into a thick leather belt. "For the sheep?" I asked, gesturing to the knife. He nodded solemnly but, befitting one who cut off balls for a living, would make no conversation. I looked across at the fibreglass sculpture. Diyarbakır really needed a good PR company: watermelons alone were never going to be enough to sell this town.

The mini-bus was an unusually cheerful affair, each seat sporting a bright yellow cover printed with a 1950s comic book woman pressing a row of sharp red nails to her face. Ringing the three ceiling lights were long green tassels, strung with beads and multi-coloured plastic jewels tied at their ends. In the front seat by the driver sat a pair of silent Kurdish sheikhs in matching outfits who, although possibly not related, had by dint of time, and a no doubt limited gene pool, been granted an eerie symmetry. As we moved off the jewels clinked together, the sonic booms moved through us, the sheikhs stared mutely at something unseen and the journey acquired a certain hallucinatory quality not wholly inappropriate for the leaving of a city as disquieting and inscrutable as Diyarbakır.

The landscape to Siverek was familiar: once-dead fields lush with melon vines and cotton, the monotony enlivened by the pickers who rose and fell in the distance like Japanese water features. The wait in town for my connecting bus was mercifully short. A dusty strip of profound ugliness, Siverek's relentless desolation was enlivened only by the juvenile compensation of a large sign at the garage advertising "UFUK PETROL". Eventually, the bus did come; the landscape around Siverek revealing a barrenness unmatched by anything else I was to see in Turkey. On either side of the road empty brown fields were punctuated only by a hail of melon-sized stones. Some had been gathered and piled into walls or little pyramids in the centre of the fields, in preparation perhaps for imminent irrigation from the nearby dam, although it was impossible to visualise anything growing here. Occasionally a flock of goats appeared, but what they ate in this wasteland was a mystery. In the distance, shepherds lounged in huts made of stones, small fires drawing thin trails of smoke on the blue horizon.

At the military checkpoint I handed over my passport and watched the gentle motion of a wrecked car suspended from a pole over the road, a warning to speeding drivers. By the time we reached the Atatürk Dam I was hot and the water looked cool and inviting. I considered swimming but soon the barge that would take us to the other side of the man-made lake arrived. The water was clear and mineral-looking, a striking counterpoint to the big caramel mountains that ringed us all around.

I had been warned about Khata by a tour operator in Urfa. "This town," he had said, struggling for the right words, "is a ... shit town." My arrival did little to contradict his assessment. Although it must be said that Khata was hardly a town, just a settlement that had grown, losing everything that made a small place beautiful but gaining everything that made a big place ugly. Recently, oil had been discovered nearby, flooding Khata with outside money, little of it, I surmised, utilised in any program of urban beautification. At the end of my journey through Turkey, well after I returned home, I would remember Khata as one might a period of disease or the funeral of a close friend.

It is possible that my intense dislike of Khata had been exaggerated by the difficulty I experienced in finding transport to my ultimate destination: Mount Nemrut. One of the few "sights" I was determined to see in the east, Mount Nemrut has haunted me since I was a child. Commissioned by the mad God-king, Antiochus I Epiphanes, ruler of the Seleucid Empire, a client state of the Romans, the huge stone heads staring out from the top of their mountain are among the most enigmatic monuments of the ancient world, their image adorning a thousand aging posters in the offices of travel agents worldwide.

The typical way to see Nemrut is on a dawn or dusk tour, an avenue I was reluctant to go down. Like feeding scared fish or rubbing the belly of some "lucky" sculpture, sunset and sunrise tours to mountain tops are one of the standard clichés of tourism and are, from bitter personal experience, nearly always disasters. My desire to see Nemrut on my own terms, however, was balanced by my need to leave Khata as soon as possible.

As I banged on the door of an apparently deserted hotel a man in a van drove up and commanded me to get in. We drove a few blocks down the street and pulled into a driveway. "This is my hotel," he said, unloading my bags.

"How much to take me to Nemrut?" I asked.

Without replying he led me into a grimy office and began a well-worn spiel, pointing to a map drawn on faded, curling card. I interrupted him and repeated my original question. He named an outrageous price. "You will find none better," he shouted as I walked out the door.

Several false leads followed as I ran in flustered circles around Khata. Eventually, I found a man lingering in a hotel foyer willing to take me for almost half the price. Old and thin, with one milky blind eye, he looked like the kind of guy who opened the door to haunted castles. "I cannot take you now," he said. "Do you want to go at sunrise?"

"I don't know. Is it worth it?"

In response he said nothing, only rolled his one good eye.

I gave up and returned to my smiling extortionist, bargaining him down to a modest rip-off. The sun was growing low so, without further delay, I was shoved into a van driven by a surprisingly stylish young man with a gruff manner, wearing a crisp polo shirt and designer European sunglasses.

I introduced myself.

"Hello," he said, not taking his eyes from the road, saying nothing more until we pulled into a graveyard on the outskirts of town.

"Do you mind if we stop for a moment?" he asked, a moot point, I thought, considering we had already done so. Leaping from the van he raced into the field of tombstones. With his hands held skywards he crouched on his haunches in a manner I would have found suspicious had I not known he was praying. The day was Friday, the holy day and reserved for remembering the dead. All across Turkey people were praying for their ancestors in the same way. As he got back in the car he thumbed behind us, towards the tombstones. "That's my brother's grave," he said, revving the engine. "He died in a car crash last year. And that," he said, pointing to the other side of the road, "is my uncle. He was trampled to death by a horse." With that he jammed a tape in the stereo and the bus filled with whatever the Kurdish equivalent of *You Picked a Fine Time to Leave Me, Lucille* is.

We drove through the craggy countryside, the mountains like coffee ice cream. On a back road we passed a bleak village of little white concrete cubes. In the distance a young man crouched among the tombstones of a cemetery, his red shirt bright against the brown ground. "That's mine," he said, pointing to the village. "I know everybody there. They're all my family and this is all our land." He said it less with pride than as a subtle warning, as though I were a wily real estate developer looking to build a resort.

We passed a Roman bridge and rounded some spectacular cliffs. The earth here was utterly desolate. The dam had yet to reach these areas and there were none of the signs of progress or industry that had touched the land further south. It reminded me vaguely of Australia, but the desolation was of a different sort: not the untouched wastes of the millennia, more as if a nuclear bomb had gone off at some point in the distant past and everyone had forgotten.

As we ascended the road to Nemrut even the modest scrub began to give way to stones and yellow dust. Here and there, tiny shepherd girls appeared from between boulders, whipping flocks of goats and a few thin, lanky cattle. The scattered homes clinging to the mountain were wretchedly poor and ill-equipped, save for the rusted satellite dishes and the occasional carpet, bright against a concrete wall.

The air became colder and the landscape nothing but stones and tufted grass. An eagle circled overhead. My driver stopped the car and got out. Together we stood on the road. "See," he said, "it is amazing." For a moment we watched the eagle coil down the narrow valley. "Will you go to Hasankeyf?" he asked, without warning.

"I don't know. What's it like?"

He gave a disdainful snort. "It is beautiful, the most beautiful place in Turkey."

"What's your name?"

"My name is Arivan," he said, the window closing on this tiny opening of intimacy. "Come, we are running out of time."

At a work site by the side of the road a well was being drilled. The water spilled up and came in a torrent across our path, washing away the dirt and leaving a stony obstacle course in its wake. Lounging by their truck, watching the workmen, were a couple of dozen soldiers. "Why are they here?" I asked. He made a gesture that meant, simultaneously, "I don't care" and "Stop asking questions", and said, "I don't like soldiers." They stared in a bored way as we passed.

The road became narrow and very winding, to one side a sheer drop. The surface was very rough and some half-hearted efforts at re-paving were underway. Finally we reached the car park at the top. The journey had been much longer than anticipated and by now the sun was a tail-light on the smoky horizon, the air biting.

"Didn't you bring a jacket?" asked Arivan, clearly exasperated by my lack of preparedness. Reaching into the back of the car he retrieved a spare one and threw it at me — three-quarter-length leather with a fetching paisley lining, burgundy piping and soft, broad shoulder pads. For a moment I stared at it. There was a distinct whiff of the Baltic about this coat: Estonia, Latvia or some other country where the women were beautiful but Joan Collins was still on the cover of *Vogue*. The woman who had left it there was called Labinka or Tatiana. She had met a German fiancé over the internet. He was disappointed to discover that she was fatter than her picture, but he was poorer than he'd claimed. In protest she had spent their entire honeymoon in Turkey sulking in the back of vans, drinking duty-free vodka and making sarcastic comments about his mother.

Believe me when I tell you it was that kind of coat.

The trail was a draining hike, made worse by the thinness of the atmosphere and the loose, shoe-sized stones, slipping underfoot. Arriving at the top of the mountain I was a moist, panting wreck in my leather jacket, the presence of an elderly Dutch tour group, including a woman of more than sixty with a club foot, only adding to my already considerable humiliation.

The more I do it the more I realise that travel is as much about the gap between expectation and reality as anything else, and that to demand travel-as-spectacle is only to set yourself up for a fall. I consoled myself with these thoughts as I stared at the monumental heads of Mount Nemrut, which are less a triumph of ancient engineering or artistry than a testament to the genius of the Turkish tourist board. Without any scale comparison, an image of Nemrut gives the impression that the sightseer can walk in solitude among a field of heads the size of wheat silos. In reality, most are not more than six feet tall and are lined up in a sad little row behind a chain fence, toppled from their blocky bodies like fairground skittles.

It was not merely their proportions that were disappointing. The carving was wooden and uninspired, the faces frozen in a single expression of mild shock, as though they had just been fired. They looked more like giant plaster garden sculptures, so loved by Turks, than anything else.

Behind the sculptures rises a huge cone of stone, an artificial mountain believed to be a giant funerary mound (although excavations have, thus far, failed to reveal any evidence for this). Its scale is astonishing and it is, in its way, far more impressive than the sculptures. One could marvel at the magnitude of the project — the blocks for the heads had been quarried many kilometres away and brought up this huge mountain — but looking at it I felt not merely underwhelmed but oppressed. I was reminded of my reaction upon seeing the terracotta warriors in China: that this was not the work of a great civilisation, only an ancient dictator with bad taste and an undiagnosed personality disorder.

The Dutch tour group hobbled away to the other side of the mountain to watch the rapidly sinking sun. I stood on the edge of a cliff and surveyed the landscape, the great compensation of this journey. All the way to the horizon, Martian hills rolled out in red, grey and lilac. The silver tendrils of the Atatürk Dam inched inevitably through the valleys, turning the mountains to islands. A couple came to share the view. They were Argentinian, very cheap and asked boring questions about my budget.

"They gave us a good price to come to Nemrut because we are not Americans," said the man, triumphantly.

"You paid as much as I did," I said.

"Oh."

I gave them some chocolate and lent them a map. "Are you not fasting for Ramadan?" he asked.

"No," I said, "there are some advantages to being an infidel."

"This," he said, gesturing to the heads behind us, "is a little bit …"

"Disappointing," I suggested.

"Yes," they said simultaneously.

Looking behind me, I realised we were the only ones left.

At the other side of the funerary mound a small crowd was milling around a second set of heads quarantined behind chain fencing, their cameras fixed in anticipation of the imminent sunset. Behind the seated stone torsos, a couple of archaeologists took measurements, oblivious to the German in a bandana who roamed boldly within the enclosure, snapping pictures. Dusk neared. Dutifully we stood and watched the sunset. A twinkle of pink, a flash of gold, and it was over. The geriatrics began their descent; the woman with the club foot overtook a man on a donkey. The Argentinians and I lingered behind, as if waiting for some revelation. Finally, accepting defeat and in virtual darkness, we made our descent, following the light from the car park for guidance. Arivan was in the souvenir shop, breaking his fast. He said nothing but signalled across the room to the cook who produced a bowl of salad, some soup and stale bread. By the time we left it was dark and very cold. I pulled my lady's jacket tight about me as we began our perilous descent down the mountain. The road was surfaced only in cracked stones and as we slid about I stared with alarm at the blackness of the sheer drop. Arivan put on a new tape. "Ibrahim Tatlıses," he shouted over the chorus of bereaved ululation, "the Michael Jackson of Turkey."

Music in Turkey is a source of some distress to me. Whether it was Turkish or Kurdish was entirely irrelevant; everything was, to my ears, nothing but a kind of endless, orchestrated lamentation, a wall of tuneless sobbing that assailed me in every cab and mini-bus, on every street corner and in every shop. The further east I was to venture the grimmer the soundtrack, and Ibrahim Tatlıses was one of the main offenders.

Tatlıses is a cultural icon in Turkey but any comparison with Michael Jackson ends there. A native of Urfa, Tatlıses was born into a homeless family, working his way through the wedding singer circuit (after being discovered singing on a construction site) to become the biggest performer in the country and the most famous Kurd in Turkey. As the country's biggest-selling artist, his ubiquity is relentless. Tatlıses TV, his cable station, provided one of my favourite Turkish shows — in which Ibrahim mediates between feuding family members, uniting them through tearful song at the climax — but the

Tatlıses empire reaches beyond entertainment to encompass hotel development, a small airline and even a chain of restaurants. If Tatlıses was anything he was the Sinatra of Turkey, complete with schmaltz and heavy mob connections.

Ibo, as he is known affectionately, is an immense source of pride to Kurds, a fact vividly illustrated by the postcards of him you could buy all through the southeast: pictures of Ibo lounging around the house in his socks, smiling warmly in a turtleneck sweater and fisherman's vest or, as in one particularly enigmatic image, posing by his air-conditioning unit. The fact that only Tatlıses' mother was Kurdish — his father died while Ibo was young and may have been an Arab — or that he has publicly declared himself to be "a Turk and a son of a Turk", seems to concern nobody. His ethnicity was a moot point anyway because, like almost every other famous performer in Turkey, he rarely sang in Kurdish, doing so on television for the first time in 2004. For this he was threatened by extreme nationalists who paraded through the streets with signs reading "We will hang you!" and "Don't try our patience. We will come and visit you in the middle of the night." In Turkey no one bothers with anything so quaint as, say, a letter to the editor.

As we drove down the mountain, Ibo's merciless wailing continued, resistant even to the ringing of a mobile phone. Arivan answered; steering down the twisting road with one hand he spoke in a high, excited tone. Clearly agitated he hung up and began to dial. Several more conversations in a similar vein followed.

"Is there something wrong?" I asked as he hung up for the fourth time.

"No, nothing. Nothing is wrong." I felt enough of an authority on the subject of mysterious, late-night phone conversations in Turkey to know he was lying.

Through the dark we drove at great speed down steep hills and around sharp bends. When a fox appeared on the road, only the second wild animal I had seen in Turkey, my ominous portents of motoring carnage were almost realised as we skidded into the opposing lane and the path of an oncoming truck. At a tiny village, consisting of little more than a few concrete boxes and a petrol station, we stopped. "Wait here," said Arivan, parking in front of the petrol station. "I won't be long."

"What's going on?" I asked. He didn't reply, just slammed the door of the van and crossed the dark road to a camouflaged military barracks. Over the fortified entrance, flanked by guard posts and garlanded by a spiral of razor wire, was a sign with the word "jandarma". The jandarmalar are the paramilitary police. In urban areas they are the frontline troops in the battle with Kurdish separatists which, out here, could mean almost anyone. They have a reputation for being ill-disciplined and antagonistic and their headquarters are not the sort of places you visit lightly. Unnerving visions now assailed me: elaborate, paranoid scenarios involving midnight arrests and bloody interrogations took root and flourished. The world became divided into layers of the seen and unseen, making me feel frustrated and useless and very much a silly spoilt tourist.

I watched the driver approach the guard post, his hands in the air, like a surrendering hostage. Slowly he reached into his top pocket and produced what must have been an ID card. After a brief discussion with the machine-gun-wielding guard he disappeared behind the trees and the razor wire. At that moment another van appeared, parking a block away. The driver approached the entrance to the barracks. I began to wait but it didn't take me long to realise I was going to be here a while. Through the window of the petrol station a soccer game was on the television, watched by a dozen old men in flat caps and dirty woollen jackets. As I walked through the door, every eye in the room moved from the television to me. The atmosphere was brooding, smoky and heavily moustached. If there had been a piano player he would have stopped. I made a hasty retreat. Outside, not far from the door, a teenage boy in a padded parka pinned with the logo of the petrol station was sitting in a broken armchair drinking tea by a horseshoe of plastic stools, an old barrel serving as a table at their centre. Noting my beleaguerment, he leaped immediately from his seat and offered it to me. Dashing inside he called for tea. Returning, he sat on one of the plastic chairs and smiled in an anticipatory manner while a mongrel puppy with a broken leg limped in circles around the barrel. The boy spoke a small amount of English and German. His name was Ahmet. Before long, a younger boy arrived bearing a silver tray balancing glasses of dark tea. Following him was another, a little older than the others, wearing a red-checked shirt which gave him a raffish cowboy quality in this bleak, frontier settlement.

Pleasantries were exchanged and for a while we played with my camera, taking photos of one another and rubbing the puppy's ears. They began to ask questions: Where was I from? Had I been to Nemrut? What did I think of it? What was Austria like? I answered as best I could with the aid of a phrase book, broken German and a few key Turkish words. Not for the first or last time during my stay in Turkey, my comparatively youthful appearance was the subject of many compliments. No matter how many times I was to be flattered in this way, it would still come as a source of enormous embarrassment to me, not because I am unduly modest but because residual middle-class guilt means I tend to get awkward in the company of people whose lives are harder than mine. Almost everyone in Turkey looks ten years older than they actually are, especially in the east where one of the only distractions from poverty, endless labour and occasional hunger is cigarettes, chain-smoked from early childhood to early death. My life of privilege was literally written on my face.

A source of equal amazement in the east was my single status. At almost thirty I was, as I had already been informed, "middle-aged" and in grave danger of never finding a wife.

"Not married?" said Ahmet, with that special blend of pity and understanding people in Turkey reserve for such situations.

I confirmed the truth of it.

My decision to keep my sexuality a cautious secret from strangers in Turkey, especially in the east, had not been an easy one. The Turkish attitude towards homosexuality is ambivalent and distinctly Asian; which is to say that most Turks are rampantly homophobic in public, while still being highly tolerant of any act committed in private. This attitude is, in some respects, at odds with the comparatively liberal history of sexuality in pre-modern Turkey. The sexual life of the Ottoman court and military was notoriously mutable, and a form of easy bisexuality was so candidly enjoyed that it can seem shocking to modern sensibilities — when Mehmed II (a.k.a. Mehmet the Conqueror) finally breached the walls of Constantinople in 1453 his speech to his men promised them many beautiful women as well as "boys, too, very many and very beautiful and of noble families". A number of later sultans were especially notorious for their homosexual inclinations, a fact left in no doubt by the erotic poems and eyebrow-raising pornography they commissioned.

In addition to beautiful boys, transvestites called *köçek* were a common feature of court life, especially as dancers and musicians, a part of Ottoman culture that has modern echoes in entertainers like Bülent Ersoy — one of the country's biggest stars and the first biological man in Turkey to be recognised as a woman — and Zeki Müren, Turkey's answer to Liberace, a symphony in sequined kaftans, rhinestone boots and *Golden Girl* hair.

Despite this history of an apparently laissez-faire attitude towards sexuality, homophobia is entrenched in Turkey, both culturally and politically, and most people's understanding of gay people is limited to a series of maddening clichés and myths. Most Turks still see homosexuality as a choice, lisping, mincing nancies are the only acceptable form of public gay figure, and the old dictum, "I'm not gay,

I'm shagging the guy who is," is quite unironically endorsed by many men keen to rationalise their extra-curricular sexual adventures. The result is that comparatively few gay people in Turkey ever have the chance of openly expressing themselves — even educated, urbanised types I'd met in Istanbul had frankly admitted that they intended to enter marriages of convenience and continue seeing boys (or girls) on the side. Very few had told their parents or friends for fear of the reaction they would get and some felt they had genuine reasons to fear for their lives. If this is what it is like for Turkish yuppies then I hated to think what the rules were out here in the Kurdish heartland, where until a few decades ago people had been living in tents, and setting your daughter on fire as a punishment for being raped is still not entirely unheard of. As a rule, I strongly believe in not patronising people, but not so strongly as I believe in not being killed.

At the news of my single status, the youngest boy grew excited. Leaning forward on his chair he made a universal gesture and began repeating a sentence, only one word of which I recognised, "sex" in Turkish being conveniently similar to the English.

I had at this point a certain instinctive understanding of what was being proposed but it was, I felt, important to be quite clear.

"Is he asking me about sex?"

Ahmet giggled.

The eldest boy said nothing, adopting that faraway, waiting-for-the-bus look that I have seen across the breadth of Asia, a dissociative technique that allowed the practitioner to completely remove himself from direct involvement in anything, while still allowing him to observe and hear all, as if he were a ghost or in a lucid coma.

"What does he want?" I asked again.

Ahmet's giggling became high and nervous. The older boy leaned back in his chair and stared at the sky, ignoring the puppy gnawing at his ankles.

"Is he asking to have sex with me?"

Ahmet held up his hand in an unconvincing display of reassurance and laughed nervously, as one with an interested eye on the outcome of the situation.

The boy remained undeterred. Sensing I had understood, he continued to jam his fist with his finger, doubling his speed as though attempting to loosen a stubborn blockage. The words "*seks*", "*otel*" and "*passif*" required no translation.

Let me preface the following by saying that I am no prude and as a homosexual am, by necessity, not easily shocked; I have been the subject of sexual advances by teenagers of both genders in various parts of the world, usually at the end of some otherwise innocent massage, haircut or karaoke duet. This exchange, however, took me aback for several reasons, not least among them the fact that he was no more than fourteen. Never have I been so bluntly propositioned, still less in such cosily fraternal company. It was the matey tone, the complete lack of shame in front of his older friends that made me draw breath: *Hey, come in. Pull up a chair and grab a beer. The game's just starting. Mind if we gangbang you?*

For a moment I sat in silence, trying to formulate an appropriate response. Ahmet shot the others sideways glances. The elder boy remained stony-faced, affecting incomprehension while the puppy whimpered and licked my boot. My paramour had ceased his pantomime and was now smiling gently, expectation playing on his face. The return of Arivan saved me any more awkwardness. "Come," he said, walking by our circle, rattling his keys. I made my goodbyes. As I shook the boys' hands they looked disappointed, as much, I suspect, at the prospect of having to return to the boredom of life at the petrol station as anything else.

Back in the van, Arivan's taciturn demeanour remained unchanged. A block away the other van began to rev, creating a Chinese dragon of dust under the street lights. Arivan started the car. I asked what the problem had been, if everything was OK. For a moment he paused, as if unsure what I was referring to, as if he had already forgotten the events of the previous hour. "The problem," he said, jamming a tape into the deck, "is fixed now." As we drove through the empty night, the mournful strains of Ibrahim Tatlıses filled the void left by conversation.

★ ★ ★

Later that evening I discovered why we had made our mysterious detour. The Argentinians, the ones I had met at the summit, had, as it transpired, not only been the passengers in the other van, parked near the petrol station, but, as the last people to leave the Nemrut car park, witnessed the incident that had prompted the visit to the barracks. They had been leaving the car park just as a truck load of *jandarmalar* arrived, probably the same ones I had seen on my ascent. Their guide, seeing this, parked the van and went, together with a small group of other guides and men from the gift shop, to meet the soldiers. The Argentinians watched as the conversation grew increasingly heated until, suddenly, one *jandarma* stepped forward and, seemingly without knowledge that tourists were watching — because he surely would have thought twice — punched a female tour guide in the face. Why? Who knew. Motives in Turkey are often deliberately obscure. Wheels turn within wheels, the onion reveals another layer and the bemused traveller is left to swing at a pinata of implication, intrigue and double meaning. The feeling of being humoured, of being an unwitting pawn in a bigger drama, dogged me in Turkey. It was an impression only accentuated by these latest events and further cemented by their explanation, which was not, in fact, an explanation at all but just another gratuitous detail in a seemingly infinite conspiracy of power and casual violence.

With the receptionist asleep on the couch, I crept out of my hotel and onto the still, morning streets of Khata. At the *otogar* the bus was delayed while we waited for the extended family of a young soldier to bid him farewell on his journey to his posting. A tap on the window distracted me from the scene, bringing me face to face with the smiling extortionist.

"Where are you going?" he asked.

"Diyarbakır."

"Do you need a ride? I can take you. Good price."

"I'm *on* the bus," I said, irritation turning to amazement, almost admiration, in the face of his near-Sisyphean persistence. He looked at me as if to say, "So you are," and, with no further pretensions to affability, retreated.

The landscape outside Khata was a scene straight from a Van Gogh: prematurely withered men cast seeds onto stony fields from sling bags hanging around their necks. Portly nannas with pickled plum faces and hands like men rode donkeys draped in carpet saddle bags, bright with patches. The bus stopped to pick up one of these impossibly weather-beaten women, pausing to allow her to empty a ballast of stones from the saddle bags. Tethering her donkey, she struggled aboard clutching an enormous sack of carrots which she held on her lap as covetously as a Tiffany lamp. The landscape was magnificently austere, the empty hills as soft and burnished as gold velvet. Occasionally we would stop in the middle of a field somewhere to drop an old man or a teenager in filthy jeans and I wondered where they could possibly be going, what there was to reach in this emptiness. The wildness of Khata appealed to my taste for the untamed and elemental. But the extreme poverty, the sterility of the land and the joylessness of the people were doing little to ease a creeping loneliness. Never did I think I would hear myself say it, but I was glad to be returning to Diyarbakır.

On the narrow road we hurtled along at high speeds, a sudden *crack* bringing our journey to a near-halt. Sketching an ominous doodle of smoke, we made the last five kilometres at a crawl to arrive at the Atatürk Dam just as the ferry was leaving, thick striations of garbage and debris arriving in waves on the shore. The driver stood on the banks and shouted across the water, pleading in turn with the ship and the ferryman who stood on the bank, making half-hearted gestures of placation. Eventually, in a tribute to either the community spirit of the Turkish people or the power of the local mini-bus mafia, the barge was turned around and we were brought on board. Not long after our embarkation a fist fight broke out between the mini-bus' co-pilot and a truck driver angry at the delay we had caused. While passengers restrained the two, our driver, oblivious to the fracas, lay under the bus performing one of those miracles of Third-World engineering, retooling the engine with only a piece of chewing gum and a biro until by the time we were due to disembark the bus was humming healthily.

Confidently we drove towards Siverek, through the ravishing moonscape of the rocky plains. Inside their stone tepees the shepherds were curled up, sleeping, like babies in rocky wombs. Almost within sight of the town, however, whatever it was that had been holding everything together failed and the bus blew up profoundly. Rolling to the side of the road we came to a halt, disembarking by a clump of abandoned sheds. The driver disappeared under the van while every male passenger slowly gathered into a close-knit circle to stare at his protruding legs.

There are, I am sure, certain parts of the world in which men do not do this. When the van breaks down in these remote regions, everyone gets out and plays hopscotch or brews palm wine. Everywhere else, however, men seem compelled to stand around the broken-down vehicle, nodding thoughtfully and making occasional, pointlessly encouraging remarks about something they cannot even see and, more likely than not, would not be able to understand if they could. Despite the best efforts of the onlookers, it was soon clear that the bus was beyond repair. Just as I was contemplating hitching a lift with a truck parked nearby, a passing mini-bus was flagged down and I, along with almost every other stranded passenger, was squeezed aboard the already fully loaded vehicle.

The scene inside was human Tetris, bodies stuffed into every available space in configurations of Karma Sutric discomfort. On a corner of a box I perched a tiny wedge of buttock and positioned myself as best I could among the tangle of limbs. Next to me a woman held her retarded teenage son on her lap, drool running down his shirt. Facing me was the young soldier I had seen being farewelled by his family in Khata, our bodies so close we were forced to interlock our legs, our faces centimetres apart. Cultivating obliviousness, he looked away, in the manner men do when they are compelled to be intimate. The retarded boy ran a wet hand down my face and his mother slapped and scolded him.

After an hour or so, like a yogi emerging from a cube, I unfolded myself from the bus into the Diyarbakır *otogar* only to trip on a freshly severed goat leg, turning the dirt black with its blood. In the blue sky the jet fighters twisted, their booms a celestial kettle drum. As tempting as another night in the sheep's head and watermelon capital of Turkey might have seemed, I realised it was time to decide my next move.

Chapter 10

Hasankeyf had been recommended to me by Arivan, its appeal lent a note of urgency by the fact it would soon be destroyed. The town was full of historical significance and, by all accounts, very beautiful; but Turkey's economic progress took priority over all else and within a few years Hasankeyf would be lost under the rising waters of a massive new dam. (Many Kurds regarded this as a none-too-subtle form of cultural ethnic cleansing because of the importance of the site in their history, explaining, perhaps, Arivan's terseness on the subject.) To reach Hasankeyf I had first to travel to a city with the unlikely name of Batman, an almost defiantly unlovable industrial town which, had the minivan not broken down — again — and I not accidentally boarded a bus bound back to Diyarbakır then spent several hours tramping the streets utterly lost, I would have skipped altogether, missing one of the most memorable events of my travels.

Until the discovery of oil in the late-1940s Batman had been nothing more than a village. Now it was a sprawling conglomeration of mobile phone shops, banks, hotels and refineries, pumping the air full of a gritty black smoke that left a taste like coins in the back of your throat. Oil pumps littered Batman. Against the purple twilight sky they were avian and menacing; Jurassic mosquitoes bowing in endless supplication, sucking nourishment from the earth. By the time

I found the centre of town, marked by one that had been decommissioned and draped in a depressing string of fairy lights, sunset and the end of the fast had arrived.

Finding a hotel, I checked in and went in search of food. In a surprisingly smart restaurant I sat on a roof terrace, watching music videos on a big screen while I ate.

Before coming to Turkey I used to regard Christian rock as the lowest form of popular entertainment. After coming to Turkey, specifically after half an hour in that restaurant, I began to realise that there was something worse, much worse: Muslim rock. For the next hour I was to endure dozens of precocious brats singing about Ramadan sweets, stout peasant choirs glorifying the name of God and a seemingly never-ending parade of near-identical flat-capped old men so maudlin and hostile to melody they made Ibrahim Tatlıses look like Elvis live at the Vegas Hilton. Crowning all this was Cat Stevens, in his incarnation as Yusef Islam, strumming a guitar for a crowd of nerdy Malaysians while a bunch of smug black guys in skullcaps tapped bongos and sang backing vocals rich in inspirational verbs: striving, seeking, hoping, finding. As I sat and listened the thought occurred to me that after decades of neurotic self-examination, military coups and pitched battles over ideologically sound headgear there could be no better argument for the separation of church and state in Turkey than the pious insipidity of religious rock.

It was difficult to reconcile this atmosphere of didactic holiness with the crowd in the restaurant. Most of the women wore no headscarf; the men were sharply dressed, their hair elegantly coiffed in a seventies-revival style fashionable that year in Istanbul. Mixed tables talked loudly and expressively in the manner no one in the east did. There was something else I hadn't seen before in the east, indeed anywhere in Turkey: tables of lone diners, all men. In Turkey nobody does anything alone. The idea that you might enjoy time to yourself is incomprehensible and the revelation that you were travelling solo produced the kind of forced, condescending pity most people reserve for the severely mentally handicapped. If you were sitting on your own in a restaurant in Turkey it meant you were either a tourist, suffering a serious disease, or a lonely businessman in some godforsaken part of the country who could only hurry through his meal, consoling himself with the money he was making and count the days until he could get back to civilisation.

The streets of Batman had settled into an after-dinner torpor. In vain I searched for a bar. The restaurants were closing and all that was still open were internet cafés and tea houses. Deciding to declare an early night I headed back to my hotel, struggling to cross a busy road, cut in the centre by a high concrete barrier planted with palm trees. As I vaulted onto the verge I noticed a teenager further down the street attempting the same manoeuvre and wondered why it was that these barriers were always erected at exactly the spot where people needed to cross, and whether the people in Batman who drove expensive European cars felt the luxury was wasted on such a miserable, godforsaken outpost as this. These thoughts, among many others, occupied me as I crossed the highway, continuing as I made my way past the tea shop, and ended only when the man beside me, in a manner that was even more shocking for its casualness, pulled out a gun and started firing.

It is a telling indication of my conditioning to the conventions of Hollywood violence that it came as a shock to see a man firing a gun without a pumping rock soundtrack in the background. It had never occurred to me that when someone began shooting bullets at another human being there was no wah-wah guitar, throbbing bassline or, at the very least, a couple of jarring piano chords to mark the occasion. The precise moment when the man drew his gun remains in my mind a question of debate. I didn't really notice the two men in the doorway of the tea house until one began to raise his voice and then, almost as if he were reaching to embrace a lover, slowly moved towards the other, lunging with what I took to be a knife. The potential victim, arching sideways, turned from his assailant in a manner I thought slightly disappointing, lacking in the kind of kung-fu elegance I associated with potentially deadly assaults. As he broke free of his attacker and began to run down the street, it was obvious he hadn't moved quickly in quite some time. In between these two events — the stabbing motion and the running — I can clearly recall my horrified queasiness at the terrible prospect that I was about to watch someone die. This queasiness turned to an adrenalin rush of survival instinct upon realising that the man had raised his gun and, not more than five feet from me, was firing it down the street.

Here my recollection becomes disjointed and uncertain. The man was shooting, no doubt, but why had he drawn his weapon for what seemed a second time: had he pulled a knife first then replaced it with a gun or, as seemed more likely, been holding a gun from the beginning which I had registered as a knife? These questions came in retrospect. In the short term I was focused more on hiding.

Diving between two white Fiats parked at an angle against the curb, I hunkered down by the front doors, my heart pounding as much from elation as fear. Crouching between the cars I was delighted to find that, from my low vantage, the angle of their rear windows formed a rectangular panorama uncannily reminiscent of a movie screen's periphery. In this hiding spot I was afforded a perfect view of the shooter, arm extended, blasting away until — and here real life did conform to the filmic template — he ran out of bullets and clicked off several empty rounds.

With that I stood up and scanned the streets, looking for corpses. Further down, the teenager who had crossed the road with me was standing on the pavement, looking entirely unfussed by the drama. The shooter, almost within reaching distance, stood as if frozen, a windvane in the near-empty street. In an instant the spell was broken and he began to inspect his gun with a look of astonishment, as if he was surprised by what it had done, having expected it to light his cigarette or turn into a bunch of flowers. This brief moment of calm was shattered with the appearance of the intended victim who emerged from between his own set of cars brandishing a pistol he had obviously set aside for just such an occasion. Seeing this, the original shooter registered a look of almost comic alarm then turned and began to run in the opposite direction. Once more I disappeared into my hiding space, watching as the victim-turned-perpetrator ran, like Buster Keaton, into, then out of, my movie screen. As he passed I stood up once more, just in time to see him fire his first, then second shot at the other man, who turned and disappeared, apparently uninjured, around a corner.

All of this took place in under twenty seconds.

With the departure of the two men a large crowd moved from the tea house onto the street. Little boys and younger teenagers scrambled on the pavement and amongst the parked cars searching for bullets. One was retrieved, bent and flat at the top, and brought to one of the old men for inspection. As the bullet was handed among the inner circle a voluble discussion broke out. Yet, even in the light of the potentially deadly commotion, emotions were restrained, as if they saw scenes such as these every day, which may not have been so unlikely. The old men stood in a huddle around the bullet inspecting it with only mild interest while the younger men milled up the back, nursing their tea glasses and affecting a casual indifference. For a moment it occurred to me that the police may have wanted me to make a statement. But, after waiting a while among the dissipating crowd, it became obvious that no police were coming and that even the thought they might was evidence of some naïvety on my part. Following the escape route of the shooters, I walked quickly back towards my hotel.

On the dark, shabby streets of Batman my heart was beating, my head spinning. Still giddy from the evening's events, I felt vulnerable and threatened. When a teenager ran out in my path to grab a soccer ball I jumped a foot in the air. On reflection, my agitation was disproportionate to the magnitude of the incident. Ultimately, it had been a rather tame affair: no one, to my knowledge, was hurt and my life had never been in any danger. In fact, the more I thought about it the more this episode had seemed an entirely calculated, theatrical spectacle. After all, if the attacker had pulled a gun from the beginning, as was likely, the obvious question was why he had not shot the man immediately — close up — rather than firing down the street. The most probable explanation seemed that the entire scene had been designed only to frighten, to create a public show of avenged honour for whatever local conspiracy had prompted this confrontation. Nevertheless, in the dark, passing the wastelands of construction equipment, abandoned petrol stations and the nodding monsters of the oil rigs, Batman took on a haunted, dangerous quality; a cowboy town of ghosts and tumbleweeds.

Back at my hotel I was still agitated. Feeling the need to share my experience with someone, I rang Hüseyin. "You saw *what*? Oh my God, Brendan!" he cried. "Be careful in the east. People out there are *crazy*. You don't understand — they'll just shoot you. I mean, this is *Turkey*, man."

I laughed. While not exactly contradicted by this evening's events, the irrational notion that eastern Turkey was wholly populated by violent psychopaths amused me. Not as much, however, as Hüseyin's unspoken assumption that I was a useless nancy-boy who had never known danger and in the face of it could be expected only to leap into the air, flap his hands and squeal like a girl. (Though, to be fair, this notion had not exactly been contradicted by this evening's events either.) He became suddenly grave. "Please, I am serious. Some very heavy shit will happen soon."

"What do you mean?"

"The US is plotting to send Turkey into a war with Iran and Syria so they can sell weapons. They are funding the PKK to plant bombs all over the country. It's in all the newspapers, man." Much of the Turkish capacity for conspiracy was built on the paradoxically naïve belief that the entire world was obsessed with Turkey and constantly looking for ways to undermine it. Trying to convince Turks that most people couldn't care less about their country and that almost as many probably couldn't point to it on a map was futile — the world was out to get Turkey but they were ready for our most cunning plans. The fact that Hüseyin was not immune to these paranoid fantasies didn't exactly surprise me but was a useful reminder that, for all his good humour, generosity and apparent reasonableness, he was in, some ways, completely fucking insane.

I decided to change the subject. "Have you seen Tevfik?" I asked. We had been texting one another intermittently but, lately, he had not been answering.

"No, I dunno anything about him, man. That sonofabitch been causing too many problems."

"What do you mean?"

"He insult my honour!" he snapped, his outrage making his English shaky. "He insult *his* honour. He says he want to visit his son in Japan, but instead he just spend all his goddamn money on drugs and being a lazy asshole. Don't believe anything he says, Brendan." Judging by his tone it seemed a little premature to hope for a reconciliation. I told him to pass on my regards to Mehmet and we made our goodbyes.

My conversation with Hüseyin had done little to settle my nerves. Unable to relax I returned to the foyer where I sat trying to read over the cheers of a visiting soccer team watching a game in one corner. After a while, my attention moved to a mysterious group of people in the opposite corner gathered around a woman with a clipboard who lectured them in a strident, didactic manner, like a high-school principal briefing a class before an excursion. All four wore identical red-and-white badges. On the desk was a new receptionist, lounging on the counter, looking bored. "Tell me," I said. "Are they members of a political party?"

He laughed. "No! They are from Herbalife. You know Herbalife? When you are fat they give you medicine. When you are thin, more medicine. You know Herbalife?"

I said I did, but had doubts about its worth.

"You don't believe?" he said, in a naughty schoolboy manner.

"No."

He lowered his voice to a whisper, repressing his laughter. "I don't think I also believe!"

Ahmet was Kurdish, green-eyed and had three children. He asked me about my impressions of Batman. I told him about the gunfight. He *tsk*ed, disgustedly. "These people," he said, "are beside their selves."

"What?"

"Beside their selves," he repeated, becoming frustrated.

"Do you mean, 'backwards'?"

"Yes!" He became solemn. "This town is not good. I hate it."

"Why?" I asked. "Batman is rich."

"Yes it is rich, but the people here are not wanting to" — he paused, searching for the words — "improve their selves. They don't want education. They don't want speak English. There is nothing here."

"Batman is a modern town," I said, meaning that it had little history and no beauty, the compensations offered by other cities in the east. The vehemence of his response shocked me.

"No! Is not modern! People here are not wanting to improve their selves."

I had, or so I was to learn, made a fundamental mistake. In Turkey, "modern" was not merely a descriptor evoking images of gleaming appliances or international space stations. To be "modern" was a civic and moral duty, an obligation to liberate your country and yourself from the dark superstitions and primitive codes of the pre-Atatürk past. It was the first but not the last time I was to hear "modern" used in this way. Later, in Istanbul, I was to meet a student from a famous family; his grandmother had been the first female bank manager in Turkey and a friend of Atatürk himself. As we walked through the streets he would point out evidence of Turkey's "progress": Ferraris, Thai restaurants and the boutiques of international fashion houses. On one occasion he was to tell me with unintentionally comical pride that in Nişantaşı, an upmarket Istanbul suburb, you could buy bacon burgers. When I asked if his parents were religious, if they prayed, he looked at me in utter disbelief and said, "No! They are modern." In a world where fundamentalists were flying planes into skyscrapers and people in India were sending prayers by SMS, it was quaint, bizarre almost, this notion that religion and the "modern world" were mutually exclusive.

Ahmet leaned over the desk and said in low, conspiratorial tones, "People here they are doing ..." He mimed tying a noose about his neck.

"Suicide?"

"Yes! Suicide. Killing their selves. Young women and men. Many, many young men."

At that moment the Herbalife people finished their meeting. The leader of the group gave money to Ahmet for their drinks and bustled out after the others, fussing with her clipboard.

Ahmet watched her exit in silence. "Herbalife people is stupid!" he said suddenly, and for a moment the soccer team were distracted from their game as we collapsed in laughter.

Chapter 11

By the time I got to it, Hasankeyf felt like an afterthought. The town lived up to its promise but after the previous evening's excitement it was difficult to be a tourist. For several hours I walked by the quick, blue waters of the Tigris, past the ruined pylons of the enormous Byzantine bridge; past the piles of goat shit and the little boys pulling wretched silver fish from nets clogged with garbage: "Please, mahnee." "No mahnee." "*Yes* mahnee." For the next few hours I dutifully inspected the graves, the caves and the monuments. Many were in a poor state of repair, worn out and vandalised, some reclaimed as squatter homes. From the top of the cliff that dominated the town, rising from the river like a curtain of red rock, the view was as desolately beautiful as anything I had seen. Down by the river I met a local crank who knew a lot about Australian politics and regaled me with incoherent internet conspiracy theories. When I stripped to my underpants and went swimming in the shallow, deceptively fast water, he applauded wildly.

The day ended at a riverside restaurant, drinking Coke and ignoring, alternately, the crank and a family of Batman yuppies who lounged on a cushioned platform above the water, eating kebabs and watching their fat children throw firecrackers at me. By the time I returned to Batman I felt refreshed and pleasantly sun-kissed. The day had been perfectly agreeable. Despite this I struggled to feel any distress for the fate that awaited Hasankeyf. The town was beautiful, and I suppose its imminent destruction ought to have roused in me some righteous indignation. Yet, old and beautiful as it was, Hasankeyf seemed to have little left to live for. To Kurds it was a symbol; to me it was nothing more than a "sight", a ruin, resigned to its doom, like a suicidal friend that cannot be helped. As I waved goodbye to the crank from the window of the *dolmuş*, I felt no pity for Hasankeyf, just a strange, incoherent melancholy that grew stronger with every day I spent in the east.

My relief at leaving Batman was only heightened by a gruelling four-hour wait in a bus company office, an altercation with a thieving cab driver and a vicious dog fight that engulfed me in a whirlwind of teeth and blood as I struggled from my hotel with my baggage. With a sensation not unlike what must have been felt by the survivors of the *Titanic* being winched onto rescue craft, I boarded the overnight bus for the far-eastern city of Van. Before I had left Istanbul my friend Charlie had given me some names of people I could contact there. Charlie was Kurdish, a carpet dealer in a small shop near Hüseyin's (his real name was Ali but I preferred the one he gave to tourists; it made him easier to distinguish from all the other Alis). With intense blue eyes and a face like an Aztec funerary mask, Charlie was an intimidating figure. I had him met on my last visit to Istanbul but found his sternness frightening and tended to make excuses every time he invited me for tea. Since that time I had learned that his grimness was mostly a façade and, after travelling a little in the east, was starting to see that some of the traits I had ascribed to his personality were in fact entirely cultural. Charlie's friends ran a carpet shop in Van, a city of which I knew nothing but for which I held great expectations, if only at the prospect of making some friends.

After several hours of thumping over potholes, we suddenly stopped at a huge petrol station on a dark, empty stretch of highway.

Grateful for the serenity I curled up into a ball and was almost asleep before the cleaner began to prod me with his brush attachment. "Eat, eat," he said in Turkish. It was 3am. There were many things I didn't understand about Turkey yet no mystery was greater than the timing of meal breaks on bus journeys. During Ramadan buses occasionally managed to time a stop with sunset. As often as not, however, breaks arrived at hours determined by methods I could only assume were entirely astrological. A bus four hours late could be within sight of its destination only to pull into an enormous petrol station on the outskirts of town, forcing passengers to spend a half-hour eating soup and bread which, given the same amount of travel time, they would have been able to enjoy in the comfort of their own home.

The cleaner continued to poke at my rump. I indicated that he should manoeuvre around me but this breach of protocol appeared to confuse him. A meeting was called with the man washing the windows. Gripping a dripping squeegee the window-washer made it plain I should leave. Once again I refused. To his credit he did not threaten me, as a man in his position almost certainly would have done back home, only eulogised the benefits of a hot meal in the small hours of the morning. I liked this about Turkey: unexpected moments of compassion, small mercies in a country on intimate terms with the concept of a bad day. Disappointing myself, I complied yet still felt it necessary to register a rather feeble protest — pulling on my jumper in an affronted manner I marched off the bus, grumbling.

Outside, it was cold; the air smelled moist and slightly alpine. Immediately I knew I was in a different place, that the east of the deserts was gone. Inside the roadhouse, men sucked soup under grey moustaches. I bought some chocolate and killed some time. Back on the bus I tried to sleep but to no avail. In the grey light we arrived in Van. The first shock here was the cold; the second, the plainness of the city. I don't know what I had expected but, whatever it was, this was not it. Van: the name sounded fantastically old, a linguistic relic from the dawn of speech, a time of single syllables. And it was. Unfortunately, almost all evidence of the city's antiquity had been destroyed during the First World War. Since then Van had been completely rebuilt, subsumed by rows of concrete apartment buildings of the sort found throughout Turkey, their utilitarian grimness only emphasised for being painted an array of jolly pastels. Especially popular was a certain shade of pink I had seen across the country, not only on apartments but schools, police stations and seemingly every council building in Turkey. Why pink was so favoured I was never to discover. It wasn't even a particularly pleasant shade; there was a hint of something uncomfortably biological about it, the colour of raw pâté or a freshly skinned knee. Whenever I saw these pink monoliths ringing Turkish cities like an encroaching cancer I thought of some general who, in the late-seventies, had ordered five billion litres of surplus Chinese paint and had been reaping the rewards ever since.

As disappointingly anonymous as much of Van was, a few notes of eccentricity were to be found. The city is home to the eponymous Van cat, a breed famous for its snow white coat and mismatching eyes: one blue, another yellow. Pictures of the animal were everywhere: on the walls of shops and restaurants, the sides of buses and, rather disconcertingly, over the bed in my hotel room. On a highway median strip on the outskirts of town a two-storey sculpture surveyed the passing traffic with a demonic gaze, only adding to the visitor's general impression of having arrived in some alternative dimension in which an alien dictator has taken over the earth, enslaving humanity.

Despite the obvious affection in which the animal is held, the real cat was almost nowhere to be seen: they are now worth so much money that they are rarely allowed out of doors, their owners fearful of cat-nappings. To make matters worse, in recent years they have fallen victim to a mysterious disease which has killed them off in massive numbers. The cause of the illness has baffled scientists, and the knowledge that the city's mascot was slowly dying did little to abate the atmosphere of foreboding that seemed to hang over Van like a nuclear cloud.

Remnants of old Van could still be found on the outskirts of town. Little remained but an impressive fortress complex that stood on a hill by the vast alkaline lake, glowing eerie, chemical colours. Dutifully I inspected the sights, noting from the lookout the difference in the landscape in this part of the country. Here the plains were very green, the distant mountains the biggest I had yet seen. Not far to the east was Iran. Further to the south, the border with Iraq. If Turkey had an epicentre of trouble, a symbol of all that might go wrong, then surely Van was it.

At the bottom of the hill by the exit, snotty boys ran through a graveyard by a small mosque, begging and tearing at one another's clothes. In the surrounding fields, hardy shepherds tapped at their flock with switches while nannas in big bloomers picked daisies for the evening meal. For reasons which were, at that time, unclear, a half dozen women sat under the portico of the mosque reading from the Koran, some wailing in a low haunting way, others hunched over their books tracing the words with their fingers. In defiance of the women's piety, the boys laughed and pointed, throwing stones at the graves and at one another. One urchin grabbed my hand and took me to the tomb of the saint. Hundreds of similar tombs are found across Turkey, their coffins draped in elaborate embroidery, lit by chandeliers and crowned by a plush turban. This veneration of holy men is a prominent feature of Turkish Islam, distinguishing it from fundamentalist interpretations with their horror of idolatry. I peered through the barred window at the coffin but it was plain and unremarkable and I wondered why it had been deemed such an attraction, why so many people had gathered to pray here. It wasn't until later that I discovered this was a pilgrimage place for infertile women.

Infertility is a fate worse than death in rural Turkey (especially in Kurdish culture) and these women were a kind of living dead, their purpose in life denied by some cruel trick of biology for which many were treated as outcasts, the victims of gossip and malignant curses. It was a desperate, unearthly scene — the mocking boys, the tomb, the wailing women — and was to haunt me until well after I had left Turkey.

Rain came; I had forgotten what it was like. My walk back along the highway quickened to a run. At a bus stop I got soaked waiting. In town I wandered the muddy streets, clutching Charlie's address. Eventually, in an alley behind a market, I found the shop. Inside two men in suits were lounging on a bench, watching television; a boy on the floor sat cross-legged, repairing carpets. I introduced myself and asked for Halil. He rose and shook my hand.

"Did Charlie mention me?" I asked.

"No," he said, and sat back down.

Like a new boyfriend in his first meeting with his prospective parents-in-law I took a seat and watched the TV with the pair. After a lengthy silence Halil pointed to the man next to him. "That is my brother," he said, as one might identify a body in a morgue. I nodded hello but my attention soon turned to the boy threading a terrifyingly sharp hook through the weft of the carpet. Scattered all around were dozens of coloured markers which he used to colour-match the wool.

"Why is it," I asked, in a desperate attempt to break the ice, "that carpets are made by women but always repaired by men?"

Halil's brow furrowed with a certain amount of genuine consternation. "I don't know," he said and the conversation ended, the silence filled only by the sound of the television.

As in so many developing countries, television in Turkey is surprisingly ubiquitous. Satellite dishes, like rusted full moons, sit atop the roofs of even the poorest households, often looking heavier than the walls that support them. For Kurds these dishes have particular significance. Kurdish language satellite channels from Denmark and Belgium are often the only source of information or entertainment in their native language, and the Turkish government has made every diplomatic effort to have them closed down. Freed of their associations with bourgeoisie ostentation, satellite dishes in the east were an unlikely symbol of resistance, a rebel flag of technology.

On the television, a documentary in Kurdish about India during the monsoon was playing. In the overcrowded slums of Mumbai men disappeared into a clogged drain, reappearing with full baskets of sewage balanced on their heads. At the sight of this there was a sudden outcry of astonishment and disgust. "They have such primitive lives," said Halil. Coming as he did from a region where, only a year prior, a family had been discovered who walked on all-fours, hailed by scientists as evidence for an evolutionary throwback, this struck me as a bit rich. I said that there were also a great many people in India who were very wealthy and very far from primitive. I told him about the Indian IT revolution and quoted a half-remembered statistic about there being more millionaires in India than the US. These facts impressed them greatly — they had previously considered such matters the sole domain of the West.

"Oh, so it is all the same everywhere," said Halil, as one speaking from personal experience. "They only show you the bad things."

This thawing of relations was soon interrupted. The Turkish Prime Minister, Recip Erdoğan, was visiting the US and his appearance on the evening news, meeting George W. Bush, drew earnest attention. Bush affirmed his "commitment to helping Turkey fight terror", ignoring the irony that his invasion of Iraq had been to terrorism in Turkey what petrol is to bonfires. Erdoğan, meanwhile, smiled and nodded, reconfirming his nation's commitment to the Israel–Lebanon war and thanked the president for his support of Turkey's bid to join the EU. These announcements prompted a sudden mocking hoot from Halil. "I'm George Bush," he announced, revealing a previously unsuspected well of irony. "I have big balls."

I asked him what he thought of the prime minister. He gave a resigned shrug.

"Don't you want to join the EU?" I asked. "You will have more rights."

"We will never join the EU," said Halil's brother, "because the military will never allow it because it will take their power away. The government can do nothing in this country. The military is everything. The government is shit."

This was a common belief in Turkey, not just in the east, among Kurds, but everywhere, and with good reason. The Turkish army is enormous and although they don't claim to have God on their side they do have Atatürk, which, in Turkey, is about the same thing. The military sees itself as the protector of Turkish democracy. Every time a government has been deemed "Islamic" or generally too big for its boots, they have staged a coup, a semi-regular occurrence during the past forty years. In recent days, the military had announced that the current government — by agitating for the rules on headscarves to be relaxed and stacking the parliament with their "fundamentalist" cronies — was becoming dangerously religious. It was clear what they were doing: sowing the seeds of doubt and paving the way, perhaps, for a possible takeover.

"So," I said, "if you cannot be in Turkey or the EU, what is the solution?"

He smiled gently and shrugged.

As darkness came the shop began to fill up. Men kissed one another and sat in groups smoking and saying little. I began to see that Halil had not been ignoring me and that, out here, there was no such thing as an uncomfortable silence. Dinner arrived and was lain out on a big Iranian carpet. Cross-legged and in silence we ate: lamb, bread, pilaf, yoghurt, roast chillies and honeycomb. People left as they finished, without a word of thanks or farewell and my neighbours took food from my plate without asking. It was all very communal and tribal and, for a moment, I got rather carried away with the romance of it all. Yet, as I looked around the room at the numerous cousins, brother-in-laws and uncles, watching their moustaches twitch as they ate, I couldn't shake the feeling that something was missing. It was then I realised that, other than Madelon, I had not had a substantial conversation with a woman in weeks. As for young women: I had not spoken to one of those since the teachers in Harran, and that had been no more than a few words. Indeed, other than the students in Van, most of whom were not local, I had hardly seen a woman who did not look like she was on a waiting list for a new lung for quite some time. All at once this relentless masculinity made me depressed and slightly panicked, as if I'd been locked in a small room — and as I looked around the circle I wondered how these men didn't go mad. The thought occurred to me that perhaps they did.

After dinner we hung around in the shop, drinking tea and looking through carpets. Business in this season was non-existent but Van was not much of a tourist centre so they made most of their money from wholesale anyway. About half the carpets they stocked came from Iran, many Iranian–Kurdish pieces. As we flicked through them I asked Halil if he went to Iran often. He did. "Do Iranian Kurds have the same problems as the Turkish Kurds?" I asked.

He smiled gently and rocked his head. "Not really."

I was frustrated by his caginess, his Cheshire Cat grin, the lack of detail he was prepared to share. I decided to broach the toughest subject of all. "And the PKK, are they still dangerous here?"

"The PKK is not a problem," he said.

"But they just killed all those little boys in Diyarbakır and put a bomb under a *dolmuş*."

"Oh no," he said, very plainly and calmly, "it is the government who kills people — then they blame the PKK."

Chapter 12

The "Armenian genocide" (always prefaced by "so-called" in Turkey) is a subject in which I have a very limited interest. As one of history's many atrocities it occupies a no more privileged position in my imagination than the massacres of the Hutus and Tutsis in Rwanda, the Indians of Argentina, the purges of Stalin or any other bloodbath in places and times remote from my comprehension. The hard part was convincing Turks of this fact.

The very mention of the word "Armenia" in Turkey is enough to elicit howls of protest which, to any objective observer, seem suspiciously, almost comically, defensive. To tell anyone that I was a journalist was to be immediately assailed with a detailed lecture on the distortions of history created by Armenian propagandists, complete with massacre photographs faked in Africa, documents forged in Russia and, very possibly, the involvement of American Zionists. During my time in Turkey, the only public discussion I saw on the subject was a television "debate" (conducted in English, presumably for the benefit of wrong-headed foreigners) in which all three panellists did nothing but agree that there had never been any such thing and that if anyone had died then they more than likely deserved it. Several equally absurd museums around the country are devoted to the topic, featuring extravagantly lopsided narratives of persecution by Armenians of innocent Turks. Some historians kill two birds with one stone and blame it all on the Kurds.

The events surrounding the massacres of Turkey's Armenian population in the period during the First World War are complex and steeped in venomous politics. Type the words "Armenian genocide" into a search engine and you will find a world of endless squabbling that would be funny if it weren't so relentlessly vicious. As depressing as it undoubtedly is, however, the Armenian Question, like a bug that has laid its eggs under the skin of the nation, cannot be ignored in modern Turkey. The fact it all started in Van further compels me to make a reluctant digression.

In March 1915, with the dying Ottoman Empire struggling on the losing side of the First World War, Russia began an invasion of what is now the northeast of the country. Hoping the Christian Russians would be sympathetic to their desires for an independent homeland, the Armenian population of Van, who had been subject to previous repressions, rose up and massacred many of the local Muslims — Turks and Kurds — killing many thousands and holding the city until the troops arrived in late April. In response, on 24 April, the Ottoman government arrested approximately two hundred prominent Istanbul Armenians, sent them to prison camps in central Anatolia and, eventually, had them executed. Soon after, a program of deportations of Armenians was enforced, spreading from Ottoman-controlled areas in the east to other regions across the Empire, with the exceptions of some big western cities, such as Izmir and Istanbul. With the institution of this new policy, many Armenians were quickly murdered in a variety of gruesome ways. Many more, mostly women and children, were taken on what were, effectively, death marches to be "resettled" in modern-day Syria.

After a convoluted series of battles, the Russians eventually conquered much of modern eastern Turkey, including the cities of Trabzon, Kars and Van. The war plunged most of the eastern Ottoman Empire into a state of complete chaos — Muslim refugees fled from the Russians, roaming bands of Armenian troops took revenge on Turks and Kurdish tribes raided and pillaged both. With the advent of the Russian Revolution in March 1917, however, the Russians began to withdraw. With them the remaining Armenians retreated, taking advantage of the collapsing Russian and Ottoman empires to create, after a series of final battles and complicated border changes, what would become modern Armenia.

Most of the major facts of this time are not in dispute. Their interpretations, however, are mired in a fog of claim and counter-claim, an infinite labyrinth of accusation, conspiracy and bias. Of all the disputed facts the central and most significant is whether the massacres and expulsions constituted a premeditated ethnic cleansing comparable to Hitler's annihilation of the Jews, a "genocide" in other words. This is, of course, to most Armenians and their supporters, an incontrovertible truth. In evidence they point to the 1.5 million dead, a figure recognised by many historians, and the fact that almost all Armenians were accused of being separatists and Russian collaborators, regardless of their age or any possible connection they may have had to seditious movements. Turks counter by claiming that genocide proponents exaggerate the number of dead (the Turkish government estimates that approximately 300,000 Armenians died, though they blame indirect causes for the casualties, such as disease and inter-fighting) and argue that many more Turks died at the hands of Russian and Armenian troops thanks, in part, to the treachery of the Armenians and their desire for a homeland. Armenian deaths were, in short, according to the official Turkish line, the unfortunate by-product of a brutal and chaotic war, not a calculated policy of ethnic extermination.

A definitive answer to such a serious allegation as "genocide" might be possible in an atmosphere of reasoned intellectual debate. The problem is that almost the only terms in which the events surrounding the Armenian deportations and massacres of 1915 are allowed to be discussed range from shrill to hysterical to outright demented. In Turkey the topic is almost impossible to raise without great trepidation, even in casual conversation, and any questioning of the official line is enough to get you jailed, as several Turkish writers and intellectuals can attest. Not only is this hardly the sign of a mature democracy looking for entry into the EU, but also tends to undermine the Turkish contention that they are merely the misunderstood victims of Western bias and Armenian propaganda. After all, what are they so worried about? What could be so terrible that to merely say a word is enough to label you a traitor, condemned to a life spent dodging endless litigation and death threats?

As ludicrous as Turkish reactions to the Armenian issue can seem, the rhetoric and extremism are hardly one-sided. Proponents of the genocide frequently speak of Turks — all Turks, living, dead and unborn — in the most unreasonable, vitriolic terms and can be highly selective of the historical evidence they present, or the violence they choose to condemn. Throughout the 1970s and early-'80s, for instance, in an attempt to force Turkey to recognise the genocide, the Lebanese–Armenian terrorist organisation, ASALA, targeted Turkish diplomats in a series of bombings and shootings that killed over fifty people, including children. Large groups of Armenian émigrés in the US and Europe are also to blame for stoking the fires (sometimes to the frustration of native Armenians, especially the approximately seventy thousand who still live in Turkey and have to deal with the consequences) with a policy of lobbying Western governments to recognise the massacres as genocide, by force if necessary. During my time in Turkey a bill would be proposed to the US congress recognising and condemning the genocide, and France would try to pass a law making its denial a crime, ludicrous proposals on numerous counts, not least because both nations pride themselves on their freedom of speech, something they are often keen to remind the rest of the world.

It's difficult not to see some legitimacy in the Armenian demands for recognition of their genocide. After all, it seems impossible to characterise any policy that marched old women and children into the desert to their deaths as anything less than ethnic cleansing. Nevertheless, there remain some legitimate Turkish objections. Why, for instance, should modern Turks be brow-beaten into apologising for crimes committed by an empire that no longer exists, especially when many of their ancestors fought to overthrow it? And what is the ultimate purpose of recognising the genocide? Even if, in some distant and unlikely future, the Turkish government did so, then what? You can't sue a dead empire and, contrary to the beliefs of some genocide lobbyists, no one's going to hand over chunks of their country because they feel bad about what happened to your ancestors. It also seems oddly hypocritical that world governments should privilege Armenian genocide claims over those of, say, the indigenous populations of Australia, North and Latin America or, for that matter, attempts to wipe out the Muslim populations of former European Ottoman territories. Ultimately, whatever terrors the Armenians endured theirs was only one chapter in a world history littered with similar atrocities in which no one takes any particular interest, the victims being generally too brown, poor and distant to elicit much sympathy.

I am not a historian and do not know how many Armenians were killed at the end of the First World War or whether their deaths constituted the definition of "genocide". Neither am I qualified or willing to wade into the quicksand of evidence that might prove it one way or another. Whatever the truth, the fact remains: there were once millions of Armenians in Turkey and now there are virtually none, a fact that Turkey has clearly yet to come to terms with.

★ ★ ★

Despite their comparatively recent troubles, Armenian and Turkish history has always been intertwined, and large parts of eastern Turkey had once been part of a grand Armenian empire. On an island in Lake Van was Akdamar Kilisesi, the Church of the Holy Cross, one of the great remaining relics of this time. To get there I had first to take a *dolmuş* to a strange little town called Gevaş, which had a beautiful cemetery on the outskirts and a plaster dinosaur on a roundabout (actually a rather inferior rendering of the so-called Lake Van "monster"), then make my way to the spot on the lake shore where boats left for the island.

The boathouse was on the side of the highway in sight of little else but a campground. The lake here was weird and primordial; the kind of water first life had crawled out from. The mountains that rose up all around were of an impressive size, their bareness lent a silvery tinge by the thick clouds gathering overhead. At the boathouse I found some men playing cards and was made to understand that I would need to wait for more people willing to share the fare to the island, or else pay the full cost. In the distance, three men stood on a beach. As I approached I realised they were actually a man and a pair of very butch women, one with close-cropped hair, the other with dreadlocks and tattoos, who had been swimming in T-shirts. It was not until later that I was struck by the irony that the first women I had the opportunity to speak with for some time I had taken for men.

"Aren't you cold?" I asked as they towelled themselves off.

"No," said the girl with short hair.

"We are German," added the one with dreadlocks, as though this explained everything.

"Are you going to Akdamar?" I asked.

"No," said the short-haired one, again.

"We have already been," said the man, who had a strange, helium voice and wore glasses so thick they made his eyes huge and googly like a shark's.

"Will you give us your guide book for Iran?" asked the girl with dreadlocks.

"I don't have one."

"I'm sorry. We must go," said her short-haired friend. "Before the rains begin."

And with that they gathered their things and began to walk down the highway, a passing bus gathering them up. It was an odd encounter and I mention it only because it would not be the last time they would cross my path.

For an hour I waited in the garden of a campground opposite the boatshed, watching the storm gather over the green lake, writing notes. No one else was around except a young man who brought me tea and gave me a plate for my biscuits. Finally, two cars arrived. A couple emerged from each BMW, walking up the path in a clink of jewellery and squeak of fine leather. Sitting at the next table the boy appeared and presented them with menus, their obvious wealth being a sure sign that these were not the fasting types. I knew they were awful, just by looking at the way the men said nothing while the women "had fun" for their benefit, reaching over the table on occasion to touch the sleeves of their pin-striped suits.

At that point I should have simply paid the money and enjoyed my time, but some vestigial backpacker cheapness would not allow it. Grabbing my phrase book I began to practise my question, repeating to myself, over and over, as I approached their table. Tentatively, I interrupted their conversation to deliver my carefully worded spiel, whereupon one of the women, without so much as looking at me, raised a manicured hand and waved it dismissively in my direction. Shocked, I returned to my bench and watched as their fish lunch was delivered. Hastily I checked my book, wondering whether I had accidentally used the phrase for "I have diarrhoea" or "Will you have my baby?" But there had been no mistake, and as I sat and watched the women laugh for their rich husbands I was reminded of Hüseyin's shop with the bricked-up door, and thought to myself that if I'd been born poor in Turkey I'd probably have bought a machine-gun and an Al-Qaeda how-to manual the first opportunity I had.

The storm clouds were gathering and soon I would have no choice: it was time to go now or not at all. Just as I packed my things, another car appeared and a pair of middle-aged men came up the path. In English the larger of the two asked if they might have my table. "Will you go to Akdamar?" I asked.

They, too, had already been but when I asked where they were from the surprise of their answer was compensation enough. "Armenia," he said.

"Really? How did you get here?" The border between the two countries had been closed for a decade.

"We drove through Georgia."

As it transpired they were from the Armenian capital, Yerevan. The large man a mathematician, the other a high school teacher. They spoke excellent English.

"Does it make you sad to be here?" I asked. He seemed confused by my question. "Because all this," I said, gesturing out to the lake, "was once Armenian."

"No, not sad," he said. "But not happy. History is ... you know" — he motioned his hand like waves — "it comes and goes. I am just curious to see." With abrupt enthusiasm he took my pen from my hand and turned my diary towards him. "Here is the name of this church." In a careful hand he wrote the word in Armenian Cyrillic script, adding the dates of construction below. As the waiter came to take their order I bid them goodbye and made my way to the boat. On the other side of the garden the yuppie women shrieked and dropped their cutlery on their plates.

By the time I reached the island it had started to rain. After the trouble it had taken me to get there I was disappointed to find the church closed for restoration. I pleaded with the workmen to let me inside but to no avail. To the foreman I invoked my status as an important foreign journalist but this produced only a weary, uncooperative "Yok". Despite this disappointment the church proved itself to be a supreme work of art. Armenian architecture was a revelation. The disproportionate height of the building, with its sharp polygonal cupola, gave it the appearance of pushing upwards out of the soil, like a growing crystal. The carvings that ringed the walls and eaves were a joy; every gesture assured and lively, every face full of character, every animal sinewy and thriving. I was particularly taken by a pair of back-flipping lions arching their necks to the feet of Christ, their little tongues poking out to lick his feet.

Scattered around the grounds of the church were large headstones known as *khachkars*, elaborate crucifixes carved into their faces, each arm bursting forth into patterns of knots and swirls so full of vitality I was compelled to rub my hand against them. As I began to walk down a path to a beach on the other side of the peninsula, the wind picked up and the rain turned from a sprinkle to a shower. The workers began to retreat to their tent as I hurried towards the boat. In the driver's cabin by the engine I sat and watched the clouds move across the mountains, earth and sky blurring into one amorphous mass.

Like the first flicker of a neon tube, lightning flashed inside shells of cloud while dark grey sheets of rain moved overhead, separating occasionally to expose patches of clear sky that cut green triangles into the lake. Looking behind me, the church had grown small and pointed: the stone a rich red against the inky clouds.

As the storm grew the boat rocked so violently I began to scan the cabin for objects that would float. As we reached the dock the full front was moments away. The Armenians' car was gone and the yuppies were running down the path, sheltering under handbags. The road was empty so I began to walk, hitching for the first lift I could find. A car stopped just as the deluge began. Two men sat in front. They wore smart suits and gold jewellery but their car was a decrepit Mercedes with a broken windshield. They said they could take me to Gevaş and indicated with exasperation the rain outside which was now falling so hard it made their conversation a mime show in the front. We stopped and picked up two more men who sat, utterly silent, either side of me, their sodden clothes seeping into mine.

"*Dolmuş!*" shouted one of the businessmen from the front. I thought it was funny but nobody laughed. Not even me.

In Gevaş I ran through the downpour trying to find the *dolmuş* that would take me back to Van. In my haste I stepped into a deep hole, sinking up to my ankle in mud. On the bus I felt my toes squelch in my sock and tried to position my shoe in front of the heater. Mournful Kurdish wailings assaulted me in stereo. The rain eased as we left and had stopped by the time we reached the edge of the lake. Between the road and the grey sand beach lay a narrow verge of grass, barely two metres wide. At intervals on the grass, facing out to the water, were concrete park benches, moulded and painted to look like logs. I was very struck by these benches, wondering who would sit on them, so near to the highway, and marvelled at the trouble someone must have taken to make them seem natural.

Suddenly, as we came to a particularly beautiful part of the lake, the purple clouds cracked in two, turning the shallows a vivid ultramarine and the rest of the water, all the way to the barren mountains, a deep bottle green. Shafts of light cut into the mountains, sending shining snakes across the ruffled water while from one shore to another arched a perfect story-book rainbow. The scene was unspeakably beautiful, yet at the sight of it, I felt unexpectedly overwhelmed by sadness and, without warning, and not entirely unaware of my own silliness, burst into tears. I do not know why this sudden melancholy overwhelmed me: something about those empty park benches facing that sublime lake, the rainbow that arched across the green water like the handle on a pot, the pathetic fake wood trying so hard to be cheerful and failing so badly. But really it was the east, the saddest place I had ever been. So sad it was as if someone had set off a nuclear sad bomb and the fallout was radiating through everything, the half-life of sorrow wearing me down until I feared that the only reason I had come here was to have a nervous breakdown.

Chapter 13

Every traveller knows the feeling: the sudden crisis of purpose, the dreaded but universal question that approaches without warning, tapping your shoulder in the boring museum, waking you at midnight, crick-necked on the airless bus or chasing you through the muddy streets of an unfriendly city at dusk when everyone else is going home and you are left, alone, to stare up at rosy windows and thin, cosy trails of smoke rising from chimneys: what am I doing here? The east was depressing me, though exactly why I could not say. In my mouldy hotel room — purple velvet armchairs, pink walls and demon cat — I realised there was at least one person I was certain could make me feel better, if only by comparison.

After a few attempts, I finally managed to get hold of Tevfik. "I have a new job, man," he announced with unexpected cheerfulness. "I'm working for a friend who has a shop near Grand Bazaar. It's fucking bullshit. No old stuff, no antiques. Nobody gives a shit. They tell tourists cotton is silk and Pakistani crap is tribal. But, you know, I need a job."

I asked if he had spoken with Hüseyin.

"No, not yet. Please, speak to him for me, man. I don't like this shit when he's angry at me. I can't handle it."

"Why don't *you* talk to him?"

"I can't, man, really. Go on … you talk to him for me, please."

The contradictions of Tevfik's character were a source of enormous frustration to me. How could someone with his almost aristocratic disdain for the rules and formalities of polite society, combined with an almost reckless indifference to his personal safety, be too scared to confront his best friend, one of the few people who might still be prepared to give him another chance? If Tevfik had a fear of anything, it seemed, it was of those who cared for him.

I promised I would try and talk to Hüseyin.

"You sound sad," he said.

"I am, a little."

"The east is not good for people who feel too much, man. You are a writer. You are a goddamn artist! You have a right to be sad in a world as terrible as this. Remember that. Don't ever apologise for your feelings."

"Um … OK."

"Power be with you, baby," he said, and hung up.

Talking to Tevfik was like consulting some Indian guru on a mountain top. The things he said didn't necessarily make any sense but they seemed to have a weird logic — a certain poetry — that you felt sure must mask some profundity. As I fell asleep that night for the last time under the demonic gaze of the Van cat, I felt marginally improved.

The next morning I visited the carpet shop, where, finding once again only silence, I succumbed to the inevitable and, hoping to cheer myself up, bought a carpet. It was a Kurdish piece; a *sofra*, or eating mat, in green and yellow, scattered with embroidered talismans, like a rock pool at low tide. "The price that I give you," said Halil, "is not business. You are a friend." It wasn't cheap but I found it difficult to bargain in the face of such apparent kindness.

From the shop I took myself off on an excursion to a Kurdish castle an hour from the city located by the hideous roadside settlement of Güzelsu, undoubtedly the most appalling village I was to see in Turkey. The setting was dramatic — the castle looming over the sterile, pastel mountains — but the filth and dereliction were exceptional. Cigarette butts and plastic bags swirled through the air. The road was lined with decrepit sheds so rough they leaned at angles like carnival haunted houses. (These, as I was soon to realise, were garages for the endless parade of petrol tankers coming from Iran, which could be seen emptying their contents into containers out the back of the village for sale on the black market.) As I crossed the bridge over the river dammed solid with garbage it felt almost cruel to point out that, literally translated, Güzelsu means "beautiful water".

My trip was not even to be compensated by a look inside the castle. I climbed the hill, above the sheds and the string of petrol tankers, only to discover the ticket office abandoned and the door wide open. Walking up the stairs I was soon confronted by a caretaker in a leather vest, dragging a teenager down by the collar. A cheerful attempt to talk my way in was met with a savage rebuke. As I retreated down the path I heard the word "*jandarma*" and turned to see the teenager burst into tears. The caretaker gave a mocking hoot and with a violent shove pushed the boy into the ticket booth, locking him in.

Back in Van, Halil insisted on taking me to the bus stop. Slinging my bag over his shoulder, the strap reached almost to his ankles.

"This strap is too long," he said.

"The strap is not too long," I replied. "You are too short."

He paused for a moment, then laughed for what might have been the first time in three days and, possibly, that year.

On the *dolmuş*, the conductor ordered me to sit in the back corner next to an enormous German with thin blond hair, intense blue eyes and skin like pink paper. In his hiking boots, Björn Borg headband and strange technological clothes — all drawstrings and zero-gravity fabrics — he was the human equivalent of one of those

Mercedes buses. "Are you going mountain climbing in Doğubayazıt?" I asked. He nodded and silently leaned over me to train his video camera out the window.

The landscape on this journey was exceptionally lush and dramatic. Waterfalls ran in steps through fields of daisies. Brown mountains rose from green fields full of fat-tailed sheep. On a high ridge an Armenian church sprouted like a crystal. The farms here seemed unusually prosperous and tidy. Their corrugated iron roofs were the only I was to see in Turkey and at the sight of them I became immediately homesick. Slowly, the farms gave way, the landscape becoming more mountainous until we began to pass fields of ancient lava. A small volcanic mountain loomed over the first security checkpoint, the rain turning the jagged stone very black and the grass that grew upon it in tufts an almost fluorescent green. As we continued, the maze of lava unfolded before us. Between the razor-like walls sheep grazed, guarded by a shepherd in a yellow raincoat.

"Look," said the German, "Mount Ararat." On the horizon, rising from nowhere, the cone of the mountain pierced the clouds. Even from this distance it was hypnotic: a candle-snuffer peak with a perfect white crown, the kind of mountain children draw, complete with a little zig-zag of snow. It was impossible not to allow myself a spontaneous exclamation of awe.

Once again, the video camera was pressed against the window. "I'm sure we'll get a better view," I said.

"Yes, but ze wezzer," he said, ominously, pointing to the gathering storm, "eez not gut."

By the time we arrived in Doğubayazıt ze wezzer was, indeed, not gut. Thick clouds obscured most of the mountain, radiating out in black bands like the arms on a Shiva. The likelihood that these would disperse in the next few days looked fairly remote, adding a sense of having been cruelly cheated to my already depressed state. Doğubayazıt itself was no compensation: the streets were muddy, the pavements broken and the only solid buildings seemed to belong to the military. Despite this there was a not entirely unpleasant atmosphere about the town. Soldiers, both in and out of uniform, filled the pavements, walking hand-in-hand. On the streets, ridiculous little tractors that were nothing more than tin boxes with a fan belt spinning at the front zipped along at furious speeds, splashing mud over pedestrians. Spilling out of the passenger seats, fat Kurdish mamas hung on for dear life, wild toothless grins on their faces, as their menfolk sped around corners.

Doğubayazıt is a border town, the crossing point for much trade between Turkey and Iran, a fact immediately evident in the rows of bootleg petrol sheds, doling out fuel into the jerry cans of queuing customers. This proximity to Iran was felt in other ways, too: petrol trucks and buses rumbled through the street covered in beautiful Farsi script, and many Iranians — traders and smugglers, I presumed — walked the streets, conspicuous for a surprising fashion consciousness, their suits and hair styled with almost Parisian flair. There were prostitutes as well, although their presence was made known only by implication. Across the city were a host of flea-pit hotels with wood-panelled walls and furniture riddled in a buck shot of cigarette burns, their windows featuring a single, apparently innocent image of a woman singing into a microphone.

The extent and variety of the smuggling was impressive. Window displays were a surrealistic garage sale, juxtaposing plastic wall clocks with giant industrial-sized boxes of plastic carnations, toaster ovens with extravagant crystal table centrepieces shaped like vases of flowers. The most remarkable evidence for this black market, however, was the cornucopia of booze on offer. Stacked in seemingly half the shop windows were bottles of every conceivable spirit and beer, including many expensive and obscure brands I had seen nowhere else in Turkey. As Iran is a dry country I could only guess that the liquor had come from Armenia or, possibly, Georgia, via Iran, making it doubly wicked.

With the approaching dusk, rain came quickly. The clouds poured over the mountain, as if Ararat itself were generating the storm which, meteorologically, might have been true. At dinner I sat in a restaurant full of single men — military and smugglers, I presumed. The atmosphere was not unlike that at the starting gates of a major horse race. Men sat fiddling with their cutlery or cigarette lighters while waiters took orders in hushed, reverential tones. (Perhaps they were conserving energy: they would be unable to eat until everyone else had finished.) After not eating or drinking all day everyone was in a thoroughly disagreeable mood, and looking around the room at the silent faces, I had the sense of having stumbled into a hospital ward full of the chronically ill and woken everybody up.

Bowls of steaming soup were placed in front of everyone's noses, like some diabolical temptation. The only person not to receive any was, of course, me, the understanding being that I had been stuffing my face all day and could afford to wait. Normally this wouldn't have been an entirely baseless assumption. Today, however, I had missed breakfast and my last meal had been almost twenty-four hours ago. To my hunger I now added resentment and a mild persecution complex.

At exactly sunset the television announced the end of the fast, a message relayed by the head waiter with a small "*Afiyet olsun*" (the Turkish *bon appetit*), and the room suddenly began to breathe as everyone tucked wordlessly into their food. This was the now-familiar evening ritual of fast-breaking. It was always the same, across the length of the country, yet the lack of ceremony always came as a slight surprise, as did the restraint and refinement with which the men would dip their spoons and take their first sips of soup; the only ones who betrayed any greed or impatience were the hardened addicts who, ignoring their food, went straight for a cigarette which they inhaled to the butt in one go with a look of opiated ecstasy.

The rain belted down. I tiptoed back through the sodden streets and retired to my dingy hotel. In the foyer, sitting in a reeking brown velvet couch, a grey-haired Englishman began a conversation.

"I have been travelling in Turkey a month," he said, raising an emphatic finger. "And I'm not impressed by the food. People say the food in England is bad. Not me. Now, for instance, you got a Chinese buffet in Nottingham off the [insert highway I have never heard of nor am ever likely to encounter] which is a very good taste and — do you know? — only four pound. Mark me, four pound! And a good taste at that."

With the greatest effort I detached myself and retreated to the grim isolation of my room. By the time I came to sleep I found myself literally praying that the weather would improve and, come morning, I would be able to see Mount Ararat. Why this had suddenly assumed such significance I do not know. Suffice to say that as I lay in my dirty sheets, listening to the rain, like pebbles in a box, I felt no surer of my purpose or any less lost or abandoned than I had that day at Akdamar.

★ ★ ★

The pink light woke me with a start. Compelled, as if someone had called my name, I leaped from the bed to the other side of the room and drew back the curtain. There, perfectly framed by the window, white as vanilla ice cream and stark against the blue sky, was the cone of Mount Ararat. Oblivious to the cold morning air I stood staring, speechless as a child at the cinema, incapable of digesting the magnificence of the scene. In the foreground the silent dilapidated townscape of Doğubayazıt stretched out before me. Flat-topped concrete boxes bristled with rows of steel cables. Flooded wastelands piled high with mounds of stagnant garbage. Rusted satellite dishes and TV antennas were a field of broken kitchen utensils. The mountain didn't just overwhelm all this but made it beautiful, as if even this ugliness and decrepitude were part of some grander plan, and as I sat and stared, inured to the biting cold on my bare skin, I felt as if I were being completely re-energised, like a flower in the sun after rain.

It was still early. The streets were empty. Downstairs in the foyer, a lone boy, no more than eighteen, sat nestled in the brown velvet couch. I recognised him as a tour guide who had accosted me the previous day but been fobbed off with vague, non-committal promises. He had obviously been waiting some time and, seeing me, flashed a rotten smile, less out of friendliness, I felt, than a sense of triumph. Feeling rejuvenated I took pity on him, taking his persistence as a sign. After a brief negotiation, I allowed myself to be bundled into a van, joining a copilot and two baffled-looking tourists.

My fellow passengers were Phil and Andy, pink-faced, red-headed Englishmen I immediately recognised. "I saw you in Mardin," I said, after our introductions had been completed.

"Did you?" said Andy.

"Yes. You arrived as I was leaving."

"Did I?" he exclaimed with what seemed genuine astonishment. "What an absolutely remarkable coincidence!"

"Well, not terribly remarkable."

He thought for a moment. "No, I suppose you're right."

Phil and Andy were likable archaeologists who had just stepped off the bus from Gaziantep, a city not far west of Urfa, where they had once lived for a year, working on an excavation site outside of the city. "They called it the Pompeii of the East," said Andy. "It had the most complete frescoes and mosaics of any Roman site in the world. Whole preserved houses. Now it's all under a dam. Still, we managed to save some of the mosaics." With effeminate manners and flaming red hair, Andy was the absolute picture of an English public schoolboy turned adventurer, the kind of man in a previous century who might have been last seen walking up Mount Everest wearing only a tweed jacket and hunting cap. He had what appeared to be an enviable unflappability, but which was in fact an absolute obliviousness to the world around him, a fact perhaps explained by his extreme poshness. Phil was also a redhead but blessed — in contrast to Andy's neat part — with a mop of red ringlets he wore tied back in an enormous waist-length ponytail. He said little but, as I was to discover, had the most to say.

As we pulled out of town the full extent of Doğubayazıt's military significance was revealed: rows of tanks and armoured personnel carriers stood ranked behind barbed wire. Between them, bored-looking soldiers milled about, machine-guns slung across their chests, fingers hooked ominously on the triggers. Above the military base Mount Ararat loomed, radiating holiness and making everything beautiful.

Our driver pulled into one of the bootleg petrol stations and began to fill the tank from a jerry can. While we waited, on the opposite side of the road, a boy carrying a steel tray full of *simitler* (a kind of Turkish pretzel) dropped them in the muddy gutter, paused a moment to see if anyone was watching, then bent over and began to pile them back onto his tray. I had come to Doğubayazıt with few expectations which, after examining the town, seemed the best attitude to have. I did not even have any clear idea as to where we were being taken on this tour, only the reassurance of our guide that we would be seeing "touristic interest sites". This didn't really worry me because like most of the relatively small number of visitors who make it to this part of east Turkey, there was only one site I was keen to see — Ishak Paşa Palace.

Ishak Paşa Palace was another recommendation of Hüseyin's hippy friend, Margaret. "I have no words," she had announced with a Bob Fosse sweep of her hands. "You simply have to see it, that's all." This turned out to be no exaggeration. Situated at the top of a six-kilometre road snaking its way up a mountain valley, Ishak Paşa Palace is undoubtedly one of the greatest sights in Turkey — it makes description redundant and kills adjectives dead in their tracks. The geometry of the building, the harmony of carving and structure are sublime. The position on a rock bluff floating over the volcanic plains and the mountain ranges, tinted in mineral greens and pinks, is so improbable that the whole thing feels as though it were floating, like a hovercraft, on an enormous bag of air. After many years of joyless tramping through hundreds of miles of corridors, under thousands of tonnes of chandelier, slavishly inspecting acres of gilding, Ishak Paşa is the only palace that didn't make me feel as though I had just been forced to suck a three-tiered wedding cake through a straw.

By the ticket booth our tour guide stood and pointed at the sign that read, with considerable rhetorical authority, "ENTRANCE TAKES CHARGE," before turning towards the courtyard and, with all the conviction he could muster, uttered the only word of information he would offer for the duration of the tour. "Ottoman," he said, pointing vaguely into the distance.

What remains of the palace is mostly a shell open to the elements. In recent years, however, it has been heavily restored and a roof erected over some quarters to protect against the snow. For a time we wandered through the rooms, our guide pausing only to insist that I take photographs of him standing in front of a tomb or ornate doorway, the worn-out brown stumps of his teeth kept self-consciously hidden in an agonising display of adolescent self-consciousness.

In a number of the rooms, forgotten pieces of scrofula clogged the corners: soft drink bottles, rotten magazines and a single condom packet, shining like a lost coin in the gloom. There was a distinct tang of urine in the air. All across Turkey it was the same — at dusk, great monuments became the secret places of the young, hideouts where they went to tell ghost stories, smash bottles against the wall and lose their virginity. Staring out at the barren mountains I was filled with a sense of inadequacy and jealousy that the milestones of my youth had all taken place in the comparatively sterile urban terrain of parks, bus shelters and the local McDonald's.

Our exit from Ishak Paşa was hurried, too much so for either my liking or that of the archaeologists. Our guide, however, was insistent. The weather, he indicated, would soon be changing and unless we began moving we would not have time to see everything on our itinerary. "Well," said Andy huffily, "I'd hate to think that out there somewhere is a carpet dealer being kept waiting." Phil laughed lowly.

As we made our way along the road towards the Iranian border Mount Ararat filled my field of vision. Also clearly visible from this vantage was the previously-hidden cone of Little Ararat, a near-perfect scale model of the larger mountain and, in its own right, a not inconsiderable peak — God's maquette for the finished product. As a tourist attraction Mount Ararat is still best viewed from a distance. Once a PKK stronghold, trekkers have, in recent years, been granted permission to climb it. Yet according to those climbers I met, the bureaucracy is labyrinthine and the cost prohibitive. But there is one thing that can guarantee a constant stream of visitors — the Ark.

The Turkish name for Ararat is Ağrı Dağı, or "Mountain of Pain", a fact which says much, I think, about the national psyche. The name by which it is known in English, however, has one immediate association: the place where Noah finally landed the Ark after the Great Flood. The notion that Noah landed on Mount Ararat is, in fact, a fallacy. The Bible says only that the Ark came to rest on the "mountains of Urartu", an ancient pre-Armenian kingdom, of which Ararat is believed to be a corruption. This leaves open the possibility that the Ark, assuming it ever existed, could be anywhere in the mountainous region crossing Turkey, Iran and Armenia. Despite this, every year strange men with metal detectors and degrees from American universities where they teach you Adam and Eve used to ride around on dinosaurs, arrive in Doğubayazıt claiming that, this time, they'll be the ones to find the Ark. These people appear to be greatly encouraged by members of the local trekking industry who make suspiciously regular "discoveries" of "unusual formations", able to be reached, naturally, only with their guiding services. Subsequently, Ark-finding has become an important part of the local economy and there are now several competing sites, all claiming to be authentic.

The best known of these is an elliptical stone formation — a landslide according to geologists — nestled in the mountains by the Iranian border about twenty minutes' drive from town. The site of this particular Ark is separated from the base of Ararat by a distance of many kilometres, an anomaly explained by those who believed in its authenticity as the result of sedimentary shift over the millennia. After a long, rough road we arrived at the top of the hill crowned by a concrete yurt. Painted across its front was a sign advertising "ANCHORSTONE.COM", an American fundamentalist group of professional Ark-hunters who had paid for the construction of the building, as indicated by another smaller sign by the front door. Hovering outside the building was an old man who smiled and nodded and shook our hands delightedly as we alighted from the bus. He looked ill, undernourished and a little mad. As we made our way to the top of the ridge to view the Ark he followed us, babbling excitedly in Turkish and gesticulating into the distance.

"He is at least a little more enthusiastic than our chap," said Andy.

To my surprise, the Ark was quite impressive — it really did look like the hull of a gigantic fossilised boat. Buried into the barren hillside among the scraggly olive trees, it was serene, even poignant, and I could imagine becoming quite excited if I had discovered it. I asked our driver if we could go down for a closer look. He shook his head. "Iran?" I asked pointing to guard posts topping the nearby mountains. He nodded and sniggered, as though I had said something slightly scandalous which, in a sense, I had.

Iran acts on the Turkish psyche like a sibling lost to drugs or a huge malevolent comet with a fifty-fifty chance of hitting the earth.

Whenever a secular, citified Turk wants to illustrate why it is important that the country not lift the ban on the headscarf, or allow various other concessions to religious freedom, he or she will point ominously east and cry, "Do you want us to end up like Iran!" Truth be told, I had a lot of sympathy for this view. People like me — ie. gays with big mouths — got lynched in Iran, a fact conveniently forgotten by many of those keen to decry the evils of "Western cultural imperialism" in the Middle East. Nevertheless, the chance of Turkey following suit seemed to me utterly remote, an intuition for which I have no real evidence other than the sense that the tribal instinct was simply too strong in the Turks, that they would always be a clan first and, everything else, even a religion, second.

Tiring quickly of the Ark I began to explore the grounds surrounding the Anchor Stone building. Finding out the back a natural spring I drank greedily from the spout, the coldness of the water on my hands and lips a synaesthetic metaphor for the twin white mounds of Ararat rising over the olive trees. Joining the others by the bus, I found the old man lingering hopefully, dangling a set of keys to the visitors' centre. The guide seemed anxious to leave but I insisted on seeing the interior. The old man, apparently delighted, turned to unlock the door, at which point the guide made a remark — either to his copilot or the old man, I could not tell, but clearly designed to upset and, I suspect, part of a longer campaign of ridicule. The old man turned on the boys and began to rant and rave, gesturing violently with his cigarette and spraying the immediate area with flecks of white spittle. In between their sniggers, the boys made condescending gestures of consolation.

Still shaking with rage, the old man opened the door and gestured for us to enter. Inside was a nondescript lecture theatre with plastic chairs facing a whiteboard. The walls were lined with press clippings from obscure Southern Christian newspapers, *Life* magazine articles from the sixties and, my favourite among them, a cover story for *Memphis Business and Leisure* featuring the director of Anchor Stone dressed as Indiana Jones, swinging a whip about his head. After a cursory inspection of the articles we thanked the old man who nodded dismissively and mumbled to himself, as though he knew we were humouring him. Outside, the boys were smirking to themselves. Fuming, the old man hovered by the bus while we boarded. When our guide muttered some parting shot, he flew into a rage, puffing out his chest in a threat of violence that drew only pitying sniggers from his tormentors. As we drove away the old man shook his fist at the bus and threw his cigarette to the ground in disgust. The boys threw back their heads and laughed at their own adolescent cleverness.

"He is Christian?" I asked, as we made the slippery descent.

"Yes," said the guide, barely able to speak for laughter.

"So he believes in the Ark?"

"Yes!" he said, and all at once I felt very sorry for the old man whose life seemed quite hard enough without having the compensation of his faith mocked by these little shits.

By the time we arrived on the sealed road Mount Ararat had acquired a coolie hat of cloud, pearl grey against the blue sky. In less than an hour the mountain would be totally obscured and the rain would fall steadily until morning. A brief and utterly unrewarding detour to a hole posing as a meteor crater followed. Our guides didn't even bother to get out of the van on this occasion, choosing instead to sit around smoking and turning up their wailing Kurdish music. I didn't blame them; the crater was an utter disappointment, a deep cylindrical shaft like a disused mine or a giant's golf hole. A sign tacked to the perimeter announced that the meteor had struck in 1892. "And they're still talking about it in Doğubayazıt," said Andy.

Only a few hundred metres away was the Iranian border, marked by a silvery line of wire and a few scattered huts. Watching from the Turkish side was a guard tower and a group of soldiers who sat outside a concrete bunker on camp chairs under a pair of brightly-coloured beach umbrellas, like disgruntled package tourists trying to make the best of it.

Back out along the highway the clouds were rolling in quickly, draping the bare lower stretches of Ararat in a downy grey boa. Still unsure of where we were going, I called out to the driver, but he could either not hear, understand or had now completely abandoned any pretence to guiding responsibilities. "I'm seeing something," said Andy, pressing his fingers to his temple in the posture of a ham psychic. "Is it … apple tea at my cousin's carpet shop?" But Andy had been wrong to be cynical. After a little more driving along the highway, we pulled off and began to move towards Ararat. As we approached, the mountain grew to CinemaScope proportions, its white peak electric against the patches of blue sky. Eventually we arrived in the middle of a tiny village, nothing more than a dozen cubic stone huts, their grey and white colour schemes enlivened only by flashes of blue plastic stretched across glassless windows. Disregarding the ubiquitous satellite dishes, the poverty was absolute, the austerity compromised only by a small, boxy mosque at the entrance to the settlement dwarfed by a disproportionately tall minaret, white and sleek as a missile emerging from the ground.

"My home," announced our driver, tapping his chest, proudly. He was right to be boastful: with the minaret slicing the grey skirt of the mountain, its white cone an echo of the snowy peak, the village exuded an almost heavenly peace, a serenity transcending its poverty and shabbiness and filling me, if only for a moment, with the mad misguided fantasy that I might never leave.

Hesitantly, with the guides trailing, we walked towards the houses, wary of the notorious dogs that roam Kurdish villages in the east. Appearing from the first of the huts, a small child, his clothes rubbed with grime, stood and watched, silent and wary, as our procession proceeded. The quiet in the village was eerie, the child the only sign of life. From a distant field a small figure grew larger with approach. His flock of fat-tailed sheep ran in currents about him, kicking up the dust as they crossed the road. Our driver hailed the shepherd, drawing in to kiss him on each dirt-rouged cheek. "Cousin," he grinned, forgetting for a moment his dental self-consciousness.

For a while the three conversed, ignoring us while we stared dumbly at the view. Pulling a packet of Marlboros from his pocket, Phil shook one out for himself then, much to the delight of our companions, accustomed, no doubt, to smoking the fakes sold in the stores in Doğubayazıt, began to offer them about. Without embarrassment the boys pulled a pair each from the red box, nestling one behind an ear before lighting the other. As they smoked a little boy wandered over from one of the huts. Our guides took turns stroking his hair and pinching his cheeks. The boy giggled and shyly took my hand.

"Give me one," I said.

"I didn't take you for a smoker," said Phil.

"I'm not," I said, gesturing to the mountain. "I'm just so happy I feel like celebrating."

Chapter 14

One of the great myths of travelling is that being in an interesting place automatically makes you interesting, a delusion easily shattered by a half-hour of conversation in any youth hostel dormitory anywhere in the world. People who do not travel are, I feel, often unduly impressed by those who do, regarding their anecdotes as evidence for a life richly lived. As anyone with half a brain who has done any travelling can tell you, however, the roads of the world are jammed with bores and it is perfectly possible to have lived on a mountain in Peru, in an Indian ashram or a yurt on the plains of Mongolia and still be a tedious, small-minded arsehole whose primary and all-consuming concern is finding creative ways to save five cents on a bunch of bananas being sold by a woman with a malnourished baby strapped to her back. Especially in an Indian ashram.

Jock was a museum-quality example of his kind. He was Scottish and had been travelling for two years across Asia in which time he had, apparently, never had a bath. His only conversation was of prices and when the archaeologists and I had told him the previous evening that we intended to go to the best restaurant in Doğubayazıt — picture, if you will, "the best restaurant in Doğubayazıt" — he had clicked his tongue reprovingly and said he had eaten nothing but bread and cheese for six months. (Not strictly true — he later arrived at the restaurant clutching a bunch of mouldy grapes which he ate glumly in the corner, refusing to pay for even a single glass of tea, the poverty of the professional traveller being every bit as exhibitionist as the most vulgar trappings of the Hong Kong mafia don.) Everything about Jock provoked me to the edge of violence, from his horrible wispy moustache that curled into the edges of his mouth to the way he kept saying "Fair enough" in response to anything I said, as though he were constantly adjudicating my conversation. So when I bumped into him the next morning on my way to Ishak Paşa Palace for a second, greedy look, I was consumed with the same feeling of my own carelessness that comes of being sprung by a colleague you have gone to great lengths to hide your birthday party from.

"Morning," he said. "Would you like a grape?"

"No thank you."

By his side was a slightly tedious New Zealander I had also met the night before, a man for whom the entire world was just a variation on the landscape between Christchurch and Dunedin. We exchanged some awkward greetings and I was finally cornered into a confession. "I'm going to Ishak Paşa Palace," I said.

"Fair enough," said Jock. "So are we. Mind if we walk with you?"

"I don't have enough time to walk," I said. "I'm heading to Kars and need to leave soon. I ..." — there was hesitation as I saw an inevitable chain of events unfold before me as well as if they were the frames of a cartoon strip — "I was going to catch a taxi."

Jock clicked his tongue. "A taxi ..."

"I'll go thirds in a taxi," said the Kiwi.

"A taxi ..."

The deliberations continued for some minutes while Jock and the Kiwi grew bogged down in potentially endless negotiations over the best method to split five dollars three ways. "Oh, look," I said, accepting the inevitable, "I'll just pay for the fucking taxi."

Ishak Paşa Palace was even better the second time round. At a more leisurely pace than on my first visit I could notice details previously missed: the snaking trees on the inner courtyard doorway, the way the windows had been perfectly aligned to frame the view and the reflections of those views in the still pools of water on the floor. A rich American couple with their own guide arrived and for a little while we tagged along, listening to their tour. Jock, who was still fuming after his fight with the ticket collector over his refusal to admit him for a student price, was obviously keen to squeeze some value from the expedition. With the boldness and cunning of a starving lion he quickly separated the couple from their guide before manoeuvring the poor man into a distant corner to bombard him with questions. To their credit, the rich couple didn't seem to mind, but the look on the guide's face was one of unmistakable revulsion, the cause of his understandable distress Jock's by now almost overwhelming odour.

Filthiness is often cultivated by the professional traveller, adding, or so they imagine, verisimilitude to their role as untamed poet of the road, the wild-eyed ascetic with a staff in one hand and a *Lonely Planet* in the other. From my experience, most people in developing countries are bemused and often disgusted by this Western practice because, although poor, they are usually impeccably clean and, if they are not, are so only because they lack access to proper facilities. It must have been a matter of some amazement to them to see these people walk through their villages with the apparent economic power to take two years off work to travel the world, but not, apparently, to get a load of washing done. As we left the building and the pair announced that they were going to hike around the mountain at the back of the palace, it was with little regret that I prepared to part ways.

"Why don't you come with us?" asked Jock with what I thought to be a hint of challenge.

"I don't really enjoy hiking," I said.

"Fair enough."

"Just come up and see Mount Ararat before you leave," said the Kiwi. "I've heard the view of Ararat from up there is pretty amazing."

The temptation to see Ararat from a height was too much and, making sure I was downwind of Jock, we set out on a track leading to a tiny clump of houses on the opposite side of the ravine. Past the village the track thinned into a crumbling ridge until we were tramping along one of a maze of goat tracks criss-crossing a mountain.

My objections to hiking are well noted: I do not, as a rule, partake of any activity that could be inflicted upon prisoners of war. Yet, try as I might, every five years I seem to get sucked back into a hike, usually because I have by then forgotten how bad it was the last time. This is, perhaps, an unusual position to take as a travel writer, but I do not view it as any paradox. Nature is to me nothing more than a nice idea, pretty to look at but amoral, unforgiving and, ultimately, quite dull. My preference is for human beings and all their inventions: good, bad and indifferent. For this reason I enjoy walking, especially in cities, where I can go for mile upon mile without weariness. Hiking, however, is the act of taking something pleasant and soothing, like walking, and turning it into something exhausting and competitive, merely so that obnoxious men in sweat bands might have the chance to high-five one another on mountaintops.

The soil on the mountain was black, volcanic and as fine as icing sugar. With each step I sank to my ankles, turning my shoes and socks into sandbags. With their hiking boots and backpacks, Jock and the Kiwi soon pulled away while I struggled to cross the waterfalls of volcanic scree in my sneakers, counter-balancing the weight of my shoulder bag. An hour later, panting and covered in a fine dusting of black powder, like a burnt wiener schnitzel, I finally arrived at the ridge where the other two were lounging about, exchanging water bottles and laughing in a hearty, cliff-top manner. I collapsed beside them.

"You don't hike much, do you?" said the Kiwi rather needlessly.

"Where's the view of Ararat?" I asked.

"I think it must be round there," he said, pointing to a ridge that was so far away there was a good chance it might have been in Iran. "This looks just like the South Island," he added with satisfaction.

"I don't think I'll be going any further," I said.

"Where are you headed to after Turkey?" asked the Kiwi.

"I'm staying in Turkey," I said. "After Kars I'm making my way back to Istanbul."

"Fair enough," said Jock.

"Will you guys go to Istanbul?" I asked.

Jock made a face. "Isn't it just another city?"

Just another city? *Just another city?* Describing Istanbul as "just another city" was like calling the Vatican "just another church", *A Night at the Opera* "just another movie" or Jock's body odour "just another smell". No, it was not just another fucking city. All at once, two realisations presented themselves: I was homesick for Istanbul in a way I hadn't expected; and I'd had it with this smug, reeking bastard.

"Right, I'm off," I said, and made my way towards the ridge that would hopefully take me back in the direction of the palace.

"Well we're going to keep walking," said Jock.

"Don't get shot at the border," I called with as much sincerity as I could muster.

The second hike to the ridge and down the hill was no easier than the first, but I eventually arrived back at the palace. After walking some of the way on the road I managed to hitch a lift with four boys in a taxi, one sitting on another's lap in the back so that I might have a seat. With sign language and key Turkish words I established they were studying in Van to be teachers, though they were only in Doğubayazıt on a sight-seeing trip. I asked if they were Kurdish and the one in front laughed and said, "No! Peh-kah-kah," and mimed machine-gunning the distance. Everybody laughed, including the obviously Kurdish driver who banged the steering wheel for emphasis. It was the most cheerful scene I'd witnessed on my entire journey in the east.

Chapter 15

Still in Doğubayazıt but sitting on the *dolmuş* to Iğdır, my phone rang. It was Hüseyin. As always, I was pleased to hear from him but his tone was so grave that I immediately became concerned. Worst case scenarios began to take hold: lurid fantasies of accidents and overdoses — Tevfik dead in his grimy flat — took root and grew. I stepped off the bus and stood in a quiet alcove.

"Brendan," he said, very solemnly.

"Yes?"

He drew breath. "Did you buy a carpet from Charlie's friends in Van?"

"Ah … yes."

"Why did you do that!"

"Why not? What's the problem?"

"Oh, no problem," he said, affecting insouciance. "It's just — you know — Charlie and all his friends are coming round to the shop and saying, 'Hey, your friends betray you. They don't buy from you. Your carpets must be shit.' They are making head games, you know?"

I had to stifle a laugh; it was like soothing a jealous lover. Was this, I wondered, the dark power of the evil eye in action? "I'm sorry. I just wanted a souvenir from the east."

"Oh, no it's no problem. I don't care where you buy from. I mean, you could have got it cheaper ... but, it's no problem."

"Well," I said, endeavouring to take this as seriously as possible, "tell Charlie that the only reason I bought the carpet was to be nice to his friends. Tell him that I took pity on them because they had no business and were so miserable."

This was, of course, a complete lie, but it seemed to cheer him up marginally. His tone changed. "Brendan, I have something to ask you."

"Yes."

"Will you run the shop while I go to America?"

I had seen the request coming and had already decided my answer. "Of course."

"I can give you commission, man."

I told him I didn't want it and, with a minimum of further conversation, reiterated my promise to see him at the end of Ramadan when we would sort out the details. "Take care, bro," he said and hung up.

Excited by the prospect of my new job, and feeling reassured by the sense of direction and purpose it offered, I reboarded the *dolmuş* and waited for it to fill so that we might leave. Taking the seat next to me was a chatty Iranian, conspicuous for his fine tailoring and Cary Grant hair. On his lap sat a briefcase under which he had deposited a bag of bread. Diving into the bag at regular intervals he produced bite-sized hunks which he would surreptitiously feed into his mouth under the guise of scratching at his nose, coughing or some other contrivance. Without warning he began to conduct a monologue in excellent English. "I do business in Erzerum," he said, referring to the large city a little further to the west. "I sell computer parts." He tapped his briefcase, portentously. "This country!" He *tsk*ed, disgustedly. "They are so ignorant." He dipped down under his briefcase and produced another morsel of bread, nibbling on it behind a closed hand. Across the aisle I saw a man watching. When my gaze met his, he looked immediately away, pretending he hadn't seen.

"Why don't you just eat your sandwich?" I said.

He *tsk*ed again and rolled his eyes. "I'm not fasting. But they are," he said, thumbing to the back of the minivan. He lowered his voice to an exasperated whisper. "These Turks! Total fundamentalists!"

The landscape to Iğdır was wild and barren. Sheep lingered by a distant river from which their shepherd emerged stark naked. Overhead, hawks skipped on the currents. Not long after our first military checkpoint a startled calf ran towards the bus. Looking again I realised it was a dog, the biggest I had ever seen, barking like Cerberus, its neck ringed in a collar of spikes six inches long to protect it from the wolves. For at least half a kilometre it chased the bus with a blind rage that, even at a safe distance, was terrifying.

First impressions of Iğdır were not immediately favourable. By the entrance to the *otogar* a stray dog sniffed at a man who sold lottery tickets, his twisted legs, like dead roots, folded into a small red trailer. As I walked off through the streets to find my connecting *dolmuş* children followed and threw stones at my head. Iğdır is the centre of Turkey's approximately two million Shia Muslims, which came as a surprise to me because I had not even realised there were any Shias in Turkey, a misconception I shared with many Turks I had met.

Islam in Turkey is as fractured and complex as the country's political life (and, indeed, inexorably bound to it) and although the majority of the population are Sunni Muslims, their practices virtually indistinguishable from those of their Arab neighbours, a number of other sects exist. Most notable are the Alevi, who number approximately twenty million and are the largest of all minority Islamic groups in Turkey. Alevi Islam is loosely connected to Shia (they recognise the Prophet's brother-in-law, Ali) but so unorthodox are their beliefs and practices, with hints of everything from Christianity to Judaism, Zoroastrianism and pagan, tribal animism, that many in the Islamic world don't even consider them Muslims. Alevi women generally don't cover their heads, it is permissible to drink alcohol, folk beliefs abound and they don't even pray in a mosque, conducting instead weekly meetings (called a *cem*) where they play music, perform ritual group dances (called a *sema*), conduct community affairs and sometimes drink a ceremonial form of wine.

Alevis are sort of the Quakers of Islam, but they have a long history of conflict with conservative factions of the Sunni majority, many of whom regard them with distrust and outright hostility, not merely for their allegedly heretical beliefs but because of their heavy connections to left-wing political movements. (The Alevis were much persecuted under the Ottoman Caliphate so they have always been staunch supporters of Atatürk's secular revolution.) The most infamous incident of Sunni–Alevi violence in recent years occurred in the central Anatolian city of Sivas in 1993 during a cultural festival and intellectual conference. After prayers at the mosque, a fundamentalist mob, led by the mayor, went to the hotel where many Alevi intellectuals were staying, including the Turkish translator of *The Satanic Verses*, and burned it down, killing thirty-seven people. During the subsequent investigation video footage was released of the police watching impassively as the fires were lit.

Closely related to the Alevis are the Bektaşi, followers of the thirteenth-century Sufi mystic and saint, Hacı Bektaş. The Bektaşi are also found outside of Turkey, mostly among Albanian communities, but their beliefs and practices are so similar to those of the Alevi that the two are often counted together. In the area between Antakya and Adana there are also a small number of Alawites (often called Nusayri in Turkey), a secretive Shia splinter group found mostly in Syria. Arguably the most fascinating are a scattering of mysterious, mostly Kurdish, sects along the Iraqi border, of which comparatively little is known. Strangest and most notorious among them are the Yezidi whose principle divinity and symbol is the "Peacock Angel", Malek

Tawwus, otherwise known as Lucifer who, or so they believe, after falling from grace was forgiven by God to take his place in heaven beside him. Their worship of the divinity most Christians associate with the devil has given the Yezidi an undeserved reputation as Satanists, something they find deeply offensive. But in a catalogue of beliefs and practices that includes the notion they are descended from children grown from the seed of Adam left in a sealed jar, a ban on the wearing of blue clothes or the eating of lettuce ("We cannot even dwell in the place where lettuce is sown," announced a nineteenth-century Yezidi message to the Ottoman Caliph), Satanism barely raises an eyebrow.

There are only a couple of thousand Yezidi in Turkey and I mention them only because they are so irresistibly weird. There are, however, more conventional Sufi sects who have begun to assert themselves in a country where grassroots Islam is experiencing a revival after a long period of state-ordered subjugation. These are the Islamic fraternities known as *tarikatlar*: secretive religious organisations with Sufi roots that act as both theological study groups and community networking tools, analogous, perhaps, to organisations such as the Catholic Opus Dei. In 1925, a couple of years after the inauguration of the secular republic, fearful of their potential to undermine the new state, *tarikatlar* were banned. Yet, in defiance of their illegality, they have experienced a massive resurgence in the last few decades and now exert an increasing influence on Turkish public life. Some *tarikatlar*, like the Mevlevi (better known in the West as the "Whirling Dervishes") or the more conservative and politically influential Nakşibendi, are large and ancient Sufi orders led by powerful clerics. Their function is partly religious but is often not unlike that of, say, Rotary: initiating charitable works, creating community ties and, presumably, offering the chance for stationery wholesalers to discuss golf and tell sexist jokes in a sympathetic environment.

Despite their secrecy, often a necessity in a country where religious organisations are still looked on with suspicion by the state, most *tarikatlar* seem to be relatively benign. Yet, in recent years there has been a flood of scandals involving dodgy "sheikhs" who, in the manner of cult leaders the world over, have set up *tarikatlar* simply to exploit their members. Criminal *tarikatlar* have become tabloid staples in the Turkish press, offering a rich source of lurid stories involving luckless country folk stripped of their savings and impressionable women manipulated into kinky trysts with spellbinding svengalis. Occasionally, even murder has been known to feature. In early 2006 a mutilated and bullet-riddled body was found by a cave outside Urfa. The victim had been a member of a *tarikat* run by a fraudulent sheikh who had been threatened with exposure. During investigations, horrific video footage was handed to police by the victim's brother. It showed a frenzied mob of *tarikat* members nailing the man to the wall before stabbing his body with skewers.

Tarikat scandals aren't limited to the rural poor. Many *tarikatlar* are now quite rich and include numerous senior parliamentarians and at least one former prime minister among their number. Other high-ranking members own influential newspapers, publishing houses and TV stations. Of course, there's no reason to see anything sinister in this — the Freemason connections of American presidents scandalise me only insofar as I find it difficult to believe that grown men can enjoy dressing up as festive ironmongers and singing fraternity songs while remaining totally sober — but if you love a good conspiracy theory, and Turks do with an unyielding passion, *tarikat* politics is a tempting labyrinth. When, for example does a *tarikat* cease to be a community religious organisation and start to become a political party or lobby group? Who really controls the *tarikatlar* and what sort of ambitions do they have for Turkey's political future? In 1993 the journalist, Uğur Mumcu, who had recently published a book critical of the relationships between *tarikatlar*, big business and the government, was killed by a car bomb. In Turkey, a nation where newspaper columnists have a habit of being blown up, this is nothing unusual, and Mumcu had written about many other controversial topics (at the time of his murder he was working on a book about the PKK). But the timing was enough to make you pause for thought. As internet cranks and potheads are keen on pointing out: it's not paranoia if it's true.

* * *

After a weary wait on the step of the bus company office, the *dolmuş* for Kars finally departed. It wasn't long, however, before we stopped for our first checkpoint. This one had the most serious firepower I had seen so far: two enormous armoured personnel carriers with cannons aimed at the bus, a pair of soldiers in each, sitting behind the blast-proof windshields. When they demanded that everyone take their bags off to be inspected, there were mutinous grumbles from the passengers. Everyone was searched except for me who was waved away as I approached, leaving me a little dejected, as if I'd been picked last for the team. From here the landscape became lush, verdant and hilly. The fields were well irrigated and the houses crowded by stone fruit trees. Slowly we climbed a steep ridge. Reaching its peak, Mount Ararat appeared on the horizon, its snowy cap turning a faint blush of pink from the approaching sunset. Directly over it hung a full moon, thin and white as a communion wafer.

As we approached Kars the earth grew barren again, the fields strewn with black rocks. Young men herded sheep from motorbikes; their hell hounds in spiked collars chased the bus. Just on sunset the appearance of the pink monoliths signalled our arrival in the city.

It is always curious to see how your impressions of a place tally with descriptions you have read. If Pamuk were to be believed Kars was a decrepit, isolated outpost of fanaticism, a paranoid nest of spies and fanatics who sat around all day plotting destruction and ruminating on what it meant to be a Turk. For all I knew it probably was. Physically, however, my immediate impression was of a cute provincial centre in Eastern Europe, minus the nuclear power station and women in leopard-skin tights.

Kars is very old. After the usual millennia of death and destruction it was rebuilt by the Russians during their brief takeover of the region in the late nineteenth century. It was hoped that the city would be a major centre for the empire, these grand plans echoed in the surviving buildings which, although not in universally good condition, were well made and decorative. Built of a dark stone, many of the larger mansions and public buildings were painted about their windows in blocks of jolly colour. Others reversed the order: their walls in yellow and pale pink and the chequerboard of stones about the windows left bare. A number were ringed by elaborate wrought-iron balconies, mostly made by Armenian metal workers, famous for their craftsmanship during the Ottoman period. Their European character seemed oddly alien in the east, their solidity and grandeur a welcome sight in a part of the country where almost everything else looked as if it had been built for as little money as possible to be used only until it fell apart.

Kars seems to hold a special place in the Turkish psyche, which is why, I suppose, Pamuk had decided to set his novel here. It is, in many ways, the forgotten city; the little town that couldn't. When people in Turkey talk about "the boondocks" or the "back of beyond", I am sure it is Kars that they imagine. Once it had been a trading post with Armenia but after the closing of the borders the city had lost almost all its, already small, purpose. (A few days after I left, the mayor caused a minor national stir by demanding that government reopen the border.) Walking about the town, I began to suspect that Kars was the subject of an urban makeover, spurred on, perhaps, by the bad press the city had received in recent years. The cobblestone streets were clean and well lit with restored Russian carriage lights. The parks and trees were well tended, the new pavements sturdy and public sculptures unusually competent in a country where a fibreglass watermelon was often the best you could hope for.

Cheese and honey are both specialties of Kars and many pretty shops featured surprisingly stylish window displays of honeycomb and cheese wheels the size of car tyres. The night was colder than it had been elsewhere, but not especially so, and packs of students wandered the streets, hand-in-hand, in various gender combinations, or congregated in the *pastane* (pastry shop) drinking tea and eating profiteroles swimming in chocolate sauce. The headscarf, the central motif of Pamuk's book, was not unduly represented and for every group of *türban* girls strolling the streets in long, unflattering raincoats there were just as many in the current street uniform of hip Turkey: jeans, Converse sneakers and thick black eyeliner, as if half the country were continually heading off to a Ramones gig. Later, I met the only woman I had ever seen in Turkey eating on her own in a restaurant. For all I knew, Kars may well have been a hotbed of terrorism, it being in the interests of fanatics to remain undetected, but compared to, say, Batman, it felt like Paris in the thirties.

Soon after my arrival I had met the archaeologists at the hotel and we had ventured out to find a meal. We settled upon a surprisingly upmarket restaurant but dinner was a strained affair, conversation made almost impossible by an amplified serenade performed by a man plucking a type of *saz* and singing utterly miserable dirges at a truly unreasonable volume.

"Oh, I do hope they bring some razor blades with the after-dinner mints," said Andy.

After dinner we wandered the streets where we found a solitary but promising Tuborg sign glowing out the front of a backgammon parlour. At the entrance a man sat guard on a high stool. After some negotiation we were ushered into a bootleg room out the back.

"Oh, our trip was frightful," said Andy as we were led out past the room full of backgammon-playing old men, lost in a permanent shroud of smoke.

"How did you get here?" I asked.

"We paid this awful little man to drive us. Well, I mean to say he virtually abducted us from Doğubayazıt and is threatening to take us to Ani tomorrow. Perhaps you could come with us."

"I've already been bullied into booking a tour, I'm afraid." The moment I had walked into the hotel a phone had been pressed against my ear and a reasonable offer made.

"Oh well," said Andy. "I dare say he'll find you sooner or later. His name is Jalal but we call him Jellied Eel. If you want a laugh, ask him about his sex life."

The bar was a horrendous Formica and neon box, enlivened by empty bottles of Grant's Whisky and a fading Swiss alpine scene on the wall. Strange, I thought, these Swiss alpine scenes everywhere when Turkey had perfectly lovely mountains of its own. We ordered drinks, but it was soon apparent that I was the only one participating. I begged and cajoled: after not having touched a drop for weeks I was feverish for booze. Finally, Andy relented but Phil remained resolute.

"I can't drink," he said in his shy mumbling way.

"Are you an alcoholic?" I asked, hazarding a guess.

"Yes. And the rest." He took a hard, compensatory drag on his cigarette. It was then that I noticed the scarring on his arm; running along both sides, front and back, like pink train tracks. I tried to pretend I hadn't seen.

"You're looking at my scars," he said, exhaling a curling cloud of smoke.

"Yes," I confessed.

"I used to be a self-mutilator." He traced the ridges of skin with a finger. "But I've stopped now." I was slightly taken aback by his frankness, but grateful for it.

"Why did you do it?" I asked.

"I dunno. Depression, I suppose. I was bullied quite horribly at school." He drew on his cigarette. "In Turkey self-mutilation is a plague. The other day we went hiking to a castle outside Van. A guy saw my arms, pointed to them and started laughing. Then he pulled open his shirt and his entire chest was covered in cigarette burns."

This was, naturally, in Güzelsu, land of the beautiful water.

"It's not the first time I've seen things like that here," continued Phil. "When we lived in Gaziantep it happened all the time. East Turkey," he said, pausing to suck on his cigarette, "is not a place to have a mental health problem."

Back at our hotel, Jellied Eel was holding court. "I lived in Holland ten years," he said, continuing a monologue to which I had been listening patiently for the last ten minutes. "On my satellite I have eight hundred channels. I get porno from Spain, Denmark and Italy, but there is none on any of the Dutch channels!" He *tsk*ed loudly and made a gesture of flabbergasted disbelief. "This is a problem, because I like Dutch porno very much." Jellied Eel was by his own account "one of the premium business identities in Kars", which may not have been an exaggeration because he appeared to run the city's tourism industry almost single-handedly, aided only by an extensive network of hotel receptionist spies.

"As I have said before," he continued, "my wife is a very understanding woman. So when I set up house next door with my mistress she did not complain. I said to her, 'Yes, my darling, I love you. Can you not see it? But is it not possible that I can love her also?' Well, she cried very much. But eventually she said, 'Go to her. If it is as you say then I cannot stand in the way of your love.' I tell you, I love my wife very much. It is most unfortunate that she has these" — he paused — "nervous problems."

"Well, that really is terrible," said Andy, nodding in sympathy.

"You," said Jellied Eel, suddenly turning his attention to me. "Are you going to Ani?"

"I'm sorry. I've already arranged a tour."

"Did you book it this evening?"

"Yes."

"Ah good," he said, smugly. "You booked it with me."

★ ★ ★

The next morning Phil, Andy and I sat in the foyer of our hotel, waiting for a pair of elderly backpackers I had seen checking in the night before. I had taken them for Germans but according to Jellied Eel they were Israeli, a fact he shared with barely concealed antagonism. "These people!" he snapped. "What are they doing?"

While Jellied Eel fumed I read the local newspaper. The front page featured a photograph of some local worthy presenting a woman in a slum somewhere in Kars with a new electric heater. The story was a follow-up from a news report I had seen on the local TV station the night before. The woman was caring for her severely retarded son but would have no heating for the winter. An appeal to charity was issued and, apparently, answered. I took an unusual interest in this story because both the newspaper and TV station feature prominently in the plot of *Snow* and, for once, Pamuk's description seemed remarkably accurate. I showed the report to Jellied Eel.

"Ha!" he scoffed. "So she has a new radiator. Pity she doesn't have any electricity."

Finally the elderly couple arrived, straining under the weight of their enormous backpacks. Together we piled into Jellied Eel's car, the Israelis sitting on one another's laps in front. "How long are you in Turkey for?" I asked.

"Four days," said the woman.

I expressed surprise. I had taken them for hardy old hippies, the sort of kibbutzniks who had travelled through India during the seventies on nothing but hash cake and anti-diarrheal medication.

"We would have stayed longer," said her husband. "But our son was invited to participate in the Lebanon war."

"'Invited to participate'," whispered Andy. "So that's what they're calling it these days."

The hills on the way to Ani were bare and green, speckled with hardy mountain flowers. A large eagle sat on a fencepost, like a sculpture on a plinth. In the distance, Mount Ararat played peekaboo between the hills. After a half-hour drive, passing only a handful of remote villages, we arrived. The walls of the city were surprisingly massive, hulking circular battlements curved off in both directions over a distance of what must have been at least half a kilometre. Impressive they undoubtedly were but had obviously been heavily, and rather unsympathetically, restored.

Under the enormous Aslan (Lion) Gate, between the two layers of walls, Jellied Eel delivered an unmodulated and obviously well-worn speech. "Ani is situated on the border between Armenia and Turkey. It is, therefore, considered a region of high security. As you walk into the site you will see to your left, at the bottom of the gully, a large fence. You are never to approach this fence. You are never to go into the gully. You are to look at the structures in there only from a distance. Likewise, you are not to approach the Citadel at the southern end of the site. Please, we are not joking. There are guards with guns on the hills" — he gestured into the distance — "and they are trained to shoot. Are there any questions?"

"I vont to buy a Coca-Cola," said the old Israeli lady.

Jellied Eel's eyes narrowed. "There are no such facilities here," he said, and stormed off back to the car.

Ani is a city with over 2500 years of history. It is best known, however, as the capital of an Armenian Empire which hit its peak in the eleventh century under the reign of King Gagik when the population of the city reached between one and two hundred thousand, making it one of the medieval world's largest. Although almost everyone has had a piece of Ani — including the Byzantines, Seljuks, Georgians, Kurds, Mongols and Ottomans — few structures other than Armenian churches survive. Ani was a well-defended city. Its massive double walls shield a naturally impregnable peninsula, bordered on one side by a river gorge, shadowed by the cliffs of Armenia, and on the other by a rocky rift, the stone walls cut with ancient cave homes. Stepping through the gate, the ruins of the city unfolded before us. The desolation was magnificent. Silence sat like a blanket over the fields. In the distance, sheep moved white across the yellow meadows and the ruins were brown building blocks against the blue sky. Looking around, it was as if we were the only people in the world, the last survivors of the apocalypse, the absolute serenity of the scene broken only by a sudden barking in what might have been Russian, the words "Coca-Cola!" punctuating the Slavic tirade like an aural karate chop. Leaving the Israelis to struggle with their backpacks and their bickering, I moved off with the archaeologists and headed along the walls towards the nearest ruins.

Possibly the most striking building in Ani, the Church of the Redeemer, is an undeniably moving sight. Once a perfect cylinder topped by a dome, like a fat bullet, the structure is now a precarious cross-section, shorn in half by a lightning strike in the early-1950s. When Armenians complain that Turkey is not doing enough to care for their heritage it is to this building that they point.

The apparent reluctance of the Turkish government to care for the Armenian buildings of Ani was bewildering but was, in fact, a partial blessing. The only two standing Islamic structures have, like the walls, been heavily restored with wildly varying results. The Seljuk mosque, believed to be the oldest Turkish mosque in the country, still retains some dignity but the Seljuk palace is a disaster. Hulking and square amongst its fragile neighbours it now resembles a large public toilet block or small Soviet power station and sections of the original walls have collapsed under the rebuilding. All across Turkey one saw this mania for "restoration", which was not restoration at all but the archaeological equivalent of cleaning the Sistine Chapel with a high-pressure hose and a bottle of Ajax. It was a mark of insecurity, the sort of thing one saw a lot in countries like China where the past was not allowed to be merely the past but forced instead into the service of the glorious present.

Taking our time among the ruins, we wandered to a nearby ridge overlooking the border with Armenia. As we walked along the edge we couldn't help but notice that for a supposedly highly sensitive border region the fence dividing the two countries was in a terrible state of repair with many man-sized holes running its length. Below us the Convent of the Virgins was tantalisingly close, its chapel rising out of a bluff above the green river at the bottom of the chasm. "Out of bounds area, bollocks!" announced Andy, and with no further debate we began to head down. The convent had once been a large complex. Now all that remained were foundations and a tiny umbrella-roofed chapel, like a fat drill-bit poking from the land, so minuscule I could only suppose that worship was conducted by a race of midget nuns sitting on pews the size of shoe boxes.

"There are guards," said Phil, pointing into the hills, "and they are trained to shoot."

As we climbed among the ruins our attention was suddenly diverted by the sound of distant voices. Looking down to the river, a pair of men — shepherds, we presumed, wrongly — were signalling to us from the other side of the fence. Cupping their mouths they cried out and waved their arms. One raised a bright silver kettle above his head. "Çay! Çay!" they called, the kettle glinting in the sun. Phil, standing on a high ridge, his ponytail fluttering in the wind, suddenly looked rather shamefaced.

"Oh, aren't they keen on you," said Andy.

"They think I'm a woman," said Phil, dolefully.

"Well," said Andy, "who are you to deny them their simple pleasures? Go on, go down there and offer yourself."

The shepherds persisted, waving the kettle and pointing to a nearby hole in the fence. "*Çay! Çay!*"

"Will you come down?" I asked.

"I don't think so," said Andy. "There's rather a lot to see. But you should. And if you don't get arrested or shot we'll meet you back at the gate in about four hours." After a moment's deliberation I farewelled the boys and began to make my way down the ridge.

The descent was not difficult but the soft dark dirt and loose stones rolled out from beneath my feet precariously. As I approached the hole in the fence the shepherds clapped and beckoned. I looked up at a distant guard post on a high hill and paused. As is my habit, I began to think in headlines: "Foolhardy Journalist Shot in Turkey"; "Young Writer's Death a Warning to Others, Says Foreign Minister"; "'He'll Always Be My Boy,' Says Dead Traveller's Mum". Reasoning that if they were going to shoot me they'd have already done so, I hopped over the low concrete barrier and was through. At the camp the shepherds stood by a small fire, keeping a battered kettle simmering. One wore a bright patterned jumper; the other was shirtless and smelled like a goat. Immediately they fetched more water to make me a glass of tea, a ritual I had been dreading for more than the usual reasons — the river water probably contained enough Soviet-era chemical waste to transform me into a mutant comic book super-villain.

With as much enthusiasm as I could muster, I sipped the glass of sweet mud. We communicated with a phrase book and sign language, exchanging the usual pleasantries and personal details. They looked in their mid-thirties but I was not surprised to learn that both were twenty-six. I asked where they were from. "Ermeni!" said the shirtless one, using the Turkish word, touching his chest and pointing across the river. The other was from a village by the gates of Ani that we had passed on the way.

Neither were shepherds. From what I could understand, the Turk was a carpenter and the Armenian was a worker at a stone quarry visible from the top of the ridge. The quarry was an idiotic nationalistic exercise on the part of the Armenian government who had established it to mine symbolic stone from a site they regarded as theirs and, at the same time, piss off the Turks. In this respect the project had been wildly successful and Jellied Eel would later spend some time ranting to me about it. The only material effect of the continuous mining and explosions, however, was geological instability that further threatened the delicate buildings, an irony apparently lost on the Armenian government for whom the petty provocation of their bitter enemies took priority, even at the cost of their heritage.

To the Armenian I made it understood that I wanted to know how he had gotten across the river. I mimed swimming. "*Yok*," he said and pointed to a big rubber inner tube that sat beached on the bank. Soon a third man appeared, wearing a red baseball cap — also an Armenian quarry worker. More questions followed: could I swim? With a hint of the rather deplorable nationalism known to stir itself on these occasions I informed them that everyone in Australia could swim — yes, even the women — and, before I knew it, had stripped down to my underpants and was wading through the reeds to prove it. To a chorus of cheers and applause I swam the width of the surprisingly strong river and emerged at the other bank, on Armenian territory, panting like a dog. It was at this point that an ulterior motive was revealed. Yelling incomprehensible instructions, the shepherds began to point over my shoulder. Looking about, I realised that not far above, hiding in the bushes by a path up the cliff, was a large white horse. For a moment the animal eyed me suspiciously then went on tearing at the branches about it. From the opposite bank it was made clear that I should bring the horse to the river to drink.

At this juncture I should explain that I had not been near a horse, outside the context of a parade, since an abortive outing to a friend's farm at the age of six. On that occasion the animal I was riding in a pen bolted and ran in demented circles for fifteen seconds, sending me into an inconsolable crying fit that ended only when my shamefaced mother came to fetch me several hours later. It's not that I don't like horses so much as I am suspicious of placing them in a privileged position relative to the rest of the animal kingdom.

Tentatively, with mud and horse shit squelching between my toes I made my way through the thick undergrowth. Never had I approached a horse before and as I did so it seemed that, for one thrilling moment, a backlog of apparently repressed *Horse Whisperer* fantasies suddenly revealed themselves. Here in the green glade, dappled by sunlight, my skin tingling in the crisp autumn air, I was at one with nature, transformed into a magical woodland sprite, a fawn with power over man and beast. This fantasy was as short-lived as it was idiotic. As I stretched my hand out to take the bridle the horse looked up from its meal and regarded me with obvious contempt. Shying off, it turned to display its rump, raised its tail and let out a steaming yellow tube of manure. Undeterred I continued, rationalising this as some sort of equine greeting, possibly a sign of kinship. Across the river I'm sure I heard the faint sound of laughter. The horse turned again and began to scratch its hind legs in the mud. Technically this shouldn't have been very intimidating — this was no proud-headed stallion. It was old; a nag, in fact, with prominent ribs and hips like anvils. Nevertheless, it was still the size of, well, a horse and, seeing it now at close range, looked perfectly capable of delivering a kick powerful enough to condemn me to a future of plastic sheets and a little round of applause every time I tied my shoelaces.

Sensing my hesitation, cries came from the opposite bank. "*Prob-lem yok! Prob-lem yok!*" Once more I approached and, once more, the horse turned, raising its hind leg in readiness. This was not an animal that looked as though it didn't have a problem.

My friends on the bank were now laughing openly, their cries of "*Prob-lem yok!*" no longer an encouragement but an ironic aside among themselves. Standing in my underpants on the river bank, my body white as bone, covered in mud and scratches, an object of derision in two nations, my humiliation was complete. Nevertheless, some warped sense of masculine pride compelled me to persist, an utterly misguided instinct that often seems to assert itself in the crowd at football matches or at the bar in country pubs. Determined that the men would come to regard me as an equal I spent the next twenty minutes conducting a slow-motion waltz across the river bank — me chasing the horse, the horse baring its backside — until we were a hundred metres from where we had started yet still no closer to the water.

The amusement of my audience soon turned to frustration. Revealing previously hidden talents, the man in the baseball cap tore off his shirt and dove into the water, swimming easily across to emerge and grab the horse by the bridle. Calmly, the animal tramped down to the water's edge and began to drink. I should, I suppose, have been annoyed by his deception. Instead, I merely gestured an entirely unnecessary apology. Ignoring this he reached down into the mud of the bank and retrieved a length of green wire, tied at one end around the trunk of a nearby tree. Hand-over-hand we pulled it up from the river bottom. Pointing the twisted end at me, he indicated that I should take it back to the other side. Determined to salvage some shred of pride, I wrapped the wire around my wrist and dove back into the water. The current seemed stronger this time and when I finally arrived at the Turkish side I was out of breath. The shirtless Armenian grabbed the wire and ran up to the fence to tie it around a steel post. It was at this point I realised that the wire was, in fact, part of the border fence, possibly a river barrier for boats. In one stroke, every pious hippy aphorism concerning the power of travel to bring people together, to make friends of enemies, was made a cruel parody.

As I watched him rebuild a section of one of the world's tensest national borders, my heart swelled with pride.

I was not even able to catch my breath before the man in the loud jumper presented me with the inner tube that had been sitting on the bank, making it clear that I was to deliver it to the other side. At this point certain objections began to assert themselves. Nevertheless, desperate to make up for the horse incident, I swam off once more, pushing the tyre in front of me. I was by now quite exhausted, but my eventual arrival was greeted with no gratitude. Seizing the tyre, the swimming Armenian jumped into the rubber ring and began to pull himself leisurely, hand-over-hand, back to Turkey.

Arriving for the final time back on the Turkish bank I was greeted by broad smiles and a glass of sweet mud. For a while I did nothing more than stretch out in the sun, drink tea and toss pebbles into the water. My new friends said little but occasionally shared a joke amongst themselves, quite possibly involving the opening line: "A horse and an Australian walk into a bar." Whatever the case, I could think of few better ways to spend an afternoon and it struck me that these were the most cheerful people I had met in east Turkey.

Once I was almost dry I made it clear that I was going to leave. I was reluctant to do so but I had spent an hour-and-a-half running errands and had only seen a fraction of Ani. As I began to dress, they expressed dismay and attempted to foist more tea upon me. Reaching into his pocket, the Turk in the jumper produced three coins and pressed them into my palm. They were not even coins, really. Just discs of metal, oxidised to a peacock green, all identifying features rotted away. They might as well have been washers or bottle caps for all I knew, and probably were. Nevertheless, I was rather touched by his gift and thanked him enthusiastically.

"Twenty lira," he demanded, in Turkish.

Perhaps he could sense my hurt but when I eventually handed him ten he didn't argue. "*Tamam*," he said, shaking my hand.

Pocketing my coins, I waved goodbye and made my way through the fence. As I began my hike back up the ridge they called out to me one last time. From behind the wire the shirtless Armenian mimed swimming then cupped his hands about his mouth. "*Çok güzel!*" he cried, meaning, literally, "very nice", an all-purpose Turkish expression of approval endorsed by the others with solemn nods and a double thumbs-up. It had cost me an hour-and-a-half, ten lira and a possible dose of radiation poisoning, but I had finally won their approval.

The walk back up the ridge was more difficult than it looked. The dirt was soft, the hill steep and my underpants were sodden. To pull myself up I clung to loose tufts of grass that came out in my hands, leaving me to perform a precarious limbo with gravity. Climbing the final ridge, I stood at the top. In the stony fields, the ruins stretched out before me, the churches a rich red in the sun. There was no sign of the archaeologists, the Israelis, Jellied Eel or anyone else. For the first time since I had arrived in Turkey I realised there was complete silence: no cars, conversations, blaring televisions or call to prayer broke the serenity. Behind me, back down the chasm, the shepherds were colour strokes against the green river. A few steps into the field and even they were gone.

Over the rocks I walked to the church in the distance. The cathedral was thickset and geometric, like a red American barn. The stones were a patchwork of reds and browns, the roof furry with grass. Overhead an eagle traced lazy circles. All at once I was overwhelmed by a feeling, an illusion but palpable nonetheless, of being the first person to have seen this. As I drew closer the cathedral loomed and I realised it was larger than I had thought. Inside, this deceptive size was fully revealed. Arches in the centre reached up to frame a perfect circle of blue where a dome had once been. On the rim of the circle doves sat in silhouette, swooping occasionally to cast shadow vultures across the wall. From the slitted windows, beams of light wrapped bright ribbons around the pillars. For a long time I did nothing more than sit inside the church, watching the doves and the surf of dust play in the light, drinking the solitude like clear water and thinking how happy I was. Then, taking the coins from my pocket, I dug a small hole in the ground with my heel and dropped them in, one by one; a meditative offering to the gods of history interrupted only by a sudden scuffling outside the entrance and a loud bickering in what might have been Russian.

Chapter 16

I did not leave Kars immediately. For two days with the archaeologists I walked the streets and the surrounding countryside which had, it seemed, reached a seasonal peak of prettiness. Seemingly overnight the trees had changed, splashing reds and oranges against the blue skies and painted houses, making even the most decrepit buildings cheerful. At the Ottoman fort on the hill overlooking the city we met a marine engineer from the western city of Izmir and his sculptor girlfriend. They had come to Kars specifically because they had read *Snow* and had also been surprised by the pleasantness of the city, a reminder that the east was as alien and forbidding to most Turks as it was to me. The caretaker allowed us onto the roof and showed us the panorama. Below us, down the hillside, the *gecekondular* were being demolished. All that remained were foundations and a handful of recalcitrants, their houses nothing more than blue tarpaulins stretched over shattered walls. The site, he informed us, was being prepared for "hotels and historical attractions", a fact which caused the brows of the archaeologists to furrow.

I asked the guard what he had thought of *Snow*. He said he had never heard of it, or its author. The sailor, however, told us that everyone he had met in Kars had been angry about the book; that they had taken it literally, failing to see its allegorical qualities. The hotel in which he was staying was the one where Pamuk had lived while researching, using it as the basis for one in the novel. The female manager had been mortified by the romantic plotline that had taken place beneath its roof. "She is religious lady," he said, laughing. "She don't have sex with men!"

After leaving Kars I had spent the night in Erzerum, my final destination in the east. The city was surprisingly large and modern but remarkable only for a group of imposing Seljuk buildings and the fact that everyone seemed to be either a student or soldier. On a street corner a group of teenagers in green headbands — a symbol of militant Islam — were staging an exhibition detailing atrocities committed against Muslims during the Chechnyan war. Taped to a fence in the park were pictures of women with their faces burnt off. Overhead, banners with images of various Islamic martyrs flapped in the wind. A market stall had been constructed to raise money for the Muslim victims, selling, without any apparent ideological contradiction, stacks of fake Levi's.

In the *otogar* the next day I bumped into the archaeologists. "Fancy seeing you here!" exclaimed Andy. "What an incredible coincidence."

"Not that incredible," I said.

"No ..." he said, considering for a moment. "I suppose not."

Together we travelled to the Black Sea port city of Trabzon. The change in atmosphere — literal and metaphoric — was immediately obvious. For a while the landscape was dry and barren, typically eastern. Then the bus began to climb, winding up a high mountain before disappearing into a deep tunnel. Emerging on the other side the air smelled of damp and the mountains bristled with smoky pine forests. Just outside Trabzon the driver stopped at a bakery, considerately asking the passengers if anyone would like to purchase bread for their evening meal. Turkey: the land of small mercies.

Arriving in Trabzon in the evening we walked the city streets. Downtown there were chic clothing stores, a McDonald's and a pedestrian shopping mall lit with iron lamps. The apartment blocks rose up the steep hills, condensing the streets into bustling alleys. At the docks, ships from Russia and the Ukraine arrived, unloading their cargo with big blue claws. In a park by the seafront, couples promenaded, hand-in-hand, apparently oblivious to the stench of sewage. Off the sea wall boys with the immune systems of plague survivors swam in the black oily water that shimmered silver under the street lights. It wasn't just the sense of prosperity that was unfamiliar, there was something else: an openness, a sensuality that life by the ocean seems to encourage. And just like that the east was gone. I cannot recall the exact moment I realised it wasn't there, just a lost, regretful feeling of having been rudely awoken from a peculiar but euphoric dream.

The next morning, Phil and Andy were watching television in the hotel lounge. We had arranged to travel together to see the Sumela Monastery, a Byzantine structure half an hour's drive out of town and the reason most tourists came to Trabzon. CNN was playing an interview in Turkish with a pale, bespectacled man with expressive hands. "Is that Bill Gates?" I asked, impressed by the software mogul's linguistic skills.

"No," said Andy, "it seems our friend Orhan Pamuk has won the Nobel Prize."

This was big news. Pamuk was the first Turk to win the prize in any category and, even though I strongly suspected the award to be politically motivated, in a country where pop stars with top-fifty hits on the Belgian R&B charts were hailed as conquering heroes, I had no doubt that all would be forgiven and Pamuk claimed as a national icon. To mark the occasion, I had Andy and Phil pose by the television for a photo. Andy adopted the voice of an American TV announcer: "We'll be back with our regularly scheduled program of slutty actresses getting out of cars after the break."

While we waited for the bus to Sumela to arrive we watched the special report, getting the gist of the coverage which seemed to centre almost exclusively on the political implications of the award. Of particular note was the recent attempt by France to make it a crime to deny the Armenian genocide, a move that had sent protestors onto the streets around Turkey. I could hardly understand what was being said; nevertheless I continued to watch for some time, realising I was happy for Turkey, as you might be for a relative or close friend.

Phil and Andy wandered outside to wait for the bus. In the foyer, the reception desk was changing shifts. Mustafa, the boy who had manned the desk overnight, was leaving, although, technically, he wasn't going anywhere as he slept in the boiler room upstairs. The previous evening we had spent hours swapping our favourite YouTube videos and discussing his arranged marriage with a girl in Germany, his ticket out of Trabzon. This morning he was entertaining himself with a translation program, entering dirty words in Turkish to hear them spoken in English by an electronic voice with an uncanny similarity to that of Stephen Hawking. "Listen, listen!" he said as I came into the room. "Horny," said the computer voice. He bent over the desk, gripping the edge, helpless with laughter. His replacement remained impassive.

"Have you heard?" I said. "Orhan Pamuk has won the Nobel Prize."

"Who is this?" asked Mustafa.

"Threesome," said the computer voice.

The replacement stepped up. "It is terrible for Turkey," he said, in a calm and understanding way. "I don't like him. All Turkish people hate him."

I was a little taken aback. "Why?" I asked.

"He is rich. He doesn't understand the real people of Turkey. He had an easy life, a good education."

"Does that make him a bad writer?"

"You don't understand," he said. "You are not from Turkey. The rich here, they have all the privileges."

I was going to add that this was hardly a condition unique to Turkey and was still no criticism of Pamuk, but could see no point in inflaming a debate I knew instinctively would lead nowhere good.

"Listen," said Mustafa.

"Spermatozoa," said the Stephen Hawking voice.

"What do you do?" asked the receptionist.

I never quite knew what to say when confronted by this question. With only one relatively unsuccessful book published and another withdrawn for legal reasons, "writer" seemed an exaggeration. Besides, bitter experience had taught me that it tends to open you up to pitying inquiries as to what your real job is and/or highly detailed descriptions of as-yet-unwritten science fiction trilogies coupled with earnest solicitations for an opinion on their likely success, with optional requests for free editing services and/or to put in a good word with my publishers. My claim to being a "journalist", on the other hand, was justified only on the basis of a year sorting faxes and writing "Pet of the Week" for a Sunday newspaper that used to have a problem column written by a talking cat, supplemented by occasional humiliating freelance puff pieces about wine tours in Eastern Europe or factory outlet shopping in California. "Journalist" was mostly a lie but one I had embraced in a vain attempt to gain some measure of professional respect. I might as well have told everyone I was a pimp or a back-yard abortionist for all the good it had ever done me.

"I'm a journalist," I said.

"You know," he said, drawing himself up, "you must not write these lies about the Armenians. It was them who killed us."

And so we had come to the elephant in the room. "Ah, I really don't care about this," I said. But it didn't matter — nothing could convince him that I had come to Turkey for any other reason.

"Oral pleasure," said the computer.

"I have books and articles," he said in a forceful but understanding tone. "I will give them to you."

"Look, I'm really not interested." My reticence was interpreted only as an attempt to deny an uncomfortable truth.

"Anal sex."

"Do you know what they did to Turkish people?" He began to recite a list of Dantean atrocities. My patience was waning.

"Do you know anyone who was a victim of Armenian attacks?" I asked.

"No. But I read the stories. I know it is true."

He had misunderstood the purpose of my question. "What I want to know is — if it doesn't directly affect you, why do you care? Why do you care what happened a hundred years ago? Why is it important to you?"

"Not a hundred, eighty," he snapped.

Andy appeared in the doorway. "I say, the bus is here."

I pressed on. "What I don't understand is *why* you care. Of all the things that have happened in Turkish history, why this one?"

"Cunnilingus."

"Because they killed our people," he said, stepping towards me. And I saw that he had crossed a barrier, that his rage was starting to spin out of control. "They killed men and women and children. Then they tell the world we killed them. And you," he said, putting the emphasis on "you" in such a way that he clearly meant to refer to a whole host of people, foreign journalists especially, "*you* believe it!"

I decided this had come to an end. As I walked down the corridor he followed, his anger so acute I began to suspect he might hit me. Hurriedly I made my way down the steps and out onto the street where Andy and Phil were waiting in the *dolmuş*. Behind me, he stood in the doorway, out of his mind with fury but pleading at the same time, like a child whose mother won't believe something he has told her.

"They killed Turkish *babies!*" he screamed, tears welling in his eyes.

I slammed the door of the *dolmuş* and we began to make our way out of town. "What was all that about?" asked Andy as we sped away, the receptionist still fuming in the rear-vision mirror.

"Armenia," I said.

"Ah, the dead Turkish baby speech, I presume."

★ ★ ★

Sumela Monastery looks like something boys who play Dungeons and Dragons draw in the margin of their exercise books. With a barely credible disregard for gravity it clings to a sheer cliff above a forested mountain divided in its centre by a swollen river, cascading in a series of dramatic waterfalls. The current structure was built mostly in the thirteenth and nineteenth centuries but the site was almost continually inhabited from 386 by a gang of particularly hardy and wily monks who successfully fought off, or negotiated with, every invading civilisation for more than 1600 years. Despite this impressive track record, they finally vacated the premises with the foundation of the Turkish Republic in 1923, no match for Turkey's great program of secularisation.

To reach the monastery you have first to hike up a not inconsiderable mountain. Although I normally object on principle to such exertions this proved to be a memorable walk, dense with what appeared to be virgin forest, a comparative rarity in a country where the land has been used and reused by countless generations until, it often seemed, it had nothing left to give. Walking with me was a sweet, fiercely earnest Chinese–American girl by the name of Margaret I had met on the *dolmuş* from Trabzon. She had been in Turkey only three days but was already on her way to Georgia that afternoon. "From there I fly to Syria, via Istanbul," she said, as we walked past the waterfalls. "I'd like to stay longer but I don't know if I'll make it to Jordan on schedule."

Margaret was only nineteen but we got along well and I was grateful for female company. She was, however, remarkably tense with a horror of the unplanned so powerful that the word *schedule* coming from her lips — which it did often — sounded very much like a euphemism for a terminal illness or a man in a leather coat pointing a machine-gun into her back: as in, "I have a schedule" or "My schedule won't allow it." In keeping with the spirit of her schedule Margaret was an enthusiastic travel blogger, a hobby that gave vent to both her obsession with order and her tendency for self-flagellation. "I've been so lazy keeping my blog updated," she said, mournfully. "I haven't added anything since Finland."

Margaret seemed to regard travel as a kind of educational penance, its only purpose to make her a better citizen. Her life was a tyranny of downloads and updates, of Wi-Fi and USB. As we walked through the forest she lamented broadband speeds in Bulgaria, corrupt files in Croatia and CD-ROMs left jammed in stubborn North African disk drives. I did not feel superior to Margaret, I was doing much the same thing as her with pen and paper, but it was the spirit in which it was done that bewildered me, as if it were homework or court transcripts. She seemed to get little joy from this obsessive communicating and I wondered to what degree it was all part of an attempt to force order on a world that secretly terrified her.

Panting and damp we arrived at the top. The air here was wet and much colder than the lower altitudes, seeping right through our clothes. From here Sumela looked, if anything, more precarious than it did from the ground, the steps to the monastery rising from a thin wedge of cliff. An impressive construction it undoubtedly was, but the interior was an anti-climax. Large sections were closed for restoration and even the frescoed ceiling of the chapel was mostly nineteenth-century over-painting. My opinion was perhaps coloured by the presence of a busload of tourists, all on some sort of academic tour, their matching T-shirts advertising some obscure mid-Western university. After weeks of having historical sites to myself I suddenly felt rather claustrophobic and, after a brief inspection of the frescoes, feeling I had fulfilled my obligation to culture, left. Margaret joined me but Phil and Andy remained behind, examining in detail the frescoes and the restoration work, tut-tutting darkly to themselves. All that was missing were the pith helmets and the letter from Queen Victoria.

On the way back down the mountain, Margaret and I talked about our travels. She asked me about the east and when I told her about Ani and how beautiful it was, she sighed. "Oh, I'd love to go there," she said. "But, you know, I've got a schedule."

I encouraged her to go. "Isn't it better to see more of one country than little bits of many?"

"I suppose. But is the east dangerous?"

"No. Although I was in the middle of a gunfight in Batman."

"Oh, what a coincidence," she exclaimed. "I know somebody else called Brendan who was also in a gunfight in Batman. Well … I don't *know* him but I was in this carpet shop in Istanbul run by this really funny guy …" etc.

She had been there when I had phoned Hüseyin. No shit. I can give you her email address and you can ask her yourself.

Back in town I reluctantly bid Margaret farewell — she was off to meet some locals she had found on an internet site for travellers before taking off on her overnight trip to Georgia. "The website is great," she said. "You should really try it. The people are really nice and the experiences are so authentic. Well, except for this one time in Sweden when I turned up to a guy's house and he was wearing nothing but a bathrobe that was so short it almost showed his … well, you know. While we ate dinner he kept crossing his legs and I could see his … well, you know."

"You ate *dinner* with him?"

"Well," she said, very seriously, "to tell you the truth I didn't think it was very appropriate but I said to myself, 'Margaret, you're in a different country with a different culture and you don't know what's right here.' But I have to say," she said, with no hint of irony, "it *was* quite a good dinner."

By the time I lost Margaret it was getting dark. All around the city people ran, frantically buying bread for the Ramadan meal and the bust of Atatürk in the park had been lit from beneath, giving him an eerie, Vincent Price-like quality. I had long since lost the company of Phil and Andy who had taken up with a pair of Swiss brothers staying at our hotel. They were adventure tour operators who had been cycling across the world for three years, their sandal straps tattooed across their feet like the aftermath of an atomic flash. They were as fit as they were boring — which is to say very — but Phil and Andy had an almost homoerotic fascination with the pair, constantly asking to be shown their bicycles or making concerned inquiries into matters of hydration and nutrition. The only source of amazement to me, however, was the fact that anyone could have done anything so apparently remarkable yet have nothing more interesting to talk about than the difficulty of finding quality inner tubes in remote regions of the Himalayas. Perhaps I was just jealous that they had stolen my friends.

Reluctant to go back to the hotel for fear of bumping into the deranged receptionist, and with nothing better to do, I decided to join everybody else and eat. Choosing a restaurant at random I sat down with my soup in front of me, waiting for the signal. The atmosphere was, as always, tense, expectant and very solemn; the only sound, the ubiquitous harangue of the television. Turks didn't seem to speak much while they ate, still less laugh, so the sudden intrusion of laughter into this scene struck me as jarring, almost sacrilegious; especially a laugh of this sort, which was high, fluting and unrepentantly decadent, like dubbed laughter in an Italian movie.

I walked to the other side of the room, behind a small partition. "Oh, how fanny!" cried Madelon as I tapped her on the shoulder.

From across the table Pieter bowed in the slow, gracious manner of a medieval knight.

The head waiter stepped into the middle of the room and gave a little gesture of commencement. Prayers wailed over the television. Moustaches twitched over soup spoons. The insectival clicking of cigarette lighters filled the air. Eating together we talked about our respective travels. They had taken a similar route to me but had spent more time in the northeast, near the Georgian border.

"We were in a village in the mountains," said Madelon. "And as we went walking among the trees we looked above us and there were girls in the high branches picking apples. Oh, it was so beautiful, like in a film by Foo-lee-ni!" She rocked her head back and gave a long peal of her musical laugh. Everyone stared.

"How much longer are you in Trabzon?"

"Oh, I'm afraid we are being picked up to go to the airport. From here we fly back to Istanbul and then back home."

"What, right now?"

"I am afrait so," said Pieter.

I found myself deeply unhappy at the prospect of not being able to see them again. I asked if there was a chance they'd be in Istanbul for a while.

"No," said Madelon. "We have both been there many times and, besides, we have to go back to work."

Together we ate kebabs and drank a jug of *ayran*, a salted yoghurt drink. "In Holland we also drink milk with dinner," said Madelon. "Once, the French ambassador caused a huge scandal because he would not drink buttermilk at a state function. There was a major diplomatic incident," she said, her laughter pressing against the words, "because he would not drink our *milk*."

Soon the mini-bus arrived to collect them. All at once a host of questions I had been dying to ask came flooding back: What was Madelon's life story? Was she single, married, a lesbian? Did she have children? Why did her friendship with Pieter have to be on neutral, alien ground? If they met in their home countries would they still be able to enjoy one another's company? But it was all too late. Pieter was already loading their bags while Madelon dawdled in the restaurant.

"Mard-e-loon!" he called from the doorway. "Would you please hurry oop. The bus is now leafing."

"Goodbye," said Madelon as she made her way to the door. "I do hope that you have a splendid time in Turkey. It's such a beautiful, sad and *fanny* place."

Chapter 17

After another day in Trabzon I bid farewell to Phil and Andy. Ramadan was almost over and Hüseyin would soon leave for America. We didn't indulge in the farce of exchanging contact details — our relationship was the travelling equivalent of casual sex, and we all knew it. "Maybe we'll come and see you in the carpet shop when we reach Istanbul," said Andy. But they never did, although it's just as likely that they got lost trying.

Leaving Trabzon gave me few regrets, not merely because it meant the end of the game of hide-and-seek I was forced to play with the deranged receptionist. The closer I looked the less charming the city became. The region around Trabzon had once been the centre of the country's hazelnut production. But when the bottom fell out of the market in the nineties, thousands of unemployed labourers flocked to the city. Further out of town, away from the shops and the harbour, the streets grew crowded with derelict tenements. Under a high bridge, on the banks of a fetid gully, a burning avalanche of debris sent an inky plume into the sky, old tyres and the remains of makeshift homes succumbing to the flames. In internet cafés, young, unemployed men sat all day, looking up conspiracy theories and playing violent computer games. Earlier in the year an Italian priest had been shot in the head by a sixteen-year-old boy in retaliation for the Danish cartoon scandal. There was a lurking menace to Trabzon, a quality that would make itself horribly apparent in the light of certain tragic events that would engulf Turkey not long after I had left the country.

My journey along the Black Sea coast, back to Istanbul, was hurried but rewarding. Although I didn't linger, and it rained the entire time, the region proved to be one of the most unexpectedly pleasant in Turkey. The Black Sea landscape was lush, misty and abundant, the trees full of cherries, the pebbly coves ringed by gentle green cliffs. The atmosphere was calm and liberal. Many bars were still trading, a book shop in a petrol station sold copies of *American Psycho* wrapped in plastic, and in the city of Samsun I saw a lonely, dreadlocked transvestite shuffling up and down the edge of a park on white platform moon boots, clutching a red vinyl briefcase.

Even the most unfamiliar scenes were imbued with a cheerfulness and conviviality that was unthinkable in the relentless glumness of the east. In the stunning Ottoman town of Amasya I saw a goat having its throat cut in the street to celebrate the opening of a new shop. Schoolgirls in uniform squealed and skipped over the blood as it ran down the pavement while clowns and Ottoman pashas handed out chocolates to the crowds. When I took one from a boy in a hire-shop turban he closed his eyes and, very gravely, bowed before me. After the severity of the east, it all seemed very civilised and gentle, a fact for which I was grateful, but tempered by a gnawing sense of loss.

Five days of *dolmuş*-hopping later I finally arrived back in Istanbul just in time for Şeker Bayramı, the public holiday celebrating the end of Ramadan. Şeker Bayramı is the informal Turkish term for Eid-ul Fitr, the Christmas of the Islamic world, when everyone everywhere travels across the country to see their families. The *otogar* looked like D-day and the streets were a peaceful revolution of pedestrians. All public transport in Istanbul had been declared free so the trains were packed beyond bursting. Gathering my bag in front of me and inhaling deeply I flung myself into the wall of humanity, sinking into the mass of bodies and made my way back to the shop. Inside, I found Mehmet with Mary, a regular customer with her own shop in Athens. "Hello, baby," said Mehmet, jumping up to wrap his legs around me. "Did you miss me, baby?" He began to thrust his crotch into my belly.

"Mehmet," said Mary, flicking back her purple hair, "you are a vile creature. But don't worry, one day someone will give you what you want."

I had met Mary on my previous visit. She was ethnically Greek but had grown up in Istanbul, her family some of the last to be expelled from Turkey during the pogroms of the 1970s. Like many of that generation she felt stuck between two worlds: Greece was only half a home to her and I wondered if her carpet shop was a way to reconcile her exile.

"How are you, baby?" I asked, detaching Mehmet.

"I'm OK, *abi*." He lit a cigarette and collapsed, cross-legged onto the sofa. "But I need a drink. You know, I was fasting for Ramadan."

Mary laughed.

"You were not," I said.

"Well ... I did for the first couple of days. But I swear to God I didn't have a drink."

"Only because your parents are in town," said Mary.

Downstairs, Hüseyin broke into his Groucho Marx walk and flung his arms about me. "Brah-ther!" he cried, and I felt myself being rejuvenated by his relentless energy. Sitting about on the couches was a group of athletic-looking girls, Kiwi teachers living in London. Loud, cheerful and improbably ignorant, their naturalness and good humour was infectious and I realised I had almost forgotten what it was like to be open with women. As they ate pide Hüseyin had bought for them the call of the muezzin began to float through the streets.

"What's all thus singing?" asked one.

"What?" I said.

"Thus, thus singing! What uz et?"

"You mean the call to prayer?"

"Yeah, what uz et?"

"It tells people when to come and pray," said Hüseyin, doing his best to contain his laughter. "You know, like church bells."

"Uz et! Und who sungs et?"

"Imams, like priests."

"Priests! Priests sung et!" She paused for a moment. "My word, they're good," she exclaimed. "Do they have to audition?"

We dropped the girls at a youth hostel then spent the afternoon selling to a slightly deranged Texan woman who was working for a hospital in Saudi Arabia. She wore an American flag shirt, matching belt buckle and white cowboy boots. At apparently random intervals she would slap her thigh and say, "Darn it!" as if she was constantly realising that she'd left the gas on. Within an hour she'd committed herself to buying two old pieces at a considerable price. As she walked out the door she commented on another stapled to the wall. Hüseyin ripped it off and threw it to Akil. "Wrap it up," he called.

"But I don't want to *buy* it!" she squealed.

"Yes you do," he said, staring at her with his devil eyes. "And you will, because you will never get a better price." She paused, making what-should-I-do faces at her friend across the room who could only give an it's-up-to-you shrug.

"Darn it!" she said, and I watched in amazement as she headed back upstairs and ran her credit card through the machine once more.

Once they had left, Hüseyin, Mehmet and I lounged back on the couches, drinking tea and watching the passing crowds. The streets were growing darker now, the trams full to bursting. For a while I said nothing, just watched Mehmet browse the internet and Zizou prowl back and forth, eyeing the crowds suspiciously, ready to attack. It was the first time in more than six weeks I hadn't been thinking about my next destination and I found myself going into a kind of withdrawal.

Outside, I was struck by the variety of people on the streets, the mismatched congregation of the big city, so unlike the conformity of the east. Among the crowds of young people (always I was impressed by the youthfulness of Turkey, the sense of vigour and potential) were all the marvellous incongruities that make the big city my favourite place in the world. A homeless man talking into a cigarette lighter as if it were a mobile phone, his T-shirt reading, simply, "ME". A mysterious, aged, eunuch-like creature with no teeth, a purple perm pulled into a ponytail and a walking cane that he used like an oar to push himself up the street. A girl with enormous breasts wearing a tight T-shirt printed with a logo — betraying, I thought, an unnecessary air of desperation — "I NEED BOYFRIEND". A perfect pair of little people, no higher than my hip, their tiny legs scissoring madly: he in a three-piece suit, she in full *çarşaf*, like a black traffic cone. There was also a guy selling Frankenstein masks and another with inflatable Scooby Doos. An astrologer in a silly hat wandered around with a pair of doves on a perch decorated with bits of tin foil and coloured paper. Girls in headscarfs giggled as the birds flapped their wings and cooed.

That evening, at a restaurant in the old Armenian district of Kumkapı, we met Serdar, another dealer in the area, and Sabire, a tour guide, part-time soprano and one of the most beautiful women I was to meet in Turkey. For the rest of the night we did all the things I had missed so much in the east: sat with girls, laughed loudly in public, listened to girls laugh loudly in public and drank like Boris Yeltsin. The memories divide into ever-decreasing fractions as the night wore on. After his first bottle of *rakı* Hüseyin got sentimental and hugged me while Sabire sang a sad Turkish folk song to the applause of the other diners. A Gypsy band appeared and Hüseyin danced on the table while stuffing twenty lira bills down the backs of their shirts. The restaurant clapped in time as the table wobbled ominously.

I was back where I had started; in the city, my home and natural environment. Here I could disappear into the crowds — anonymously watched and watching — sit next to a girl on the bus, drink whenever I liked and listen to music that had melody. Yet, that night as I fell asleep in the early hours of the morning, it was the images of the east that came to bed with me — the tattooed sheikh in Harran, the women wailing in the graveyard in Van, Mount Ararat in the morning. And all at once I found myself overwhelmed by an unexpected sensation of loss, made all the more acute by the realisation that I had not been sufficiently grateful at the time.

★ ★ ★

In the morning I snuck away and made a surreptitious rendezvous with Tevfik. This subterfuge was necessary. His room was only a few blocks from the shop and Hüseyin clearly did not approve of our association. I didn't want to make trouble. The door to Tevfik's apartment building looked like the entrance to a sex club or a biker headquarters: grey steel slitted by a sinister metal grate. I called up to his window and he buzzed me in. Hesitantly I made my way up the narrow, grimy passage. Having braced myself for something like Sid and Nancy's pad at the Chelsea Hotel I was pleasantly surprised to find a small but clean room with a single bed, a television and a little Stonehenge of prescription medication ringing the sink — the only real sign that anyone lived here at all.

"Doesn't it get loud?" I asked, peering out the window to the bar and service alley below.

"In summer it's worse. Soon it will be fine."

"What do you have for heating?"

"I don't have any."

I expressed dismay. The Istanbul winter could be ferocious.

"Don't worry," he said, and where others might have been fishing for sympathy I could see that he meant it.

In the corner were two thick carpets, folded into a pile. "I just picked these up from my father's place," he said, pulling the top one off. "These are the real deal, man. Kurdish, tribal Herkis. You don't get this shit anymore." He unfurled one, then the other. They were big and heavy and hit the floor with a thump. I considered them for a moment. Their designs were angular and uneven, the colours wild and garish. None of the edges were straight; they had clearly been made on rough tribal looms. Spreading from the end were tassels of ragged goat hair, strong as wire. They were not immediately appealing but were unlike anything else I had seen. "I can't keep them here, man. I need to get rid of them. This" — he gestured about him with a slight air of disgust — "is not the right place for them." He folded the carpets back up. Suddenly unsteady on his feet he sank to the bed and held his head in his hands.

"Are you alright?" I asked.

"Agh, I didn't sleep all night. I can't sleep, man. I don't know what's wrong with me." He lit a cigarette.

"Are you hungry?"

"I had anchovies yesterday."

I offered to buy him breakfast.

Down by the waterfront the sky was blue and the holiday crowds were in full force, the pavements a mile-long mosh pit. Where they could, people spilled out onto the roads, ignoring the honking traffic. Fenced-off sections became a perambulatory stalemate. Teenagers jumped over the barriers into the impatient traffic that swerved and honked around them. A man lifted his baby over the barrier, handing it to a boy who took the child in the crook of his arm, running through the speeding traffic to the safety of the opposite footpath. The father jumped the barrier and followed their path, taking the baby with a cheerful wave as the boy departed. Watching this, it struck me that the only conceivable situation in which a Western parent might hand their child to a strange man — let alone allow him to take it across four lanes of traffic — was if he was wearing a uniform and standing atop a ladder leaning against a burning building. Yet such scenes were common in Turkey, the land of the small mercy, a fact which only renewed my intense affection for this country and its people who were, underneath all their divisions, an enormous tribe, staunch and generous.

At a corner café we ate pastries and drank tea while Tevfik told me about the job he had lost.

"I was in the shop one day and I lit up a cigarette. The boss says to me, 'Hey you. What the fuck do you think this is? You don't smoke in front of customers. This is not a goddamn bar.' So I just said, 'OK — enough. You don't scream at me like that, I'm not a fucking child. So fuck you and your job.'"

"Where will you work now?"

"I don't know," he said, exhaling irritably. "There's always something." He thought for a moment. "Maybe go back to Spike's."

Spike was a dealer with a shop not far from Hüseyin's (he was Turkish but had lived around the world and nobody used his real name). A rather self-conscious eccentric who wore flowing hippy robes and told rehearsed, exaggerated stories about his time as an elephant handler in the circus, Spike was fun to be around. He gave out free beers and hash and had some of the most beautiful carpets and tribal artefacts I had seen. Tevfik had done his carpet apprenticeship with Spike and obviously still adored him, referring to him in Jedi Knight tones as "my master". This affection clearly blinded Tevfik to what I felt was a distinct streak of narcissistic coldness in his old boss, an impression not helped by the fact that he focused much of his energy on seducing the silly, impressionable backpacker girls who fluttered about him like moths. I was ambivalent towards Spike but Hüseyin hated him. He blamed him for giving his nose its current contour, naming Spike as the force behind the six guys who had turned up at the bar with baseball bats after an argument over a girl. Tevfik had denied that his old mentor was capable of such a thing, but I wasn't so sure. Whatever the case, and whoever he ended up working for, I hoped Tevfik would soon be able to find another job because, apart from anything else, he had talent, and was wasting it.

The conversation ground to a halt. Tevfik looked frail in the sharp morning light. "Brendan," he said, leaning forward and staring through his shades, "buy my carpets."

I gave a sigh.

"Just seven hundred lira," he said. "That's wholesale. I swear to you."

"I don't know, Tevfik."

"You don't like them?"

"It's not that." And it really wasn't.

"OK, don't worry."

Silence fell again. I paid for breakfast. As we made to leave he stood and turned to me. "Brendan," he said, with a perfect note of pleading, "please buy my carpets. Please … please. I need money, man. You have no idea how bad I need it."

"Tevfik, I can't do this."

"OK, then lend me three hundred bucks."

I gave him fifty.

"Thank you, brother," he said, hugging me tightly before loping off down the street to wherever it was Tevfik went with fifty bucks in his pocket.

Back at the shop, Hüseyin was leaning in the doorframe, smoking and nodding to the passing tourists. In shades and with his suit hanging loose from his skinny body, picking tobacco from his teeth, he looked like a lost *Blues Brother* or a reserve grade *Reservoir Dog*. Inside, an old man sat on a stool reading the paper over his spectacles. Zizou, lying at his feet, looked up warily with my entrance before returning to her snooze in the sun. Hüseyin kissed me and gestured to the old man. "Meet my dad," he said and called Akil for coffee.

In a country where old age is both venerated and premature, Hüseyin's father — grey moustached and waistcoated — had substantially achieved the bearing and appearance universal to all men in Turkey between the ages of forty-five and death. Unlike most Turkish patriarchs, however, he was not stern and forbidding, and with his cheeky grin and button eyes was the double of Mehmet. It was immediately obvious from where his sons had got their charm. For the next week he would hang around the shop during the day, reading the newspaper, watching the door and making hearty peasant lunches of leeks, eggplant and potato all stewed in the same oily red sauce; meals so austerely nutritious that every bite made you feel guilty for a life of wasteful Western decadence. They were a reminder of where Mr Yılmaz had come from — that between him and his sons there was more than just a generation gap but a chasm. One afternoon Mehmet showed me photographs of his parents in their youth: pictures from the village of Mr Yılmaz riding a donkey in his suit, sitting in the doorway of a barren hut or submitting to the ritual shave before his wedding. The images were very touching and the poverty of the world they depicted shocking — if I had been asked to guess I would have said they were from the 1930s, not the late-'60s. They were a reminder that, in defiance of the complaints of its citizens, Turkey had made much progress and that the prosperity and stability it craved were tantalisingly close.

Without saying anything we sat and drank our coffee, watching the holiday crowds. I found I was becoming more accustomed to the long silences of Turkey and began to see the need to fill the void with trivial conversation as a kind of cultural neurosis. A brief interlude broke the peace. A man, obviously quite drunk, opened the door and stood swaying at the step. Zizou, a confirmed racist who only ever barked at Turks, ran up and stood inches from him, her back arched, making a sound like bones being ground. In horrible slow motion, the drunk, grinning idiotically, reached down and went to pat her snarling snout. Howls of pain followed, the retreat of the pet lover sketched out on the pavement by a trail of bright, sticky blood. While I restrained Zizou by the collar, the drunk stood on the street, clutching his dripping hand and screaming at Hüseyin, who screamed back. For just a moment, Mr Yılmaz looked over his paper and crossed his legs, before disappearing again behind the newsprint.

Two things about this incident impressed me. Firstly, Zizou's ability to distinguish a local from a tourist — a skill that relied, I guessed, on her sense of smell because she didn't even look twice at Mediterraneans, many of whom could have easily passed for a Turk. The other was Hüseyin's ability to remain not only unyielding in the face of cries for compensation from an outraged chorus led by the bleeding drunk and several of his friends and supporters roped in from the crowds, but positively belligerent, warning that if he should set foot again anywhere near his shop he would see to it that the dog was granted an anatomical souvenir. Slamming the door, he muttered some curses under his breath before turning to me. "So, bro," he said. "Are you ready to learn how to be a carpet dealer?"

My first lesson was cracking the code of the prices. Every carpet in the shop had a ticket attached. On each ticket was the wholesale price of the piece. Every shop in Turkey has a different system for these tickets, a code that obscures the price to give the dealer leverage when bargaining (all prices were in US dollars because that's what most dealers and middle-men dealt in, the Turkish lira being notoriously unstable). Hüseyin's system was simple enough but I could reveal it only at the risk of writing all future books from the comfort of a wheelchair so it shall remain, like so much in Turkey, in the realm of mystery.

Bargaining is, of course, the essential skill of the successful carpet dealer but the prospect terrified me, partly because taking liberties in someone else's shop made me uncomfortable but mostly because I have an attitude to money not unlike that of an eighteenth-century English aristocrat: which is to say that I feel it should be given to me for no reason and as a topic of discussion consider it in much the same category as my parents' sex life. In addition to the art of bargaining I also had to learn, very quickly, as much as I could about the various types of carpets on offer. Hüseyin's range represented a large cross-section of Turkish carpets, a world of infinite depth and variety and the subject of endless scholarly debate. At its most basic level — the only level at which I'm qualified to speak — Turkish weaving can be divided into two main categories: carpets, which have a pile, and flat-weaves, which don't. The most common variety of flat-weave is the *kilim*, but there are dozens of variations, including the *cicim* and *sumak* techniques. (Often included in the category of flat-weaves are items like donkey or camel bags, pillow covers, baby's cradles and various other hangings and bandings used by nomads to decorate the interiors of their tents.) Carpets are less varied in technique, limited for the most part to the double knot, favoured in Turkey, or the single, favoured in Persian weaving. Within these basic techniques was, of course, an incomprehensible variety of styles, patterns, materials and iconography — varying from village to village and family to family — and the constant promise of some undiscovered masterpiece, lurking neglected and forgotten in a family chest or dealer's store room, could inspire a particular kind of madness in collectors.

The shop's stock was divided into carpets and flat-weaves, then into the new, semi-old and antique, each with their own profit margin. Antiques had the biggest mark-up although weren't necessarily more expensive than a good new one because, having been made in people's homes for non-commercial purposes, they had none of the taxes or labour costs that came with the modern, mass-produced product. Almost all the woollen carpets were made in Turkey, although Hüseyin did stock a limited number of Afghani,

Iranian and Pakistani pieces. Some of this was junk, especially the Pakistani stuff, which was a wool and nylon blend, often sold to unsuspecting buyers as "lambswool" and "Afghani" only by virtue of the fact that it was made mostly by desperately poor refugees in Pakistani camps. Unfortunately it was too popular not to have: many people had seen cheap Pakistani pieces in their home countries being sold as "Turkish" carpets and had come to Istanbul expecting to find the same, the irony compounded by the fact that, because of tariffs aimed at protecting the Turkish industry, they were about twice the price you could expect to pay at home.

The most expensive new carpets, comparatively, were the silks. These came in three kinds: Hereke, Kayseri and Chinese. Hereke were the finest. First commissioned during the mid-nineteenth century during the last gasp of the Ottoman Empire, the Hereke carpet was named after the village, not far from Istanbul, in which they were originally produced. These days, however, although the town still produced them in a Ye Olde Factory, Hereke had come to refer to any Turkish silk carpet with a knot count of ten-by-ten per square centimetre or higher (they were also produced in wool with a lower knot count). Even though they were now made everywhere and had long since lost their status as unique imperial objects, the craft and technique were impressive. A good size Hereke took a year to make and anything less than a couple of thousand dollars was definitely a fake. Cheaper than Hereke were Kayseri silks, named for the big carpet-producing city in central Turkey, the largest in Cappadocia. These were, generally, eight-by-eight knots per square centimetre and came in a wide range of inoffensive patterns and pastel, grandmotherly colours. Kayseri silks were the Volvo to Hereke's Mercedes. The Chinese silks were the cheapest. Unlike many dealers, Hüseyin sold them for what they were: competently crafted, hideously ugly pieces of decoration. But others weren't so principled and every year, especially after the cruise ships returned, carpet dealers across the world braced themselves for a flood of hopefuls trying to unload ten-thousand-dollar Herekes which were, in fact, two-hundred-dollar bathmats produced in a sweatshop in Shanghai.

Other than knowing the rough age, price and type of each piece there weren't many other skills I needed. The language barrier was not a problem. We only sold to tourists, and the majority of those could speak English. Turks, on the whole, did not buy carpets and most seemed to regard them in much the same way the English did Morris dancing — although I met numerous Turkish passers-by, in all the months I spent sitting in Hüseyin's shop I only saw one lot of Turkish customers, an engaged couple looking for expensive wedding presents. But she was *Almanca* (German–Turk) and they didn't buy anything anyway.

With a quick lesson in how to use the credit card machine my training was over. "Is that it?" I asked.

"You will be fine, *abi*. My brother-in-law will be here sometimes to check on you and, as you see, Zizou will be there for security." He gave his jungle bird laugh. "I just hope you don't get bored, man."

This, or so I was to learn, was to be the least of my problems.

Chapter 18

A few days before he was due to return to Cyprus Mehmet got sick. After sleeping two days upstairs he appeared one morning in the shop wearing a T-shirt printed with the word "ANTISOCIAL" and spent the rest of the day lying on the couch, shivering and moaning. "No wonder you're sick," I said. "You've been partying so hard."

"Nah!" he said. "I just drank a glass of cold water." This common Turkish medical superstition was a source of bemusement and frustration to me, supposing as it did that the health hazards posed by going out every night for two weeks, consuming hundreds of beers, smoking two packs a day and having various sexual encounters with a transient backpacker population paled by comparison to the horrors awaiting anyone foolish enough to ingest a slightly chilly glass of the substance constituting 70 per cent of our bodies. The rest of my day was spent nursing Mehmet, our relationship having become, by now, ridiculously homo. Many days it was not unusual for us to sit around giving one another shoulder rubs while discussing topics as diverse as nineteenth-century economic theory, the psychology of fashion branding or the merits of Indonesian vampire movies. All that was missing were the cricket flannels, bottle of house sherry and a bout of guilty sodomy by a roaring fire. When he finally left for Cyprus to start his university exams I took to moping about the shop with a wilted rose in my lapel, writing poetry in the manner of Verlaine.

Not long after Mehmet's departure, his brother began to prepare for his trip to America. On his final day, while Hüseyin and his father ate lunch (cabbage in red sauce), I sat with Akil, drinking coffee and waiting for customers. Without warning, the door opened and a strong breeze sent an autumnal ripple through the shop. Zizou, recognising the intruders as senior members of the family, stood to attention, doing her best to look as though she was contributing. In the doorway, Hüseyin's sister supported her mother, waiting patiently as the old lady made what was an obviously difficult step inside.

Hüseyin's sister I had met before. She was beautiful but possessed a certain ferocious look common to many Turkish women, whether by nature or cultivation I could never tell. Whereas she looked more like Mehmet and the paternal side of the family, her mother was the image of Hüseyin: that same strong nose you saw often in Turkey — big but not hooked, long and downward pointing; the same eyebrows, like thick black ticks above each eye; the angry arrow of muscle just above the bridge of her nose. As she sat silently on the couch, staring intently into the distance, my immediate impression was of a battle-weary matriarch, stern and liable to queenly proclamations. With a hint of trepidation I asked whether she would like some tea and, all at once, her face broke out into a disarmingly impish smile, melting the illusion of ferocity to reveal a kindly woman who was merely in a great deal of pain.

I made myself scarce for the family farewell, standing out the front of the shop to make vaguely sleazy, ultimately fruitless, overtures to passing tourists. As pathetically inept as my attempts to lure customers were to prove, I did, in that brief introduction to the carpet dealer's trade, learn a very curious fact: that if you stand in front of a Turkish carpet shop people will assume, in defiance of all evidence to the contrary, that you are a Turkish carpet dealer.

This observation was to be confirmed, time and again, during my brief career in Istanbul, and never failed to baffle me. It was as if I was the subject of one of those sociological experiments in racism where they show you a flash card of a black guy and you say "Drug dealer", except here a 6'3" blond, bespectacled Australian in an Iggy Pop T-shirt was, by virtue only of his environment, suddenly transformed into a leering bazaar crook who could use terms like "I swear on my honour!" without a hint of irony. (Of course, during my stay in the country I saw a few blond Turks and a few who were 6'3". Yet, even allowing for the surprising physical diversity of the population, I doubt there are many who are both *and* speak with a broad Australian accent.) Walking down the street I was just another tourist, but put me in front of a carpet shop and suddenly little old ladies were asking for directions and tourist girls were running past, calling me a pervert. It was like putting a ballerina in a tutu in the middle of a steel works and fooling everyone into thinking she was an industrial welder.

Not long after they arrived, Mr and Mrs Yılmaz left the shop, shepherded by their children to the taxi that would take them to the airport. Hüseyin's patience and gentleness, his protective arm around his mother, were quite unlike anything I had seen in him before, and I began to realise how close he kept his emotional cards to his chest. An hour later, with his parents gone, he was preparing to leave. I was given instructions on the operation of the alarm and the tricky hot water system. My bedroom was upstairs, the one that Mehmet used, littered like a hobo's camp ground in a scattering of papers, Coke cans and underpants. As Hüseyin dropped his bags by the door I began to grasp the reality of the situation, surveying the shop with the eyes of a guy who has been on a week-long bender only to wake up and realise he's joined the army or there's a horse in his back yard.

"Hey, bro, don't worry about it," he said, kissing me. "I totally trust you." And with that he was out on the street, in a cab and gone, leaving me to assume the role of Turkish carpet dealer. On his stool

Akil cracked his neck. Under the coffee table, Zizou looked up and beat her tail excitedly.

★ ★ ★

When I came downstairs the next morning Tevfik was already in his soon-to-be-customary position, reclining on the couch, a cigarette in one hand, his shades fixed to his face. In one corner were the pair of Herki carpets, folded into a bright cube. "What are you doing, man?" he said, an agitated Morse code of smoke tripping from his mouth. "It's almost ten o'clock. You gotta get up earlier if you wanna run this shop."

I wasn't in the mood for his provocations. The previous evening I had met up with an acquaintance from Sydney who was teaching English in Istanbul and had ended up drinking until five o'clock. The inside of my head felt like New Year's Day in Russia. Like a lot of foreigners she was based on the Asian side of the city, which, contrary to the assumption of many tourists, is richer and better ordered than the European half and, despite there being little left to show for it, far older.

Istanbul's Anatolian shore was inhabited for almost five thousand years by pre-Hellenic civilisations, including the Phoenicians and Thracians, until the Greeks in the seventh century BC, led by King Byzas, took over the region and established the settlement of Byzantium on the European shore where the Topkapı Palace now stands. (Legend has it that the Oracle of Delphi told Byzas to build his city across the shore from "the blind ones". Byzas, seeing the infinite superiority of the European shore, decided that these people must be blind for wanting to live on the Asian shore — an observation I regard as still holding true almost three thousand years later.) For centuries the Anatolian side was relegated to a shipping port and farmland until late in the life of the Ottoman Empire, when it was reclaimed as a residential district. These days much of it is highly fashionable and prosperous, a conglomeration of smart apartment buildings, fine restaurants, fashion boutiques and enough Starbucks outlets to satisfy even the most ambitious globalisation protest. It is also extremely boring so when all the bars shut down we bought as much alcohol as we could carry and headed back to someone's apartment.

The party didn't last long. At the stroke of midnight the cops began banging on the door. At the mention of the words "English teachers", passports were called for. Almost every English teacher in Turkey works without a permit, staying in the country on a tourist visa and travelling across the border every three months to renew it. This is, essentially, illegal but tolerated; unless, that is, a pushy policeman decides he wants a bribe or simply to make life difficult. I didn't have my passport and they wouldn't believe I wasn't a teacher. Threats were made; I would have to come with them. I did my "me-speak-a-no-Turkish" routine and hoped they'd drop it. They didn't. After some tense argument I was eventually saved by the residents of the apartment building who began to appear in the stairwell, screaming at the police and telling them that they were now making more noise than the party. While the police argued with the neighbours I slipped downstairs and disappeared into a side street.

In my hurry I lost my friend but quickly teamed up with another refugee from the party. Alice was a London girl with cropped hair and the kind of working-class accent you could tell was making a point. With her tartan skirt, Doc Marten boots and taste for protest folk music she seemed to be living in her own personal Thatcher Years. Together we sat in the gutter and cracked open a beer. Alice had been in Turkey for almost seven years, but had finally decided to get out. "They're the most miserable people in the world," she said, by way of explanation. I could, perhaps, see what she meant but was there in her tone, I wondered, the tell-tale hint of a relationship gone sour? "Yeah, I had a boyfriend," she said, swigging from her can. "His mother used to call me *pasaklı kadın* which, by the way, means filthy whore."

As we sat in the gutter, the unthinkable happened: a second lot of police pulled up in their car and demanded to see our passports. The same farce was repeated.

"Give them your driver's licence," she said. "They're too dumb to know the difference." Alice was getting angry. Two weeks before, she had been picked up by a cop car coming home from a bar. They had thrown her into the back, telling her it was illegal to drink during Ramadan. She knew this was a lie but was in no position to argue. They drove her through the suburbs of Istanbul, saying they were going to arrest her unless she had sex with both of them. For half an hour she argued and pleaded until they finally got an emergency call and took off, dumping her on a street somewhere in the middle of distant suburbia.

I recognised the Turkish word for "fuck off".

"Please, Alice," I pleaded. But I needn't have been concerned. It soon became obvious that the cops were bored more than anything, taken with the novelty of a *yabancı* (foreigner) girl who could speak their language. After some time spent solemnly examining the old student ID card I had given them, they handed back our documentation and drove off.

"Fucking bastards!" she screamed, as much at Turkey, I suspect, as anything else. The rest of the night was spent at Alice's place, drinking until the first ferry of the morning.

I told Tevfik the story. "No way!" he said. "Fucking arsehole cop motherfuckers!" He shook his head. "Man, you are going to be tired today."

Feeling very near death, I collapsed in the chair by the door and promptly fell asleep. For an unknown time I sat in full view of the passing crowds, splayed out like some performance art installation, my mouth gaping, Darth Vader noises filling the room. An uncertain amount of time later I awoke to a blast of cold air and a pair of eager smiles, large as boomerangs.

"Oh, we're sorry," said the woman, with exaggerated timidity. "If you're sleeping we'll come back later." They were Canadian, a fact betrayed as much by their high-waisted jeans and matching fleece tops as their accents and apologetic, slightly insincere manners.

"Don't be ridiculous," I said, wiping the sheen of drool from my cheek and rising unsteadily to my feet. "Come this way."

Doing my best to appear the boss I sent Akil to fetch some tea and shoved Tevfik aside. He sat up and lifted his shades onto his head. "Welcome," he said in his vampiric tones. They giggled uncertainly.

My carpet spiel had been gleaned from my time observing Hüseyin but was still far from perfect. The idea was to unroll a dozen or so pieces to give a rough guide to the various types on offer, then, in a process of elimination, remove each one until they arrived at the carpet — preferably carpets — they wanted.

When presenting carpets it is important to impart a theatrical aura, a sense of revelation — as if you were unveiling a lost Raphael to the world press rather than a piece of Pakistani junk that was available next door for half the price. The unrolling of a carpet is an art in itself and I had been practising for a week. The rolled-up carpet is held high, against the chest, then tossed outwards with a strong flick of the wrists, the aim being for it to hit the ground with a smack and unravel with a good speed along the floor. Throwing the carpet to illustrate the play of light on the pile is also important. The technique involves grabbing one corner then flicking the carpet back quickly in such a way that it gives a whip crack before spinning through the air and coming to rest in front of the customer's feet. Silks, especially, change colour dramatically under the light and Akil and I spent many hours frisbeeing thousands of dollars worth of Herekes from one side of the room to the other, trying to improve our skills and make the colours flash like opals in the sun. This was not a technique I ever mastered, there being children who wear crash helmets and callipers with better fine motor skills than mine, but

Hüseyin could lift huge, room-sized pieces into the air and send them spinning over his head to land with a gentle puff of air that never failed to elicit appreciative exclamations.

One carpet after the other I rolled out, each producing the same reaction: "Well, that is gore-jus." Meanwhile, Tevfik prowled through the patchwork of colour and patterns, making impresario gestures and announcing, "Now this, *this* is the goddamn carpet for you." The Canadians gave scandalised giggles.

After laying out the carpets there was an uncomfortable silence while the Canadians considered what they had just seen. This was a crucial time for a sale. At this point, many dealers would start to ratchet up the pressure. Hüseyin, more subtle than many, would call for more tea then insist he buy lunch. It was all part of making the customer feel connected, obligated even, to the dealer, to create a narrative and give the sale a sense of inevitability.

"Well these are all just gore-jus," she said, and from her tone I could tell immediately that they didn't like anything and would now put all their efforts into finding a polite way to leave. Canadians are like that; they always have to compensate you for their opinions.

"Well, I think we'll definitely come back, won't we, Terry?"

"Oh, yeah. They're all just so ... gore-jus."

"But we need time to think."

"Sure," I said, "there's no pressure here."

"No pressure," said Tevfik. "We're not like those assholes in Grand Bazaar."

They gathered their things and began to head towards the door. When they left I collapsed gratefully onto the couch and watched Akil roll up the carpets. "They were nice," I said. "Maybe they'll come back."

Tevfik *tsk*ed. "Missionaries."

"Really, how can you tell?"

"Oh, I know. They were too nice. Even for goddamn Canadians."

He was right, of course: there were a bunch of them in town. They'd been moving their way through the Middle East, spreading the good word, for quite a while.

Missionary activity does not inspire in me any particular horror — the Jehovah's Witnesses have the same right to knock on my door as I do to slam it in their face. Being a missionary is something I regard as little more than a slightly pitiful anachronism, the very word conjuring in my mind images of safari suits, leper colonies and *ooga-booga* dances about the cooking pot. Such a view was not generally shared in Turkey, however, and when, a few months after I left the country, a German missionary and two local converts in the eastern city of Malatya were tied up in their office, tortured and their throats cut, one stabbed 150 times, I thought of those sweet, artless Canadians with their blonde hair and bright Reeboks and wondered how they got on.

There was only one other lot of customers that day, a pair of middle-aged Spaniards. I did my best but it was soon obvious that my efforts were futile: they could speak virtually no English and when I asked which part of Spain they were from she had replied, slightly snippily, "North. Basque."

"Huh!" exclaimed Tevfik, derisively. "Basques. The Spanish PKK."

The woman looked at her husband and made a gesture of bafflement. "*Que es pee kay kay?*"

By the end of the day we had, of course, sold nothing. "Akil!" called Tevfik. "Close up the shop. Brendan, come upstairs." In a room out the back Tevfik sat on the window ledge, rolling a joint. "You want some chocolate, man?"

"Where'd you get it?"

"Don't ask."

Together we smoked the hash by the open window. The weather was still fine and for a while we sat in the breeze, listening to the sounds of the evening: the zing and rumble of the tram, the muffled footfalls of the pedestrians and the whoopings of the cranes from their big shaggy nests in the tree tops. The tombs in the graveyard below were silver in the night; the tall marble headstones topped with their little turbans a field of wonky paddles.

"How is Hüseyin?" he asked.

"OK, I suppose. I met his mother yesterday."

"Oh," he said excitedly, "how is she?"

"Frankly? She looks like she's going to die."

He exhaled deeply. "Aw, shit, man! This is bullshit! This is no fucking *good*." He was shaking as he spoke and I could see that his distress was genuine. "She is a good lady, a kind lady. She doesn't deserve this shit. Why is the world like this?" He punched the window frame and the glass rattled.

We finished the joint and went back downstairs. A little stoned we began to rifle through the carpets, Tevfik pulling out one, then another. "This," he said, "is a good carpet. Nice and healthy, good colours. I like it. This," he said, pointing to another, "is a piece of shit and I would be embarrassed to have it in my home."

I asked him to explain the difference, how you could tell a good carpet from a bad one.

"There is really only one thing you have to know," he said, kicking open another piece that unravelled on the floor with a satisfying flutter. "Colours. Good colour is everything. Good colour is poetry. Without it nothing else matters. People who talk about the number of knots and iconography and all that shit — forget about it. Colour is the number one."

He dropped to his knees and began to pull apart the pile on a magnificent Kurdish piece. "Yellow should be bright as daisies. Blue should be a little bit washed out, and green too, but a dark emerald green is good. Orange is often chemical but natural orange is like bright clay mud. Pink is disgusting — it's nearly always chemical. Natural pink is pale, like roses, but it's hard to find. You can only learn perfect colours by looking at thousands and thousands of carpets. There is no other way."

Dragging a carpet either side of him, he ran his hand through the pile. "The second most important thing is the quality of the wool. This one," he said, gesturing to his left, "is made with unbelievably beautiful wool. This one is shit, which is why it has worn down so quickly. You gotta learn to feel like you see. In winter the sheep have more lanolin in their coat and it ages the wool more quickly. The dyes rot the wool, too. They are made with all sorts of crazy mysterious shit — beetles, flowers, rocks, horse piss. Look, here," he said, pointing to two different parts of the black border. "The black in this part is slightly shorter than in that part." I peered closely. "The blacks and dark browns age faster than the other colours. They oxidise and eat into the wool. You can date a carpet by how much the black has worn down. These are not old enough to have this much wear. Someone has trimmed the black down" — he mimed cutting with scissors — "to make it look older."

"Surely not Hüseyin?"

"No, not Hüseyin. He doesn't do that. Probably whoever he bought it from, or whoever *he* bought it from."

"Shouldn't we tell people then?"

"No. Why should we? These are beautiful carpets, man. What difference does it make if they're ten or fifty years old?"

"Have you told people that cotton is silk and stuff like that?"

"Sure, I gotta make a living. But you know, Brendan, people don't care. You tell them it's silk, they're happy. What do they know? They live their whole life with this carpet and they love it. Who cares? None of these people are buying a real carpet anyway. It's just furniture and they'd be better off just going down the street to some Iranian rug guy. But most people aren't buying a carpet here because they want a *carpet*. They're buying so that they can take it home and tell everyone a story. And it's our job to give them a story. The rest is bonus."

Chapter 19

Overnight the weather grew bitter. In the graveyard the snapdragons dropped fat lips against the white stone. After a few more days the first snows came. The falls were furious and heavy but the ground was still warm, so all that remained in the streets were big dirty piles of slush. Tevfik had been missing for two days now. He wasn't answering his phone and when I went round to his place the lights were off and he didn't answer my cries up to the window. It would be an exaggeration to say this alarmed me but it did fill me with a certain sinking feeling, an intuition that events were moving towards an unhappy conclusion.

With Tevfik gone the peace and calm were almost eerie. I realised that, even though we did, essentially, nothing all day — sitting and waiting, harassing people out the front, drinking coffee and smoking — without him I suddenly had free time. I caught up on my notes while Akil set about improving the window display, boldly contrasting the tribal Turkmen pieces, embroidered in their fetishes of buttons, coins and seashells, with the refinement of the silks. His eye for colour and pattern revealed a remarkable aesthetic sensibility.

"This is beautiful, Akil." In response he just rocked his head slightly and gave me one of his blooming flower smiles.

The display was not only visually pleasing but popular with the public. There were not many tourists but all who passed stopped to look. The Turkmen pieces Hüseyin bought from some Uzbeks in the Grand Bazaar were particularly popular. We didn't sell many, they were window dressing mostly, but people were taken by the tribal romance of it all.

"These are circumcision jackets," I explained to some elderly Canadians who had stopped out the front. "When the boys are circumcised the whole village comes to sew these talismans on the jacket to ward off evil. Like a family quilt."

"Oh, gore-jus!" she exclaimed.

"Just gore-jus," he echoed.

I was, of course, making most of this up. In fact, after only a week of being a carpet dealer I had not only given up all pretence to the truth but was now concocting blatant and outrageous lies. For this I now felt no conscience. Being a carpet dealer, I had decided, is like being an evangelist preacher who claims he can cure the sick. It seems like an evil way of fleecing people of their money but if they were happy, felt better and had something to talk about for the rest of their lives, then you couldn't help but feel some good had come of it.

Inside, Akil brought tea and I began my pitch. I rolled out the piece Tevfik told me had been trimmed.

"And what do these symbols mean?" she asked.

"Ah ... this is a horse's hoof. Back in the village a man would dance, pretending to be a horse, and the woman would pick him for marriage."

"Well, isn't that gore-jus."

"Gore-jus."

"And how old is this one?" she asked.

I hesitated. "About fifty or sixty years. Can you see," I said, getting on my hands and knees, "that the darker colours have worn down over time. This is how you can date the carpet."

There were exclamations of disbelief. They were clearly interested. Drawing herself up, she grew solemn and businesslike.

232

"Now I want you to tell me honestly," she said, "do little children make these?"

It was a question I had been asked many times and which had started to annoy me, not because it was entirely unwarranted but rather because of the hypocrisies and presumptions it betrayed. A few big scandals in India and Pakistan — not traditional carpet countries — have permanently associated the carpet industry with rows of bent-backed little boys going slowly blind in filthy sheds run by heartless Fagins. These practices, I'm sure, still go on in parts of the subcontinent. During my time in Turkey, however, I visited many carpet workshops and saw only one — in Doğubayazıt — that was employing children. The girls were young teenagers, thirteen or fourteen I estimated, but their conditions seemed good and they weren't doing anything different from previous generations of girls in that part of the world. Of course they should have been in school, but so should the thousands of other working children I had seen across Turkey: kids who picked melons, sold roses, cleaned shops, carried vegetables, pushed wheelbarrows, herded sheep or shined shoes until they fell asleep, slumped over their little boxes of polish in the same spot they had been sitting since the morning. Many who profess to be horrified by the possibility that a child might have made their carpet are, apparently, untroubled by, or completely ignorant of, the fact that children make their shoes, pick the tea they drink, the fruit they eat and the cotton they wear. Western economies — by which I mean Western luxury — are, to a large degree, reliant on cheap labour of the Third World, and sometimes that means children. This is obviously not a good thing but when you are poor and hungry outraged sermons from the rich and well fed concerning the value of education can sound not merely hollow but arrogant. Seeking reassurance that your carpet was free of child labour was often just a way to assuage your guilt for living in a world that was not.

"No," I said. "Little children didn't make these."

We continued to talk, and the more we did the more I liked them.

"We're from Regina." She held up a hand. "Don't make the jokes because we've heard 'em all."

He nodded. "Heard 'em *all*."

I asked if they were enjoying Turkey.

"Oh, it's just gore-jus. And the people are so *nice*."

"Really nice."

"But when we said we were going to Turkey people were shocked."

"Shocked."

"'What about the terrorism?' they said. And I just said, 'Well, nobody's telling us not to go to New York, are they? And I heard they had some problems down there.'"

He chuckled, knowingly. All at once she grew very serious. "Do you wanna know the most dangerous place in the whole world you could go now?" She leaned in, portentously. "Disney World. If you wanted to do something really terrible — I mean horrific — imagine the carnage you could cause if you set off a bomb in the EPCOT Center?" She shook her head. "I mean, think about all those hundreds of innocent children you could slaughter. I mean, it would be *horrific*."

"Horrific," he said.

In the end they left without buying anything. "We'll come back, won't we?" she said. "Oh, we'll come back," he said. "You can bet on it." By which, of course, they meant I would never see them again. I fell back into the couch, feeling dejected and futile.

The next morning, Tevfik appeared. He was unsteady and a little manic, alternating from hypochondriacal moanings in a supine position on the couch to agitated monologues, conducted while pacing the room, concerning his financial affairs, the imminent social collapse of his country or the wall blocking the door. He was, in other words, essentially unchanged.

"Where have you been?" I asked.

"I had to see my family," he said, taking a glass of tea from the silver tray Akil had set before us. "I went to my dad's house and gave him some carpets and then I went to visit some friends."

"Which friends?"

"Oh, just some friends."

For a while we sat in the customary silence, Tevfik smoking while Akil ran around sweeping up his ashes. The atmosphere seemed back to normal, but the gnawing sense that something was amiss would not leave me. "Tevfik," I said, "where is your coin?"

"Oh," he said, glancing down at his chest, "I gave it back to my father. I went round to his place and while we were talking I put it down on the table. He got angry at me and started saying, 'Hey, you treat my gift like shit.' I just picked it up and gave it back to him. I said, 'Here, take it. I don't want it if you are always going to hold it over me.' Just threw it at him."

It was difficult talking to Tevfik sometimes. On the one hand I felt instinctively that this story was nonsense — he had sold it, of that I was almost certain. On the other, he was crazy enough for there to be a margin of reasonable doubt. "It must be hard to be a son in Turkey," I said, in an attempt to mollify him. "There are so many responsibilities."

He got up and began to pace the room with manic energy, shaking as he smoked. "Brendan, you people have no idea. Each new generation in this country is the property of the last. You know, I went to visit my uncle in the summer, back in the village. When I had a glass of water he started to scream at me, 'Hey, why are you disrespecting me in this way?' Do you know why he was angry? Because when I am with him I have to drink water with the proper, old manners. I have to get on one knee" — he did the actions as he spoke — "and turn my head from him. Then I can drink." He stood up and dropped his hands to his sides with something between exasperation and despair. "Brendan, I am a 45-year-old man and I cannot drink a glass of water without being made to feel ashamed."

★ ★ ★

We spent the rest of the day as we would so many others: sitting by the door waiting for customers that never came, drinking tea and listening to the percussive accretions of the shop and street — the tinkle of spoons in glasses, the low rumble of the tram, the scratching of Zizou's nails on the floor — until they became a rhythmic and indivisible fabric of sound, a tone poem in the void. Late in the evening, Tevfik called me upstairs where we sat by the window and smoked a joint — a gift, perhaps, from his friends. Stoned and bored, we were about to close up for the evening when Erkan appeared with a wealthy looking couple in a promising procession behind him.

Erkan ran a little gift shop up the street. Sometimes he brought customers to us but at this time of year no one was getting much business, so this was the first time we had seen him since we started.

Immediately I did my best impersonation of a stoned guy who's not stoned. "Would you like some tea?" I said. "It's really ... amazing."

They were rich. We could see it. He was the caricature of a Jewish New York real estate agent, which is precisely what he was. She was blonde and fat lipped with wide staring eyes, her features so blank and expressionless it was as if she had been cryogenically frozen and was staring out through a thick wall of ice.

I did the usual spiel, rolling out the carpets. They were curious but not much more than that. Tevfik, with excellent timing, took the opportunity. "Brendan, put this junk away," he commanded. "We are going upstairs to see the good shit."

The antique room was smaller and more intimate than downstairs, the lighting lower and the furniture more expensive. There was an air of having been allowed into a privileged space, like the back room at Studio 54. Akil brought more tea as Tevfik began to pull pieces from the pile. Some he threw dismissively to one side, others he lay out before the Americans with the careful gestures of a man covering a corpse. "Here is one of the most beautiful grain bags you will ever see," he said, and he was almost telling the truth. The bag was exceptional: a soothing chequerboard of green, blue and white, bordered by a subtle red. Seeing it by the others its quality was obvious. The woman pulled out a pair of thick, saucer-sized glasses from her bag. Banished by vanity, they explained much about her odd frozen expression. "So, wait a minute," she said in her honking New York accent, "this is just ... a *bag*?"

Tevfik's tone was not impatient but his eyes were almost fevered. "Yes, it's a bag," he said, stroking the piece, as if it were skin. "But it's not just a bag, it's a message. A message from her time to ours. It's a message from a woman who didn't have anything else. Would the grain grow? Would her children eat tomorrow? Would she make it through the winter? She had all the same hopes and dreams as we do, but all she had was this bag. That's it. So she put everything into it, all her love for her family, for her children. Her hope that they would have enough to eat. This is not just a *bag*, it's a prayer — a prayer and a message. And for you to own that is a privilege."

Maybe I was stoned but I could feel a tear welling up. The woman, meanwhile, was enraptured. You could see it in the way her strange blank eyes grew big behind her glasses.

"Maybe we'll think about it and come back later," said her husband.

"OK," said Tevfik. "No pressure."

I couldn't believe what I was hearing. Even as she stood up, the woman continued to stare at the bag, almost unable to look away. But before any more negotiations could be entered into her husband had taken her by the arm, led her downstairs and out the door. Tevfik fell down on the couch and lit a cigarette. "Tevfik," I snapped, "what are you doing!" He seemed genuinely confused. "They were going to buy that and you just let them walk out."

He *tsk*ed dismissively. "They love it, man. They cannot do without it. They are in *love*. They will come back. You will see." Pulling his shades down, he leaned his head back and began to snore softly.

Chapter 20

The day they invented hot Coke I sold my first carpet. Strictly speaking, it was not "Hot Coke" as Mehmet had envisioned; rather a cola-based doughnut smothered in warm Coke syrup, a revolution in confectionery showcased at an American rural fair and reported with much amusement by the world's media. When I rang Mehmet in Cyprus to tell him, he was furious. "I told you!" he cried. "No one thinks my ideas are good. Now, what about this: a restaurant in the back of a semi-trailer that goes from town to town."

The morning had not looked promising. On the street, hunched pedestrians walked slant-eyed into white bullets of sleet, their umbrellas squashed into Christmas trees by the wind. Tevfik, meanwhile, lay on the couch in the corner, eating cheese rolls I had bought for breakfast and complaining loudly. "There will be nothing today, man. Nothing! I can tell. It is hopeless, really hopeless." For a while I stood on the step, wrapped in my coat, squinting into the weather, pretending to smile. I did my best but it seemed Tevfik was right: there were few tourists left and those that were had retreated to the comfort of museums or the Grand Bazaar. At last a middle-aged man — obviously European — stopped and stared into the window. "Please come in," I said, and perhaps he detected the note of desperation in my voice because, after a brief hesitation, he did.

As it turned out, he was a Swedish crime writer in Istanbul for a book fair that was being held on the outskirts of town. He had just won a Turkish distribution deal for his latest novel and was, I gathered, in a celebratory mood. "It's actually a children's book," he said, taking his tea from the tray. "It's about a group of boys who take over a school and kill all the teachers. They have very high hopes for it in Turkey." Akil brought tea. On the opposite couch Tevfik lay down, his head resting on a rolled-up Hereke.

"Oh hello!" said the crime writer, in that unflappable Swedish way. "Are you the boss?" Tevfik gave a scoffing snort and folded his arms across his chest.

I decided to attempt the "bait and switch", a technique that relied on a customer's interest in a cheaper carpet which I would then talk down while presenting something of higher quality, making them greedy in increments.

Pulling a Kayseri silk from the window I rolled it out in front of the Swede. "Now this is a good carpet," I said. "You're right to have noticed it. It's the best Kayseri we have. But this" — I snatched the Hereke Tevfik was using as a pillow, sending him into an upright position — "is a work of art."

For a while I eulogised the benefits of the Hereke but it was soon apparent he was not listening. My heart sank as I watched him glance distractedly about the room. I carried on, but he quickly interrupted me. "This," he said, pointing to a Kayseri stapled to the wall. "How much is it?"

"For you, because I know that Scandinavians don't like to bargain" — I was full of friendly banter these days — "a thousand dollars." I'd have taken eight hundred but I was counting on some haggling. He considered for a moment, drank his tea and said, "Well, if you say that is a good price, then I believe you."

And just like that, he bought it.

"Look me up if you are ever in Uppsala," he said as he walked out the door.

For the next hour I was the Prodigal Son. Hüseyin's brother-in-law, Hazım, shook my hand. A phone call was made to inform Hüseyin. "Brother!" he cried from Tucson or Wilmington or wherever he was. "You are bringing good luck!"

Triumphant and nursing fantasies of selling a silk every week for the next three months, I spent the rest of the afternoon visiting some of the other dealers in the area. The shops on Hüseyin's block constituted a little community, a village of carpet dealers, complete with gossip and in-breeding. All day they criss-crossed to one another's stores: dropping in to play backgammon, drink tea and sit in conspiratorial huddles designed to give the impression that they were concocting some world-shaking Machiavellian scheme when they were, in fact, discussing football, the weather or, for all I know, which they liked better: Coke or Pepsi.

On the corner were Charlie and the Kurds. They hung out the front all day on chairs, petting a cat in a meditative fashion, drinking tea and asking girls to sit with them — a simple tactic with a higher success rate than you might imagine. Further down was Ibo, a backgammon buddy of Hüseyin's. He wore soft-shouldered leather jackets and had a smile like a Komodo dragon. I liked him very much but he asked me so many questions about my sex life that I began to suspect ulterior motives. Further up the street was Ahmet, an old friend of Hüseyin's from Cappadocia who once told me bananas were a vegetable and was stoned a lot of the time. Most of the rest were just faces to me. They weren't only carpet dealers but hotel receptionists, gift-shop guys, kebab makers and an old gardener who tended all the graveyards in the area and would constantly kiss my hand, making long strings of spit between it and his lips — a practice I found, frankly, revolting. (Perhaps he realised how I felt because one day he started ignoring me when he came by the shop, and I found myself more hurt by that than grateful for a dry hand.)

Of all the other dealers on the block, Bull Ant was the only one I knew particularly well. "Ah, yes," he said when I told him about my sale. "Swedish people is like this. Once they say they buy, they buy. But you cannot make they buy, no matter what." Alongside Tevfik, Bull Ant had also worked for Hüseyin during my last trip to Turkey, although only on an occasional basis. There had, however, been some sort of falling out. Exactly why, I was never to discover; their stories were so wildly conflicting that I soon gave up and consigned it all to the realm of Great Turkish Conspiracies.

Bull Ant was everything tourists fear in a carpet dealer. His sales techniques exhibited a degree of shamelessness that was considered extreme even by other carpet dealers, men with a fairly high shame threshold. His approaches to prospective customers on the street were awe-inspiring in their brazenness and he would do anything for a sale: cry, beg, cajole or, as in one memorable incident, call a soft-hearted French woman, sobbing, to claim that he would be fired if she didn't buy the thousand-dollar silk she had been deliberating over. Bull Ant's real name was Belant — common in Turkey — but when I told Hüseyin about a particularly aggressive form of Australian ant that was so stubborn, once it had bitten, you had to twist its body from its head to pull it from your flesh, the name had stuck.

Bull Ant also had a reputation for sleeping with customers and was notoriously flexible in matters of looks and age, a fact which made him the butt of many jokes among dealers on the street. Every other day, it seemed, he had to make a trip to the airport to wave goodbye to some "girlfriend" with whom he had spent the last week, cadging little gifts and making hollow promises to stay in touch forever. From Copenhagen to Colorado there were literally hundreds of middle-aged women who couldn't look at the rug at the bottom of their bed without getting a little misty-eyed over their summer in Istanbul with Bull Ant.

As we sipped tea I asked how business was. He sighed heavily. "I meet one woman. She is from Belgian. She is little bit older. I put in much work. I buy many beers. Many meals. Sleep with her." He shook his head, despairingly. "She buy only one small item."

Carpet dealers in Turkey are regarded by tourists with near-universal revulsion — jackals with apple tea. On every corner of every tourist town in the country they wait: leaning in doorframes, lounging in chairs on the pavement or chasing pretty girls (actually, any girl) with pick-up lines that went out with Bruce Lee movies and velvet tuxedos. Almost every foreigner I met was to complain to me at some point of being "harassed" or "pressured", of feeling "violated" or "threatened" by their behaviour. These complaints, even before I started working in a carpet shop, struck me as bizarre, but after having done so seemed almost offensive. Not because carpet dealers aren't pushy or don't harass tourists — they do, although compared to their counterparts in, say, North Africa they are a model of apathy — but because such cries of outrage — the wounded, indignant pleas to be *left in peace* — are predicated on the assumption that these men, merely through the influence of words and a free glass of tea, have the power to force you to buy thousands of dollars of carpets.

Buying a carpet sent tourists into a panic. It was as if people didn't trust themselves; as if they were so crippled by their sense of social obligation that to accept a glass of tea or exchange a word of greeting was to enter into an eternally binding Faustian pact. It was a source of continual amazement to see the trepidation with which people approached carpet shops, as though they were buying weapons in Chechnya or cocaine in Colombia and might at any minute find themselves in the centre of a blazing gun battle. I could never quite understand what it was that instilled such fear. It wasn't just spending money: people who would happily pay a 500 per cent mark-up on a pair of jeans made in a factory in Bangkok found themselves suddenly panicked at the prospect of being "ripped off" on a carpet that cost less than a new mobile phone and took a woman bent over a loom a month to make. It was the sale process itself that terrified, the blurring of boundaries between customer and salesman, the lack of fixed rules for the transaction. Buying a carpet was like pushing someone into a form of theatre sports. As if they had arrived at the mall only to discover that they had been asked to do some impromptu public speaking.

The sale itself was only one of the carpet dealer's many skills. I was frequently astonished at the ability possessed by Hüseyin, Tevfik and every other dealer on the block to spot the most apparently imperceptible details, allowing them to distinguish a Spaniard from an Italian, a German from a Dutchman, a Belgian from a Frenchman. For the most part, however, we didn't bother trying to sell to European customers, preferring Americans instead. Not because they necessarily spent more than the Europeans, although they often did, but because they were generally more trusting and friendly with a genuine cultural curiosity. This was a quality common to colonials — Australians, Canadians, New Zealanders and South Africans — perhaps because they had been exposed to indigenous cultures at home, but probably because they had made a bigger effort to get to Turkey and were, therefore, more inclined to make the most of it.

Choosing your dealer was an important part of buying a carpet, and not just for the buyer. Customers were under no obligation to buy directly from the boss or the guy who'd dragged them into the shop. Mary, for instance, bought from Mehmet because she felt more comfortable haggling with him than Hüseyin. So, much to his older brother's chagrin, he was forced to pay Mehmet commission on everything she bought. Every salesman in the carpet shops worked solely for commission. Generally speaking, the person who brought the customer had the first go at selling. If somebody else ended up making the sale, however, then the per centages were divided: he got a cut but so did the guy who brought the customer into the shop. This was factored into the price but, not unexpectedly, this system often led to endless behind-the-scenes arguments and the dividing line between where the "sale" began and ended, or who had officially introduced the customer, was fine and often fraught with tension. (These principles did not, of course, apply merely to carpets, but everything: from dinners to hotels to paragliding. When I asked Hüseyin why it was that the buses sometimes stopped for meals in the middle of the night he just shrugged, as if I was asking why the sky was blue, and said, "Because the restaurants pay them.")

Sometimes shops employ freelance touts who approach people in the street or at tourist sites. These guys are universally despised by tourists, sometimes for good reason, but they had a rhinoceros hide and chutzpah that I couldn't help but admire. (Hüseyin told me he had been a tout once, after arriving in Istanbul for the first time as a teenager: "But somebody yelled at me and I ran away and almost cried." Which only went to show that, contrary to the belief of many tourists, touts were not impervious to unkindness.) Most shops, however, rely on a more subtle approach: a network of people in hotels, gift shops and restaurants who befriend tourists then take them to the "best" place to buy a carpet. Their commission could vary but a hotel receptionist could make as much from this, if not more, as he did from his wage and tips.

The biggest earners were the tour guides, who could sometimes earn thousands of dollars for themselves and tens of thousands for their company, just from one bus load of wealthy tourists. These relationships were, of course, heavily controlled by the biggest operators and protected as fiercely as similar associations in the drug trade. It was not uncommon for shots to be fired or serious beatings to be administered in the interests of protecting their turf. The politics and conspiracies of the trade, as with seemingly every facet of Turkish life, were an infinite labyrinth of conspiracy.

Carpet dealers were not, contrary to popular opinion, avaricious swindlers who made obscene profits on every sale. If they had put their skills of salesmanship towards, say, real estate they would have been rich. Most of the owners of shops in Hüseyin's area had reasonable incomes, but were no more than middle class and their business was highly precarious. Many of the guys who worked for them lived barely above the poverty line. Their homes were sad little bedsits with no heating and communal toilets, or a basement room in the shop — even the shop itself where they slept on a couch out the back and brushed their teeth by the tea urn. A number of them supported a widowed parent and most of them were single, hiding like recalcitrant teenagers from arranged marriages back in the village. Few girls in Istanbul would have looked at them twice anyway.

Very few carpet dealers get rich. They do what they do because carpets are their craft and their trade and often all they've known. The difference between carpet dealers and used car salesmen was that a used car salesman didn't care who he sold the car to. But a carpet dealer couldn't help himself: he had to know that it was going to a good home. Theirs was not a logical business; it was a labour of love and I have loved, in some way, every carpet dealer I have ever met — every greasy, sleazy, lying last one of them.

★ ★ ★

Back in the shop, Tevfik was pacing about with his slope-shouldered walk, his hands jammed deep in his pockets. His hair had begun to get long and wild so that when he put his glasses on his head it stuck out in a peacock's fan. "Where have you been, man?" he asked, curtly.

"Hanging out with Bull Ant."

"Hmph. That bastard. Still telling old ladies lies?"

"He sells stuff."

He *tsk*ed. "And gives us all a bad name."

"You already have a bad name."

Ignoring me, he rocked his head back, as if in pain. "Oh, where are my Americans!" He headbutted a big stack of carpets and his sunglasses flew off his head, skittering across the floor. "Where are my goddamn rich Jewish real estate asshole Americans?" In one movement he scooped up his glasses and collapsed on the couch, lying with arms outstretched like a consumptive Edwardian actress. "What are you holding?" he asked.

On my visiting rounds I had stopped by Charlie's shop. Before leaving Van I had arranged to have my carpet sent to him. It had been sitting there for a week and I had almost forgotten about it.

Tevfik snapped his fingers. "Come, let's see it."

I cut open the tight brown paper package and rolled it out. Secretly, I found myself nervous. For a moment I entertained absurd fantasies of having unearthed some rarity. Heads would nod in respectful recognition. Arcane texts would be consulted. Perhaps there would be a small article in some modest academic journal.

Tevfik got up and began to pace around the piece, his hands behind his back, like a sergeant at a parade ground. He kicked up a corner of the *sofra*, examined the underside and flipped it back down. Finally, he broke his silence. "How much did you pay for this?"

I told him.

"Ha! Why?"

My heart sank. "I like it and I wanted something from the east."

He waved a regal hand in its direction. "You got ripped off, man."

I was not entirely surprised. Yet, even though I had no real right or reason to be, I was hurt. Not because I'd been swindled or because I felt betrayed by Halil, but because, odd as it may seem, for all his faults and madness I envied Tevfik and longed for his approval. Tevfik was the cool friend I'd never had and, in some ways, the man I wished I could be. I coveted his autonomy, his autocratic manner, his indifference to convention, the way he could sit in silence for hours on end if he thought he had nothing important to say. If I couldn't be like him, I would settle for his esteem.

He continued. "Wholesale this is a quarter of what you paid. Look at it," he said, scornfully. "It has no good colours, no age, nothing. Brendan, I am disappointed in you." He flung out his hands towards it. "This is a pile of shit."

Doing my best to hide my dejection I rolled the carpet back up and packed it away, never to be seen until the day I left.

Chapter 21

"Look at this! Look at this fucking shit!" cried Tevfik. "Can you believe what these assholes have done?" With one hand he held up a newspaper; with the other he gesticulated wildly, slicing the air with his finger and pointing to the front page. "Do you see?" I peered at the paper, uncomprehending. "This is the biggest religious newspaper in the country. The paper our goddamn fascist prime minister reads. And you see what they have done. Look!" he screamed, pointing. "They have blurred out her legs."

I looked again. The front-page photo was of a little ballerina, no more than six or seven, her face set in a caricature of childish concentration, her arms braced in an awkward arc above her head. Below the tulle cloud about her waist her legs were a pixilated blur.

"These fundamentalists, man, they make me sick. They may not know it but they are committing a big sin ... a *big* sin! They are making a little girl sexual. I mean, these people are sick! Seriously, somebody call a psychiatrist." He kicked the couch, very hard.

I had to admit, it disturbed me too, but not as much as the squirrel in my head using my eyeballs as kettle drums. The day before, I had met a Spanish couple. They had bought nothing so I closed up early and went out to Taksim. The night had been unremarkable but we had still managed to come home as dawn broke, the mist sitting heavily on the streets, the street dogs weaving through the rubbish bins and graveyards.

Oblivious to my tender condition, Tevfik continued. "A few weeks ago a policeman comes up to a girl who is wearing a short skirt and slaps her across the face. 'Go home and put some pants on, slut,' he says. Earlier this year a judge made a decision that it was not the right of teachers to wear a headscarf to school. A young guy goes into the courthouse and shoots him dead. This," he said, raising a finger, "is what happens when you give these people an inch. These people are smart, Brendan. Smart! The headscarf is the Trojan Horse."

"But, Tevfik, you will only make people more angry by not allowing them to wear the headscarf. It's just one little thing."

"Let them be angry. These people will be angry until Turkey is Iran."

"Tevfik, I don't think Turkey is ever going to be Iran."

"Yes, and do you know why? Because in 1923 Mustafa Kemal Atatürk declared that Turkey was a secular country." He raised a warning finger. "And it will stay that way."

It was odd to hear this quotation of policy from the 1920s, as if it were infallible. No odder, I suppose, than hearing people quote religious scripture in the same way. But the suggestion that the two were essentially the same raised more questions than I was prepared to answer.

The Turkish veneration of Mustafa Kemal Atatürk is probably the closest thing you will see in a democracy to the kind of great-leader worship normally associated with African pillbox-hat dictatorships or secretive post-Soviet oil states with public holidays in honour of the general's pet llama. His image stares down at you from every wall in the country. His statue stands in the middle of every town square. His name adorns the main road of every city and town in the country. His profile sits on mountain tops, picked out in lights at night. To not have a picture of Atatürk somewhere on public display, even in your home, is to immediately make you a suspicious figure. Cab drivers tuck little postcards of him into their sun visors. Teenage boys write poems about how much they love him. "He was so handsome," said one woman to me, rolling her eyes back into her head, as if she was fifteen and at a roller disco, rather than forty-five with a Masters in economics.

To see this kind of cult of personality in a developed, (relatively) free and westernised state comes as a shock. But Atatürk was no ordinary founding father and there are few other modern leaders whose influence on their nation has been comparable. Almost single-handedly he established the borders of the modern Turkish state — salvaging it from the ashes of the Ottoman Empire and kicking out the encroaching colonial powers — rewrote the Turkish language, gave women the vote (ten years before France), westernised the education system, separated church and state and even decreed the institution of surnames. (Before this innovation, as in parts of Asia today, Turks did not have surnames. Most chose their own but Mustafa Kemal's, "Atatürk", was conferred upon him by the Turkish parliament in 1932. It means "Father of the Turks", an appellation nobody else, even his own adopted daughter, was allowed to share.)

Atatürk is supposed to be a symbol of everything post-Ottoman Turkey should be: secularised, westernised and very *modern*. Yet much about the cult of personality he has inspired looks anything but. In a country where many forms of public religious observance are vigorously repressed, Atatürk worship has achieved the status of a pseudo-religion, complete with holy texts, relics and secular priests serving in institutions with creepy, vaguely Orwellian titles like the Kemalist Thought Association. There has even been talk of divine apparitions: near the northeastern town of Ardahan a tourism industry has been born to cater for pilgrims who have come to see a shadow on a hill which, at a certain time of day, forms his unmistakable silhouette.

Atatürk wasn't just a Mao or a Fidel; he seemed to have been subsumed into something deeper and older, something that went to the heart of Turkish culture, reaching back to the time where all the spooky stuff came from: the amulets, curses and prayers in graveyards. Hüseyin, who was both highly superstitious and part-time religious, kept his picture in a little nook surrounded by evil-eye charms, like an ancestor shrine. Once I saw an episode of a TV show featuring home videos of ridiculous things people had seen in Turkey, usually with an emphasis on bureaucratic incompetence. One featured a mechanic using an earth mover to lift cars; another a stop sign planted in the middle of the road. But the footage that got the biggest laugh was of a mosque that had been erected without a permit and deemed unsafe by the council. When the wreckers came to knock it down they found themselves confronted with a huge image of Atatürk painted on the side of the building. The council workers, terrified of the consequences of destroying it, refused to do anything and the mosque was saved. This is the kind of voodoo power Atatürk still exerts.

The reforms of Atatürk were, for the most, far-sighted and necessary for the survival of a modern state. To this day their daring is astonishing. But they demanded the Turkish people give up almost all their old ways and dedicate themselves to the construction of a totally new identity. Considering the scale of the enterprise this has been achieved with remarkable harmony, but it asked more than could ever be expected of most ordinary people without creating a sense of loss, a yearning, even if only sentimental, for things as they had been.

Atatürk's vision was too radical for compromise. He was the Father of the Turks but, like the archetypal Turkish patriarch, he was stern, demanding and not open to negotiation — of all the thousands of pictures I saw of him on public display, airbrushed and unreal as an Orthodox icon — I cannot recall seeing one in which he was smiling, his expressions ranging only from stern to very stern to downright menacing. There was nothing tender or approachable about Atatürk.

He was the long-dead father, staring down from the mantel, a powerful ghost, alive in legend but becoming more and more of a symbol with every passing year, his authority as oppressive as it was liberating for the millions of people who, just over eighty years after he gave them a country, still counted themselves his children.

Tevfik began to march up and down. He was on a roll now, flinging his hands into the air as he spoke. "How can they do this to a little girl? These people are obsessed. Obsessed with sex. Do you know why these fundamentalist guys wear the long coat, the one that goes to their ankles? So that when they bend over in the mosque they are not tempted by the arse of the guy in front. I mean, seriously, man, call a goddamn psychiatrist." He pulled open the door and screamed into the street. "Call a goddamn psychiatrist!" A group of teenagers waiting for the tram turned, momentarily startled, before continuing their conversation.

The next fortnight passed in much the same way. On his good days Tevfik was animated, answering all my questions about Turkey with remarkable accuracy and lack of bias. Without prompting he would launch into stories of Turkish history, full of colour and detail: the intrigues of the Topkapı Palace where jealous harem mothers would strangle dozens of infant princes to ensure the succession of their son; stories about the Janissaries, the imperial guard made up of captured Christian boys raised as soldiers; or the private lives of the Byzantine emperors. "Did you know," he announced one day, "that Theodora, the wife of Emperor Justinian, used to perform sex shows in the circus? She would put grain in her pussy and geese would come and peck it out."

Tevfik's bad days, however, were becoming increasingly frequent. Sometimes he would disappear for hours or even days at a time, returning like a mad aunt escaped from the attic to break the peace with his rants about the state of the nation, his financial straits or the wall blocking the door. The fact we weren't selling anything frustrated me, but with each passing, fruitless day, I began to grow less concerned and, slowly, found myself slipping further and further into a seductive Turkish laziness.

In Turkey, doing nothing all day is not necessarily something to be ashamed of. It's not that Turks are lazy — they are not, as a walk through any village will confirm — it's just that they can't see the point of doing unnecessary work if they have the means to do nothing more than socialise with friends and family, drink tea and watch the world go by. This prioritising of leisure over work had my full approval but was for many Turks I met a source of intense mortification; long homilies concerning the laziness of the Turkish people (a favourite topic of Hüseyin's), peppered with heartfelt apologies on behalf of the nation, were to be a regular feature of my time in the country. Despite my protests to the contrary, nobody seemed willing to believe that I regarded this kind of civilised laziness to be the mark of a superior culture and no cause for defensiveness — every citizen of Turkey could spend the rest of their lives eating pot noodles in front of daytime TV for all I cared. As one who had spent the last year doing pretty much that, I was in no position to judge.

With indolence normalised, I no longer felt guilty about not selling. Nevertheless, the quiet of the shop often made me restless. Some days I would hang around on the pavement in front, touting for business, chatting with passers-by. Others I would take a few hours "off" and go wandering through the endless back alleys of the Egyptian Bazaar, among the stalls selling toys, embroidery, glass beads or guns. One day I held an impromptu yoga class: Tevfik and I doing stretches on silk Herekes worth ten thousand dollars while Akil watched with smirking bemusement.

In an attempt to make the long hours shorter I rigged up the shop's stereo system to play music from my MP3 player. Unfortunately all it seemed to contain were albums by depressing English bands from the eighties — The Smiths, Joy Division and Echo and the Bunnymen. The music did little to raise my spirits but Tevfik seemed quite taken with its suicidal gloominess and would often pace up and down by the glass, nodding his head frantically and singing the wrong lyrics to his favourites: "Love, love will tear out our hearts …" Yet, for all my best efforts, most of our days were the same: seemingly endless hours of sitting around, doing nothing but drinking tea, watching people walk by the windows and wishing, like starving castaways on a desert island, that someone would come to rescue us from our boredom.

Sometimes we had visitors: fellow dealers or Tevfik's mismatched menagerie of acquaintances. One frequent guest was his friend Yavuz, a dealer who worked in a shop by the bazaar selling fake Herekes to tour groups. (One day he came while his friend wasn't around and I showed him the two carpets Tevfik had been bugging me to buy. "You should buy these," he said. "They are real tribal Herkis from the southeast. You can't find them anymore." It made me look at them in a different light but I suspected this endorsement was merely an attempt to do a favour for his friend.) Another regular was Adalet. She was a quiet hippy chick who wore Thai fisherman's pants and layers of ragged ponchos teamed with knitted gloves, scarves and a beanie pulled loosely over her dreadlocks. Over the course of my time in Istanbul I was to see her often: sometimes at the shop, where she would sit in a corner, bundled up in her ponchos, sipping a glass of tea from her mittened hands; or on Istiklal Caddesi where she played bongos and sang with her hippy friends. Adalet was part of a "Whirling Dervish" troupe, and one afternoon she came to say goodbye before leaving on a tour with them.

"Adalet's group are going all round the country for a couple of months doing meditation and whirling and having workshops," said Tevfik. "They are going to finish in Konya for the Mevlana festival in December. Every year on the 17th they have a big religious festival. It's the day Mevlana died." Mevlana was a mystical poet and founder of the so-called "Whirling Dervishes". When I told Tevfik and Adalet that my birthday was 17 December they were insistent I should attend the festival.

"Konya is very beautiful on this day," said Adalet. "Many Sufis come for the festival."

Tevfik encouraged me with this plan, claiming Hüseyin wouldn't mind if he ran the shop while I went away. I had my doubts but, as it happened, fate was to intervene and Adalet and I would meet again in unexpected circumstances.

One of my other activities was to sit about making lists of Turkish words I liked, consulting with Tevfik on the subtlety of their meanings. Modern Turkish is another product of the reforms of Atatürk. Before he Romanised the alphabet and purged the language of "foreign influences", Turkish had so many Persian and Arabic words that Atatürk's speeches cannot be understood by modern Turks and have to be "translated" (more than once, in fact, as the language has rapidly evolved since the 1930s). The result is that modern Turkish is, technically, a fairly easy language to get a basic grasp of. The pronunciation is totally standardised and the vocabulary relatively small. The tenses and plurals are simple and, like Finnish, to which it is distantly related, there are no gendered pronouns — which is why Turks speaking English will often confuse "he" and "she", making cross-cultural dating a potential minefield. The definite and indefinite articles, too, do not translate well, encouraging many Turkish English-speakers to merely put one in front of everything, just to be on the safe side, as in: "I like the Coca-Cola" or "Oh, you are a gay?" or "I will kill the Tevfik".

This simplicity is, of course, deceptive. Many words in Turkish have multiple definitions, relying heavily on context for their meaning. I cannot speak Turkish so the following short list should be read only as it was written, informally and with a hangover:

Tamam: Meaning, essentially, "OK", but also "finished" or "It's done!". I swear I have heard entire conversations in which this was the only word used.

Güzel: "Beautiful", "good", "nice", "excellent" and almost every variant thereof. This is a fun word to say because you can really draw out the syllables to show your appreciation: "Ah, *gooo-zell!*" Also, the most common sentence asked of any foreigner in Turkey is, "Turkey *güzel?*" For the appropriate response see below.

Çok: An all-purpose word for "big", "great" or "very". Whenever someone asks you "Turkey *güzel?*" you are supposed to respond with "*Çok güzel*", as if you were telling an annoying, nationalist knock-knock joke with no punchline. It's worth the bother, however, because simply repeating it is enough to make people clap their hands in delight and feed you.

Kıro: Usually translated as "redneck", kıro seems to me closer to the English "chav" or Australian "bogan". According to Tevfik and others I spoke to it was originally intended as a derogatory term for Kurds. But these days it was used to describe a particular kind of hair-gelled lothario seen frequently on the streets of Istanbul. Associations include: a mullet haircut, open-necked shirt, pointed black shoes teamed with white socks and a Conan moustache. *Kıro* is, basically, an urbanised redneck who has adopted the trappings of the city while retaining the mentality of the village, which makes it, for my money, *the* Turkish word of the new millennium. (NB. Carpet dealers are often a bit *kıro*.)

Alıngan: When I asked Akil what he thought of Turkey he said, "OK, but people is *alıngan*," meaning "touchy", "sensitive" and "easily offended". Having been threatened in Turkey more than once with violence merely for "looking" at someone's girlfriend, this was a characterisation I would not debate.

Saf: This can mean naïve, artless and gullible but also pure-hearted. Tevfik used it to describe Akil.

Bebek: By far my favourite Turkish word and possibly the best word for "baby" in any language. Just saying it makes me want to pinch fat cheeks and blow raspberries on tummies.

Ufuk: It means "horizon" but every time I saw it I felt like a kid who's just discovered that "bitch" means female dog. When I later found out there was a candidate for the Turkish election called Ufuk Uras I was insensible with delight.

Canım: One of the prettiest words in Turkish. It is used in much the same manner as "my dear" or "my darling" although it can be shared between good friends as well as lovers. Literally, however, it means "my life", "my soul" or "my very being" which is a lot more romantic and gives you some insight into why carpet dealers get laid so often.

Dönmek: Slang for a transsexual, derived from one of the official meanings of the word "to change one's mind".

Hüzün: A word central to Turkish culture. An inadequate definition would be melancholy, but it is, essentially, untranslatable. At heart it is a philosophical and religious concept and appears, in an Arabic form, a number of times in the Koran. *Hüzün* is the sadness that comes of knowing we are both part of and separate from God; of being able to see the beauty and perfection of the world yet being at a remove from it. The east, I thought, was the centre of *hüzün* and I'm sure I had felt it that day at Akdamar. One day, when he was in a particularly miserable mood, Tevfik announced, "I am what they call a *hüzün bey* [man with *hüzün*]." A statement which, like much he said, I thought rather melodramatic but also, probably, true.

★ ★ ★

The evenings in the shop were often as uneventful as the days. Sometimes I would go out with local friends or customers I'd met. Mostly, however, my time was spent with Akil, which at least gave me an opportunity to get to know him better.

Silent and inscrutable, Akil was a source of some fascination to me. "He is very strong in his mind," Bull Ant had once said of him. "He know everybody secret. He is always thinking, thinking." Conversations with Akil were like Beckett dialogue and facts about his life were wrung out slowly and with caution. Of his background in Afghanistan I knew very little. Only that he was a Tajik from a large family in a province near Kandahar, that his parents were educated but his sisters wore the burqa; only, he said, because for them not to would be dangerous. He hadn't been home for more than five years and I suspected he had skipped the draft. His views on religion and politics were elusive. I knew that he was moderately religious but I never saw him pray, although I suspected he did so in private. In keeping with his principles, he had never tried alcohol but did not seem disapproving of the almost constant inebriation of all those around him. (He once cautiously inquired if my parents knew I drank. When I told him that everyone in Australia drank, even my grandmother, his eyes widened into a rare expression of astonishment and he said, "Your *grandmother* drinks?") When I asked what he thought of the Taliban he said he hated them, though as they are constituted mostly of the rival Pashtun ethnic majority this was to be expected. For the most part, however, he never spoke of his homeland and its state of perpetual war, keeping his feelings on it, like everything else, to himself.

Akil worked constantly, the thump of weights coming from his room signalling that he was enjoying some of his very rare free time. I worried that he was lonely and bored, but it was difficult to tell. He seemed to have no complaints about his employment although he confessed to knowing nothing about carpets and was, besides, a terrible salesman (as tourists walked past he would simply open the door and say, "Yes please, car-pit," the carpet dealer equivalent to "How about a shag?"). His physique was Herculean and he was very good looking but had no girlfriend and was never invited on the nights out, a fact he didn't seem to resent. His professional duties were simple but demanding: all day, every day, he spent in the shop, unfolding and refolding carpets, cleaning, fetching tea and leaving only to run errands. Occasionally, on his monthly holiday, he would make an excursion to some distant pink monolith to visit his Afghan friends, some of the thousands of Central Asian exiles and refugees sheltering in Istanbul. More often they would come to the shop where they would sit in quiet circles on the floor around a sheet of newspaper, drinking tea, eating carrot pilaf and having whispered conversations about their visa troubles.

Generally I didn't press Akil for information or opinions. His manners were so refined and his demeanour so noble and dignified I felt guilty, like interrupting a monk at prayer. There were, however, little surprises, unexpected intrusions of playfulness and humour that made his company easy and enjoyable. Aside from his gifts in window display he was an excellent calligrapher of Persian script and had won prizes at school — occasionally I would pick up my morning newspaper to find a corner embellished with some exquisite felt-tip doodle. To my surprise he hated watching soccer and supported no one, a fact I took as evidence for a heartening iconoclastic streak. He was always impeccably groomed and took great pride in his appearance — when he bought a new pair of jeans from the market he brought them to me for inspection. "Is it good pantaloon?" he asked, as though I were the editor of *Vogue*. When I asked what he thought of Turkish music he gave a rare, impish giggle, his eyes darting, and said, "It so boring."

He also enjoyed cooking — possibly because it represented one of his few creative outlets — and had surprisingly frivolous taste in television. At nights we took turns making dinner for one another which we ate huddled around a radiator while watching soap operas or shows like *Survivor: Turkey vs Greece*, a program that, despite its occasional vicious racism, had done more to heal the rift between the two countries than any diplomatic effort of the last fifty years. Akil's and my favourite show, however, was *Oryental Star*, a talent contest for belly dancers. In a television culture dedicated to either the rich and famous or endless turgid soap operas about bare-foot peasant girls being vigorously dishonoured, *Oryental Star* represented one of the few opportunities to see real people: hard-arsed Gypsy chicks with nose rings and four children; secretaries paying their way through business school by dancing at shady nightclubs; delusional sixty-year-olds in low-cut leopard skin blouses.

The audition process was hosted by a cruel blonde wench with a ponytail on top of her head and eyebrows like two grim little mouths, her speciality cutting remarks like, "This isn't the sticks anymore, honey. This is *Oryental Star*!" One evening a hopeful was being auditioned. She was close to fifty and dressed like the wife of an armed robber making her yearly conjugal visit. Either confused by or oblivious to the point of *Oryental Star*, she skipped the belly dancing and went straight to a toe-curling rendition of some mournful tribal ballad that had plucked eyebrows arching and ponytails swishing disapprovingly in response.

Upon seeing this, Akil — for the first and last time I would witness it — broke into howls of laughter so shattering that for a brief moment I thought he had been bitten by something poisonous.

"What is it?" I asked. "What's so funny?"

Barely able to get the words out, he raised a shaking finger towards the television and, with his deep voice raised to a helium pitch, said, "She is from Azerbaijan!" This unexpected moment of Central Asian snobbery was one of the few times I was to see him break his façade of stony self-possession.

Sometimes after watching TV with Akil I would wander downstairs and study some carpets, read or take notes by lamplight. By night the shop took on an unmistakably eerie quality, as seductive as it was unsettling. Many nights I would do nothing more than sit in the darkened shop, looking at the street outside, stroking Zizou and thinking. On several occasions Hüseyin had told me, in all seriousness, that a ghost lived here, and with the streets empty and the security grill sending a shadow web of silver moonlight across the room, it was difficult to dismiss his warnings as mere superstition. Alone among the stacks of carpets it was impossible not to feel the presence of the long-dead: of the graveyard with its turban tombs; of the little green coffins of the infant sultans strangled one-by-one in the Topkapı Palace; of all the kings and emperors that had gone before and of all the hands that had made all those carpets, anonymously, without reward and forgotten now in the night.

Chapter 22

Every year at 9.05am on 10 November, the anniversary of Atatürk's death, the nation of Turkey comes to a complete halt. Traffic stops, men stand in the street and salute, some in the path of city buses, just to make sure everyone gets the message. In Ankara, the capital created by the great man, Soviet-style military parades mark the occasion — rows of frozen soldiers stare stoically into space while their superiors move through the ranks, armed with tissues, dabbing at the tears on their handsome faces.

Since my arrival in Turkey I had been curious to see this phenomenon. Unfortunately, I had not been paying close attention to dates and when the day finally arrived slept through it. The previous night I had gone out with Alice — the English girl I had met at the party — and a Turkish jazz musician friend of hers. Together we had met some Russian prostitutes in a bar and they had taken us to a transvestite club where we had ended up dancing until 4am. The girls — the real ones — had proved to be an enormous hit, both with us and the nightclub crowd. Vastly well-educated, fluent in several languages, outrageously funny and with dance moves that were the subject of much envious congratulation from the trannies, they were quite the reverse of the buck-toothed Chernobyl babies I might have imagined would end up working as hookers in Istanbul. In Australia they'd have all been celebrities and married millionaires. It was a good insight into how bad things must be in Russia.

Now, from somewhere at the end of a dark dance floor, through a blur of rouge, sequins and plastic moon boots, someone was calling my name. With a dreamer's logic I declined the dance but she wouldn't take no for an answer. Her voice was familiar and mannish. I peeled open one eye. By the bedroom doorway Tevfik stood, white as clay and shaking uncontrollably. He had been missing for three days and when he stumbled into the room with marionette steps, his shades black against his sallow cheeks, it was immediately obvious that something was terribly wrong. I rubbed the sleep from my eyes. "Brendan, Brendan, Brendan!" he cried, collapsing onto my legs. "Please, brother. Please help me!"

Suddenly fully awake, I sat up in bed. Tevfik began to roll over me. "Please, Brendan, we need to talk some business," he wailed, grabbing me around the legs. "Please, please, please buy my carpets." He stood up and began to walk in disoriented circles about the room, ranting and begging. I was appalled but realised that a cool head was called for.

"Tevfik," I said, very clearly, "go and wait for me downstairs. Have a cigarette and try to relax. I'll be down in a minute."

"OK," he said, turned and walked straight into the doorframe, his head bouncing off like a ripe coconut. With uncertain movements he straightened his sunglasses and headed off.

Downstairs, he was sprawled out on the couch, a pale shivering wreck. I was horrified by his appearance and all at once felt much recovered. On the opposite side of the room, Akil sat on his stool, his arms crossed, unable to hide his alarm. "Oh, Brendan ... Brendan," panted Tevfik, his hands clamped on either side of his head. "You have to help me, man."

"What's the matter? What's wrong with you?"

"Oh, Brendan. I haven't slept in three days. I can't sleep. I can't think. I can't do anything. I need money, man. Please, you gotta help me."

"Do you need food or something?"

"I need my medicine, man. Please, I gotta go to the hospital. I need to buy my medicine. It calms me down. Please, Brendan, please, please, please buy my carpets. I need the money for my medicine."

I was at a loss. One half of me wanted to stay strong — to deny him what I felt certain was money to fuel his habit. The other, more powerful, half wanted his pain to end; whether for his benefit or mine I was unsure.

"Tevfik … I can't do this."

"Why? Come on, man."

"Please, Tevfik, you know it's not a good position to put me in."

Shaking, he sat up. "OK, if you won't buy them then I know someone who will." He gave a command in Turkish. With his usual duteousness Akil rose and gathered the carpets that had been sitting in the corner for weeks. Carefully he folded one and put it into one of the nylon carry bags we gave the customers. Before he could zip it up Tevfik brushed him aside and lifted the package onto his shoulder. Shaking under the weight he began to rise to his feet only to collapse in a heap, his head cracking against the floor, his glasses skidding across the room.

"Tevfik, please." I went over and tried to take the carpet off him. "Please have a rest. Calm down. You can hardly walk."

"Please, Brendan," he said, still lying on the floor. "Buy my carpets."

It was all too awful, like watching a dog in pain. What was I to do?

"Alright," I said.

"Oh, thank you, brother." Akil, with perfect courtly timing, bundled the carpets off and folded them up in the corner.

"I need 350 dollars."

It was a suspiciously specific amount and I noted that the price had dropped by half. I felt terrible, as if I were bargaining with him. I offered him the original amount but he wouldn't accept it.

"I still owe you money, man. Just gimme the three-fifty."

"OK," I said. "Let's go to the bank."

Outside he was moderately more composed. He began a monologue: "Thank you, man. I mean it, really. I gotta get my medicine, but it's so expensive, you know. I'm just gonna get on the train and get out there and I'll be back this afternoon, I promise you."

"Tevfik, I think it's best if I come to the hospital with you."

He stopped in front of the graveyard, his eyes flickering behind his shades. "Oh come on, man. Why do you want to do that? It's way out in the suburbs. No one will be there to mind the shop."

"Akil will mind the shop."

"What's the matter — why do you want to come with me?" He paused. "Do you think I'm not going to go to the hospital?"

I was silent for a moment. "Tevfik, please, tell me honestly. Will you use this money to buy drugs?"

"No!" he cried, karate-chopping the air and narrowly missing a pedestrian. "Crack and heroin are out of my life!" His whimpering resumed. "Please, please, please, man. You have no idea how bad I need this." His eyes were pale circles through his shades.

It was all upsetting me too much. I decided I didn't care what he did with the money. At least it would mean me not having to watch this. I took him to the ATM and handed over the cash.

"Oh, thank you, *abi*," he said, hugging me tightly about the shoulders. "You are my brother, man." And with that he lurched off and stumbled down the road.

Back in the shop, Akil was neatly rearranging everything, his face impassive. Seeing me he gave a sympathetic smile and continued about his work.

For the next few hours I stood out the front, trying to entice customers. But it was an automatic effort, drained of enthusiasm by the events of the morning and a growing sense of regret. Finally I managed to snare a couple of middle-aged Americans. At first they seemed promising, the mention of "Colorado" ringing dollar signs in my eyes. But it was soon apparent that my hope had been premature. Refusing tea they settled into the couch. "I want," she announced, as one accustomed to using those words, "a blue carpet that is no more than two-and-a-half feet long by one-and-a-half feet wide and no more than a hundred dollars."

"Honey," he said, as one who had already seen the inside of a lot of carpet shops, "I don't reckon you'll find anything like what you want in the whole of Turkey for less than a hundred dollars."

"Be quiet, you," she snapped. Then, turning to me, "Second husband, same bullshit."

Prepared to abase myself for even this fishwife, I dragged out every cheap thing we had and much of the expensive stuff in the hope of igniting her interest. But it soon became apparent that nothing was good enough, a principle I suspected she extended to all areas of her life.

Having exhausted our entire supply I asked her why she wanted something so specific.

"Because I need something to stand on while I do the washing up."

"Then wouldn't it be cheaper and easier to just buy something in America?"

"But I don't *want* an American carpet. I *want* a Turkish one."

Several hours later, Tevfik reappeared, wild-eyed and agitated but on the road to normal. On the couch he held his head in his hands. "Oh my God. That hospital, man. You gotta line up for hours. You have no idea what it's like in this country if you are sick, man. No one cares! Doctors, nurses, no one."

This was partially true: in Turkey as in many other countries, there was no expectation of care. Everyone assumed that's what your family was for.

He sat back up and pushed his shades onto his head. "Here, check," he said, throwing the medication packet at me. "You see: 350 lira. Thirty-five bucks a tablet, man."

He was telling the truth. The price was there on the side of the box. It seemed I had been wrong to mistrust him and now began to feel a twinge of guilt.

"Why did you doubt me, man? That really hurt."

"Sorry," I said and threw the packet back but not before the thought crossed my mind that, just perhaps, it was an old one.

"Have we had any customers?" he asked.

"No."

"Oh, where are my Americans?" he moaned for a final time before rolling a Hereke under his head and, spreading his long body across the couch, falling asleep.

★ ★ ★

In the morning there was an atmosphere of eerie, expectant calm in the shop, a strong contrast to the previous evening which had ended with a classic Tevfik performance. After a fitful slumber on the couch interspersed with occasional demands for food and beverages, he was finally forced into an upright position by the ringing of his mobile phone. Pulling his shades onto his head, he looked at the caller ID, sighed and answered. For a while he conducted a mumbled conversation, punctuated by exasperated exhalations. "Julie … Julie! I cannot do this shit." Quickly he grew louder. "Enough, OK? Enough! I cannot do this with you anymore. Don't call me! I don't wanna hear from you, OK? Enough is enough!"

He held the phone away from his face and screamed into the mouthpiece. "STOP CALLING ME, YOU CRAZY BITCH! ENOUGH IS ENOUGH! UNDERSTAND? I DON'T WANNA HEAR FROM YOU ANYMORE. I DON'T WANNA HAVE YOUR BABY! YOU ARE CRAAY-ZEE! THIS IS OVER, OK?"

Without bothering to hang up he threw the phone across the room where it hit a wall and exploded into half-a-dozen pieces. By the front door, Akil's eyes grew bright and wide with uncharacteristic glee. "Tevfik is crazy!" he said, speaking for us both.

There was a distinct sense that things were coming to a head and when Hazım appeared later that morning, I knew immediately what was in store. For a while he just smiled at me awkwardly as he mentally rehearsed his English, but when the lecture came it was emphatic and ever-so-slightly infuriating. "Brayn-dan," he began, "don't listen Tevfik. He is *liar*. He don't work. He only smoke and take drug. Don't give money to him for medicine. No money for hospital. No money. Don't give him."

At first I wondered how he had discovered the previous day's events. Suspicion immediately fell on Akil who, affecting obliviousness, busied himself, folding carpets in the corner. Then again, the whole street probably knew by now. But the specifics were really of no matter. My relationship with Tevfik was reaching an impossible impasse. It was clear that Hazım, the epitome of the small businessman, despised him, the two being less chalk and cheese than nitroglycerine and a long bumpy ride in a truck across a mountain road. It was also clear that my influence was the only reason his presence in the shop was being tolerated: I was a guest and Tevfik was the stray cat I was feeding, much to everyone's disgust.

Half an hour later Tevfik arrived. He was agitated and manic. Hazım stared with barely concealed loathing.

"Did you manage to sleep last night?" I asked.

"Yes! Much better. Now, what's for breakfast?" Hazım shot me a knowing look.

Things got even worse when an old man I recognised turned up. He was a part-time hash dealer and, I suspected, full-time local mafia don, who kept a little shop by the Egyptian Bazaar. I had already been there with Tevfik. It was a shabby, mysterious place — a spy novel rendezvous. In the centre of the room was a huge brass incense burner; covering the walls were glass cabinets full of dusty junk: beads, opium pipes, cigarette lighters, boxes of ivory combs, little digital scales, sculptures of Atatürk, jars of evil-eye beads and a Zeki Müren record — the Turkish Liberace — in pride of place next to the Turkish flag. Through the window, the rooftops and minarets of Istanbul were a postcard from the past.

Tevfik kissed the don on both cheeks and called Akil for coffee. Hazım, furious, disappeared upstairs.

Outside, there was some activity. A new American cruise ship was in town, the first in ages, and all the shops were on high alert. In contrast to the usual bovine herds of floral-printed sumos sprouting black erections from their chests, these passengers were all very young, teenagers in fact, but obviously rich: the girls wore oddly conservative, breakfast-show-host clothes and burn victim make-up. The boys were enormous in all directions and loped through the streets in finely embroidered jeans and basketball shoes like space pods. Seeing them next to other passengers on the tram — talking at the tops of their voices, high-fiving and comparing jewellery — was as unnerving an experience as if a gang of African tribesmen had boarded the New York subway and broken into a war dance. They made the Turks look like a race of glum dolls by comparison.

I accosted a passing group and asked them what their story was. "We're on Semester at Sea," said Cindy brightly. "It's totally awesome! We go around the world on a cruise ship and it counts to our study.

We just came from Egypt which was totally awesome." The other two nodded in agreement.

"That's awesome," I said. "Would you like to come in?"

Inside, I asked Akil to fetch tea which they accepted with exaggerated reverence. Tevfik, lying on the couch, raised a hand in greeting. I had high hopes for making a sale and for a while I rolled out carpets, giving my spiel and concocting a series of increasingly outrageous lies. It was soon obvious, however, that they didn't want to buy anything and, like so many others we had seen, we didn't have the heart to push them: they were rich but they were also enthusiastic, curious and utterly artless.

For a while we talked, drinking tea and watching Zizou prowl up and down, barking at the crowds. Tevfik in his position on the couch issued an occasional rejoinder but mostly just dozed under his sunglasses, removing them every now and again to massage his eyes and temples. A group of little boys walked by the window and began to tease Zizou. She flew into a frenzy, fogging up the glass with savage barking. Tevfik bristled, his fingers pressed more deeply into his temples. "There is a word in Turkish," he said pointing towards the dog. "*Işgüzar*. Look it up in the dictionary please and tell me what it says."

"It says, 'conceitedly officious'."

"Thank you," he said, rising and moving towards Zizou who was still barking, pacing up and down to follow the startled pedestrians. "*Işgüzar!*" he said, raising an accusing finger. Zizou, startled, looked up at him with her melting brown eyes. The Americans giggled nervously. "Yes, that is you. 'Conceitedly officious'!" All at once his voice grew to a roar. "What's the matter! What do you want?" He bent down and held her by the muzzle, screaming into her face. "Are you a homosexual? Is that it? Is that your problem? Are you a goddamn lesbian dog? No? Then why don't you just shut the fuck up, you stupid fucking animal! SHUT UP! SHUT UP! SHUT UP!"

Freed, Zizou slunk backwards under a chair, her eyes fixed with terror on Tevfik. Before she could attempt a few face-saving grumbles he turned, silencing her immediately with nothing more than a finger and a glare. He pointed towards me. "Please add *işgüzar* to the list."

The Americans looked at one another, then announced that they really had to be going.

"Oh please," I said. "Have some coffee."

"Yeah, come on, stay," said Tevfik, spreading back out on the couch.

But our pleading was futile. After a taxing round of enthusiastic farewells and promises of return, they fled down the street, never to be seen again.

Over the course of the rest of the day Tevfik grew increasingly agitated. Rising from the couch he began to storm about the shop, kicking stacks of carpets until they wobbled, screaming, over and over again, "Where are my Americans! Where are my goddamn Americans!" Turning towards me he raised a finger. "They never come back, Brendan! They say they will but they don't!" He punched a stack of carpets. "And those Canadians! Those lying Canadian missionary *motherfuckers*! They are goddamn Christians, for Christ's sake. When a Christian says he will come back, he should come back! Don't they know about *sin*?" He collapsed on the couch and pressed his fingers to his temples, his tone barely above a whimper. "Where are they all, Brendan? Why do they never come back when they say they will?"

Coming from a carpet dealer as experienced as Tevfik I found it difficult to believe he wasn't being disingenuous. "What do you mean!" I said. "They come to us, we're too nice and then they go to Grand Bazaar where they meet a Bull Ant who screws them for thousands of dollars."

He paused for a moment, sitting up slightly, his eyes darting. I could see this was a genuine revelation. "Really?" he said. "Is that what really happens?"

And all at once I knew that for all his madness, rudeness, narcissism, callousness and self-pity I would always love Tevfik, because it was impossible to dislike someone who felt so sincerely, and despite all evidence to the contrary, that the world was, ultimately, good.

Chapter 23

As much as I loved Tevfik, something had to give. All the signs were there that the end had come. That it happened the way it did was, essentially, irrelevant to the fact that life in the shop with him was, quite clearly, over. Little things were falling apart. Zizou smelt like a drain, so dirty that when you patted her your hands came back black, as if she were a sponge for all the ancient grime of Istanbul. The hot water hadn't worked in a week and Tevfik had run out of hash, which only made him more irritable, strolling about the shop, ranting about the wall, demanding to know when I was going to wash the dog and kicking things, screaming, "Where are my goddamn Americans!"

I wasn't the only one he was annoying. Akil was a pyroclastic ball of rage. All day long he sat on his stool, like a temple guardian, rolling his neck and flexing his giant fingers, moving only to obey Tevfik's endless demands for tea, coffee, cigarettes and shoulder rubs. More than once, however, I had seen his unflappable façade crack — a certain sideways look, a snap of the neck — and, for a split-second, I could sense the raw power he possessed and the intense effort it must have been for him not to get up and tear Tevfik's head from his shoulders.

An almost terminal blow came with the appearance of the only potential customers we'd had in ages. They were architects from

Chicago, which made them, if not rich, then at least rich enough to be fair game. I fired every rocket in the charm arsenal. Paintings in the Art Institute of Chicago were discussed and when I said that Louis Kahn was the greatest architect of the twentieth century there was a little round of applause. There was only one hitch: they were looking for ethnographic stuff — tent hangings and the like — and we didn't have a great deal of it. I distracted them with some Turkmen pieces — silver bridal hats and circumcision jackets — then, while I had their attention, waved some antiques under their noses. I could sense their focus shift. The wife began to finger a big, expensive *kilim* and say things like, "Oh, now this would look great with the Rietveld chairs." But, before I had the chance to work on them any further, Tevfik interrupted the proceedings. "OK," he said, "I'll take you to where you can get some ethnographic stuff. Come, we will go to Spike's shop."

As he led them out the door I made furious faces behind their backs. "Tevfik, what are you doing?"

"We don't have what they want. Spike will maybe sell to them."

"I don't care. Let's sell them something here."

He shrugged.

Together we trudged through the streets in the pouring rain only to discover that Spike wasn't there and wouldn't be back for several days. Nevertheless, his sidekicks showed us in and we sat among the tent hangings, drinking tea and watching the architects crawl over everything, blathering on about what a nice contrast this or that would make with the Eero Aarnio dining table. Tevfik, meanwhile, had undergone an immediate transformation. Only moments before he had been the cheerful ringmaster — now he was sullen and withdrawn, sprawled out on a couch in the corner, distant from the conversation, like a child who has been denied a treat. At which point I must have realised (stupid Brendan) that the only reason he had brought us here in the first place was to score.

A few days later and things were worse. Tevfik's customary sulkiness was supplemented now by a snappishness that sometimes strayed into outright bullying. When he said he needed a belt I offered him my old one. After taking one look at it he thrust it back at me and said, "Brendan, I cannot wear this. It is dis-*gus*-ting." To make matters worse an acquaintance of mine was in town and we had spent the last three nights drinking. My head felt like a stocking full of pins.

"Brendan," he said after breakfast, "gimme something. I have terrible pain." I gave him a couple of cold and flu tablets. He downed them and asked for the packet.

Come lunchtime no one had eaten. The previous day I had promised Akil I would make spaghetti. While I cooked, Tevfik wandered through occasionally to peer over my shoulder and check on my progress. "What?" he said, sarcastically. "Are we eating it for breakfast?"

When we all sat down to eat he rolled up his spaghetti, took one bite then dropped his fork back into his plate, pushing it to the centre of the table. "I'm sorry," he said, looking pitiful. "But I'm not hungry. I am missing my son too much today." Several obvious, pointed observations immediately suggested themselves, most of them pertaining to the perils of selfishness and the consequences of our actions. It took all my willpower but I didn't say anything. Just rolled up another fork of spaghetti and muzzled myself.

After lunch we lay on the couches, drinking coffee until I was shaking, listening to Joy Division, watching Zizou pace by the window growling at the passing crowds and going slowly mad. Tevfik's moan-of-consciousness continued without pause. "There is no cure for what I have, Brendan," he announced with a quavering voice. "I tell you, if I thought it would help me" — he paused for dramatic effect — "*I* would become a homosexual."

The hours passed. No one came. Tevfik raised an imperious finger in Akil's direction. "Taliban!" he called. "Get me a cup of coffee."

Akil's brow furrowed into rope-like coils of muscle. "I don't like Taliban," he said, with chilling, primeval menace.

As Akil disappeared upstairs, Tevfik, brightened perhaps by the flu tablets he had been eating all day, sat up. "Poor guy. He is going crazy in this shop." He stubbed out his cigarette in the grounds of his empty cup. "He never goes anywhere. Just works here all day." He thought for a moment. "Will you get him a prostitute?"

"Come on, Tevfik."

"Why? I'm serious. He had an Australian girl once, I think. But he has had no sex in three years. He's going crazy in this shop, man. Go on, buy him a hooker."

"No."

"Bah. You are stingy, man," he said, returning to his reclining position. "That is your problem. You just don't wanna pay for it. You don't wanna give me money. You don't wanna give Akil money. You are just a really stingy bastard."

In the time I had been in Istanbul I had: paid for almost his every meal, bought him dozens of beers, many of his groceries, tram fares and cigarettes, purchased a pair of carpets I didn't want and lent him several hundred dollars with little expectation I would ever see it again. So it was not without justification, I felt, that exception was taken to this characterisation.

"That's it, Tevfik," I said, putting on my coat. "Fuck you. I'm leaving. You mind the shop. And try and sell something this time, you whining junkie ... cunt!"

"Hey, what's wrong with you, man?" he said, looking genuinely bemused. He sat up as I opened the door. "And how dare you call me a junkie!"

Marching outside I walked to the waterfront, burning off my rage. The weather had shifted since the first snowfalls and it was now freakishly warm. In Taksim I spent the late afternoon wandering Istiklal, watching the crowds from the comfort of a café and feeling my pulse fall. The street was always packed with thousands of teenagers: suburban boys in their best jackets; girls in basketball shoes and school ties; young lovers in matching eyeliner holding hands; buskers singing maudlin ballads with a horseshoe of respectful onlookers; crazy old men selling little postcards of Atatürk and dead film stars from a tray on wheels. It was one of the few places in Turkey that always seemed joyful and alive, albeit tinged with a familiar sepia of melancholy.

The sunset over the Bosphorus caught the autumn clouds and floated fairy floss above the golden water. In the twilight I headed through the alleys to the *hamam*. For several hours I had it all to myself, and as I lay under the rusted chandelier on the warm marble slab listening to the water drip from the ceiling — the comforting, lachrymose cycle of condensation — I felt all my tension and resentment wash away with my hangover.

By the time I returned, the streets were almost empty and Tevfik was gone. Akil sat on his stool by the door, his arms crossed. As I walked in he looked up, rocked his head slowly to one side then the other and said in the same tone he delivered everything. "Hüseyin mah-ther very sick. He come home soon."

Chapter 24

When Hüseyin appeared in the shop the next morning I was surprised, not just by the speed of his arrival but his apparent composure. We all knew by now that his mother was dying, and to see him showered and shaved, drinking coffee and making easy conversation with Tevfik, as if nothing at all had passed between the two — raising my hopes for a reconciliation — contradicted many of my assumptions of how such a scene ought to look. It was, of course, exactly as such a scene ought to look. His joviality was a carefully crafted façade, his stoicism as much for his own benefit as ours. "*Abi,*" I said, kissing him. But I had nothing else to add. There was some bright talk of possible recoveries, of twelve years fought and won and bigger hurdles having been overcome. But we all sensed that this was it. She had gone into a coma and would not be coming out. Strange the ability we have to know these things.

When the relative arrived to drive Hüseyin to the hospital in Ankara, we kissed him goodbye and waited while Zizou licked his face. "Take care," I said, theatrical partings not being one of my specialties. As he walked up the pavement, he turned and waved, his smile tight and grim.

The next few days saw an unlikely flurry of activity, almost all of it unprofitable. There was, however, some good news. Unbelievably, the elderly Canadian couple from Regina returned and bought a carpet.

"We went all over, didn't we, Jim?"

"All over."

"We went to the coast and to Cappadocia 'cause we thought they'd be cheaper, but they weren't, were they, Jim?"

"If anything they were more expensive!"

"So here we are now — our last day in Turkey and we come to you."

"Well thank you very much," I said, "you certainly have extraordinary willpower to wait this long before buying."

"Oh," she said, "we like to shop *around*, don't we, Jim?"

"Oh yeah. Lin won't be forced. You know, she hit a guy in India once. Punched him, hard too."

A steady stream of other visitors kept us entertained. A few days were spent in the company of a beefy Korean–Canadian NATO soldier on hiatus from Afghanistan. For a while I entertained the notion of selling him a piece, but he was more interested in collecting comic books, which he discussed, like all his conversation, at never anything less than the volume of mortar fire over Kabul. When he came by the shop the next day I noticed that he trembled constantly, like a chihuahua. "He is traumatised, man," noted Tevfik, and I remembered that, as unlikely as it seemed, he had also been a soldier. (For those who might be wondering, Tevfik's military service could not, so far as I could see, be blamed for any of the cracks in his fragile psyche. He never saw combat and according to his accounts had an unremarkable, often enjoyable experience, even allowing for his compulsive contempt for authority.)

The next evening a Spanish magician and his wife arrived in the shop. He was an expert at card tricks and we spent an hour staring inches from his hands as he made queens turn to kings and clubs to hearts. "No way!" screamed Tevfik, kicking bits of furniture. "No fucking way! You are a goddamn genius!" It was the happiest I had seen him in some time.

One afternoon I was sitting by the door to the shop when a familiar face passed by on the street. I called out but was ignored, taken, no doubt, for another carpet dealer who wanted to sell her something, an assumption that was not entirely unfair. "Hey," I cried, following her down the street. "Hey, I met you in the east. At Lake Van."

With that she stopped and turned, pausing for a moment, before announcing, as though she were a detective meeting the killer at the end of a novel, "Yes, it is you."

She was one of the German girls, the one with the dreadlocks I had seen swimming the day I had gone to Akdamar. On the couch we sat and drank tea for the rest of the afternoon. "Where are your friends?" I asked.

She hesitated. "They have gone home," she said in measured Teutonic tones. "I did not know the boy. He was Italian, a sociologist, studying the lives of Kurdish farmers."

"And the girl with the shaved head?"

"She has gone back to Germany."

Did I detect the hint of some secret drama, the end of a love affair perhaps? "Was she your girlfriend?" I asked.

Her eyebrows disappeared beneath the ropes of hair. "No. She lives on my commune in Germany. She is an expert in natural pesticides and fertilisation."

"Good," I said. "Unnatural fertilisation is messy and involves all those kitchen utensils."

She stared at me hard, whether in confusion or disgust I could not tell.

Her name was Liesel and we talked for hours about many things. She was quite humourless but obviously very kind and when I told her I was worried about my friend whose mother was dying she looked very intensely in my eyes and said, "That is sad. But we all must die." This struck me as a rather self-evident observation and, as consolation, fairly inept, but with her intense, hypnotic eyes and the clipped monotone of her German accent I still found myself strangely soothed.

Night came. Just as she was about to leave, a group of little boys came up the street. Thankfully Zizou was upstairs so when they opened the door and their dog nosed into the shop there was no commotion. Seeing this, Liesel cooed with delight and went to pat the animal, at which point I noticed that it was a rather scruffy looking pet and that it wasn't wearing a lead, just a rope knotted about its neck and that the boys were all wild-eyed and filthy, their mouths and noses ringed with stains from sniffing solvents, which is when I must have realised that they weren't coming to show us their dog but trying to storm the shop and rob us.

The dog barked and growled and Liesel shrieked in fright. As the boys tried to barge their way in, I rose from my chair, planted a swift kick under the animal's jaw, sending it back out onto the street, locking the door before they could make another attempt. With barely an acknowledgment that anything had happened, the boys continued to stumble up the street in the dark, trailing behind their dog, in search of another victim.

Liesel was shocked, and so was I — mostly at my own uncharacteristic quick-wittedness and coordination. More than anything though, this incident was a vivid illustration of what a strange in-between world this city — this country — seemed to inhabit. One day you were ordering frappacinos at Starbucks, getting drunk with Russian prostitutes or discussing the finer points of organic farming with German hippies; the next someone was trying to sell you a peacock in a cage, or you saw a little boy pulling a legless woman in a cart up a hill, or you had to fight off homeless demon children, high on glue — rude reminders that this was still the Third World, that nothing was certain and that chaos lurked in the shadows.

The death of Hüseyin's mother upset me far more than was logical. The night before it happened he had called me, almost incoherent with grief. We spoke for a little and I made some hollow-sounding expressions of support, the sort of things that sound woefully inadequate at the time and forehead-slappingly stupid in retrospect. "We are thinking of you," I said, and: "Everyone in the street is so sad." Despite the obvious futility of these compensations he thanked me, albeit in a frantic automatic way, repeating the words "Thank you, thank you", over and over again, like a man chanting in the back of a very deep cave.

When Hazım announced the news the next day with a sad, earnest face, almost indistinguishable from his usual, I had to lock myself in my room for a few minutes and cry. I was aware that this grief seemed disproportionate, even indulgent, for a woman I had met once and with whom I had exchanged two words. Mostly, however, it was for Hüseyin, the big brother who felt he had to keep everything together — the ringmaster who kept people at a distance by, ironically, doing everything for them — and of whom, I realised now, I knew so little.

The next day Hüseyin rang and asked if I would mind continuing to look after the shop while he was in Kayseri for the funeral and the family business that would follow. I said he should take as long as he needed.

The news of Mrs Yılmaz's death made the atmosphere in the shop even more oppressive, sending Tevfik into some sort of depressive spiral — he wasn't even ranting anymore, just lying on the couch shivering, asking for tea and whimpering. When I complained of the slow business he looked up from the couch and said, "Tourists these days, man, they don't buy anything. Why should they? This city is just another goddamn weekend getaway for Dutch dentists. Carpets are dead, man."

"But you still love carpets, don't you?"

"Sure," he said, his face screwed up, as if in pain. "Carpets are beautiful. They are life, man. But carpets are over. There are no good ones left. The Germans bought them all in the eighties, and after the Americans discovered them … well, that was it. Who cares about carpets now anyway? Nobody makes them, nobody buys them. All these ladies are dead." He gestured to the stacks around us. "It's all gone. There is nothing left now, man. Nothing."

One morning he went out to buy a Coke only to reappear the following afternoon, looking pale and shattered. The customers I was entertaining — newly-weds: he a jazz musician from Kansas, she a dental hygienist from, of all places, Turkmenistan — made quizzical faces at one another as I bundled Tevfik into a quiet corner.

"Brendan," he croaked, "gimme fifty dollars."

I'd decided that it was time to be firm. "I can't do it."

He sighed heavily.

"I could buy you some groceries," I added.

"No, I need the money." His voice was barely above a whisper.

"Sorry, Tevfik."

"OK," he said, his eyes closing heavily in despair, and left.

The honeymooners looked at one another and said, almost simultaneously, "Can we think about it?"

Later that evening Bull Ant appeared and told me that Tevfik had come to his shop asking for money. "I say no," said Bull Ant in his peg-on-nose voice. "But he say, 'Please I need money, I need money so bad.' I say, 'I don't have.' And he say, 'Oh please, Bull Ant, help me,' and he fall on floor — collapse! He is on floor, his face white. He roll on floor. 'Oh, help me,' he say. 'I die. I need money.' Finally, I say, 'OK, Tevfik.' He say 'Thank you' and we walk to ATM machine. I give him fifty lira."

Although I considered it a cheering testament to what I regard as the inherently charitable nature of Turkish culture that a guy as tight as Bull Ant would give money to a guy like Tevfik simply because he was part of the tribe, this story disturbed me, and not merely for the obvious reasons. If Tevfik had been reduced to begging from Bull Ant it could only mean that he had bled dry all other wells of support, leaving open the possibility that even his family had abandoned him. This hypothesis was lent further credibility by the discovery that he had stooped so low as to borrow money from Akil, a man in no position to be acting as lender to anyone. When I found out I was furious but Akil was philosophical. When I asked why he had given any of his meagre wage to Tevfik he looked off into the distance with saintly eyes and said, "Because he so sad."

Meanwhile, the financial situation of the shop was beginning to closely mirror that of its residents. With his mother's death, Hüseyin had incurred a massive loss on his trip to America and I felt duty bound to help out by selling as many pieces as I could before his return from Kayseri. With a final burst of persistence, I could, I reasoned, sell at least a couple of token items, even if it meant picking people up and carrying them inside. This ambition was to prove wildly optimistic. After six weeks as a carpet dealer I had come to the conclusion that most tourists wouldn't have bought from me if I was holding a gun to their head. Numerous reasons were to blame for this — including, but not limited to, the fact that I am a terrible salesman — but by far the most important factor was the very reason Hüseyin had regarded me as a good candidate for carpet dealer in the first place: my familiarity.

Most tourists claim to despise carpet dealers. In reality they feel let down if they are not harassed and dragged into shops by leering moustache-twirlers with designs on their wallet and their daughter's virginity. When people buy a carpet they fear being ripped off — far exceeding this fear, however, is the prospect of being denied an "authentic" holiday experience. The carpet dealer was local colour, a dying craft, like a candle-maker or a kid in a sombrero on the back of a donkey. Buying a Turkish carpet in Istanbul from a skinny backpacker with an Australian accent was like paying to see the Stones fronted by Leo Sayer, or turning up to the zoo only to find all the cages filled with sheep. Tevfik had been right — selling carpets was storytelling, the rest was bonus.

In defiance of this realisation I persisted as best I could, my humiliations compounding daily. For hours I stood in front of the shop, futilely accosting anyone who would look at me: mute Koreans who glanced sideways with deep suspicion before scuttling off into the distance; a pair of sour New York art-lesbians with Art-Deco haircuts and abstract Japanese tunics, who actually laughed when I invited them in; a pair of English alcoholics who despite being completely inebriated at ten o'clock in the morning had the hide to announce loudly, "Those are all made by children, anyway." It was the Germans, though, who pushed me over the edge. They were a middle-aged couple, rotund and unseasonably tanned, like glazed hams. She had a subtle beehive, like a well-made nest, and wore a string of pearls over her green canvas jacket. He had a way of pulling his coat back to put his hands into his trouser pockets to reveal his enormous stomach. They looked like communist propaganda cartoons — all that was missing was the top hat, the dollar sign on the chest and a caption reading "Capitalist Scum".

As they pointed into the window I began to prime my usual routine. He, seeing me approach, without making eye contact and with his face screwed into a look of pure disgust, began to shoo me away with two hands, as one might wave off a fart.

A dam of frustration inside me burst. "Don't do that!" I yelled. "It's not necessary." He was momentarily shocked, his chin disappearing into his neck.

"Zen why do you people always bozzer us so much? It's not nice, you know!"

"Well if you look in my window then I'll come and bother you as much as I like!" To my surprise he suddenly became shamefaced and apologetic, not, I quickly understood, because he felt any regret but because he had realised I was not Turkish. Embarrassed and flustered he began a monologue, an apology of sorts.

"I have come to Istanbul many times and bought many carpets," he said in his Colonel Klink voice. "The dealers are very rude. Always pushing." His tone grew low and conspiratorial. "This is why they will never be European. Never ever. Because they are not like us. This Muslim culture is not like ours. They are so" — he struggled for the word — "*dirty*." While he spoke his wife just stared through the window with her hands in the pockets of her coat, smiling to herself.

Chapter 25

Nothing can prepare you for the beauty of Cappadocia. It's a UFO sighting or a lottery win. It's beautiful in ways that make you want to turn involuntarily to the stranger next to you on the bus and say, "Look! Look at that!" which is precisely what I did the first time I glimpsed the Göreme Valley from the high road, oblivious to and uncaring of the fact that he didn't speak English and actually lived there. That was two years ago. This time round the same sight had lost none of its excitement.

More than a month had passed since the death of Hüseyin's mother. As soon as he and his family had arrived back from Kayseri it was obvious that I had to get out of Istanbul. Almost immediately the shop became a musical chairs of relatives and friends, a marathon of grief and condolences. Mehmet, who had been in the middle of exams when he'd gotten the news, had already gone straight back to Cyprus. Hüseyin, meanwhile, could do little but accept commiserations and walk around like a zombie, playing the host and nodding emptily when visitors said how sad they were. His only compensation now was prayer which he increased from once a week, on Fridays, to daily. "Every day, man," he announced in a haltering, faraway voice, "I'm going to mosque every day for forty days." As he sat in the chair by the door staring out at the window he looked like a leprechaun who'd lost his pot of gold.

Tevfik, in contrast, had perked up considerably, bringing to his role as consoler more energy than he had ever applied to that of carpet dealer. In the days after the family's arrival he spent much of his time playing host: organising the shop, dealing with Zizou and fetching tea, especially for Hüseyin's father, who he obviously adored. "Hüseyin is on a I-lost-my-mother trip at the moment," he said with a shake of his head. "It's a bad scene, man. That guy *worshipped* that woman."

A couple of days after Hüseyin's return, I announced my intention to leave. Hüseyin hugged me and asked if there was anything I needed. I would have said, "Yes. For you to stop worrying about everyone else," but thought that sounded rather melodramatic and, like most Hollywood lines, only occurred to me in retrospect anyway. The next month was spent travelling along the west coast, visiting or revisiting various cities and historical sites. From Istanbul I headed south, taking in along the way: Troy, where, like many visitors before me, I was disappointed to discover that the most famous war in history had been waged over a city smaller than a supermarket car park; Bergama, home to Pergamum, arguably the best Roman site outside of Pompeii; Izmir, the third-largest city in Turkey, where I spent three days in the apartment of some Bosnian students I met on a bus, sleeping off hangovers on a mattress caked in black chewing gum; and the resort town of Bodrum where I fulfilled a long-term ambition to visit the former home of Zeki Müren, Turkey's greatest and best-loved pop singer, whose death during his own 1996 tribute concert conferred his entire estate, including a fine collection of home furnishings and costumes, to the Turkish army. (This decision was, I suspect, a purely symbolic statement of his secular principles. Nevertheless, the image of some stony-faced colonel rifling through boxes of sequinned muumuus, Swarovski figurines and rhinestone knee-boots refuses to leave me.)

From Bodrum I turned east, moving along the Mediterranean, via the port of Fethiye, to arrive, once again, at the dreaded Antalya from where I flew to Cyprus to meet Mehmet. (The so-called Turkish Republic of Northern Cyprus was created in 1983, almost ten years after the Turkish invasion of the island. It is now almost completely owned by the military and mafia, gambling and maintaining the invasion force being the major industries. Yet, as fascinating the Freedonia of the Mediterranean undoubtedly is, a full account of its charms would require a greater diversion than I am willing to make in these pages — just imagine North Korea with beach resorts or the Costa del Sol if Franco had never died.) As was to be expected, Mehmet's mood was subdued. Nevertheless, we still enjoyed a restorative week of sightseeing, interspersed with long bouts of lying in bed watching TV, going to the *hamam* and generally adding new chapters to the greatest sexless homosexual love story ever told. At the end of the week, like a pinball hitting a flipper, I flew back up to Istanbul where I began a new journey with a new travelling companion, a woman held much in my esteem yet who, for the purposes of this book, shall be referred to only as Lady Penelope.

Lady Penelope was English but we had met in Australia while working together in the same menial role on the same newspaper. United by an aversion to almost all our more career-minded colleagues and a strong mutual commitment to sloth, we quickly became close friends. That was more than six years ago and since that time she had moved back to London where she was now between writing jobs. This was, of course, nothing unusual — Lady Penelope was permanently between jobs, not to mention homes, boyfriends and time zones. Her life was a series of preposterous escapades, one after the other, like a silent film heroine who runs from the railway tracks still bound in rope only to fall through the haunted disused mineshaft. Every time we spoke there was a new story about some distant part of the world and some doomed and unlikely romance: the Mongolian Sherpa, the minor Bollywood film star, the Cuban cardiac surgeon who was "six-foot-two and black as piano sharps". When I rang to ask

Mehmet

if she would like to travel with me, suggesting that she might be able to squeeze in a few freelance pieces on the way, she had said, "Of course. I've never been — can you believe it? But I did once shag a kebab vendor in the back of his van at the Reading Festival. Though to be honest, I think he might have been Lebanese."

For Lady Penelope I would do or forgive anything, even her habit of referring to me loudly and in public as "Brendychops".

We arrived in Cappadocia after a gruelling overnight journey via Ankara and Kayseri. The bus had been heated to the levels of a Victorian fern house and I had spent many hours pleading with the driver to turn down, alternately, the thermostat and the deafening volume on a film of a stand-up comedian so loud the canned laughter made the speakers fuzz, but which left the entire bus utterly stony faced — because he wasn't funny or because Turks don't laugh much in public was unclear. In the seat beside me, sweat ran down Lady Penelope's face like snail trails, matting her blonde hair to her brow. "Kill me. Kill me now," she croaked.

Cappadocia is the kind of place no one can die happy without having seen once. The area was formed by ancient volcanic eruptions: some of the most massive in recent geological history and still active until only nine thousand years ago, as recorded in local cave paintings. These eruptions smothered the entire region of central Turkey in a blanket of ash, hundreds of metres deep, which has made Cappadocia not only one of the most fertile places in the country, but has created some of the strangest and most haunting rock formations in the world, giving shelter since the dawn of civilisation to the usual bewildering succession of cultures.

These formations are scattered across Cappadocia, with the highest concentrations found in the Devrent Valley and its surrounding areas. The "Valley of the Fairy Chimneys", as it is referred to in the tourist literature, a legacy of the unfortunate influence the works of JRR Tolkien exerted over the hippy imagination of the 1970s, bristles with thousands of conical rock turrets which, to be fair to the hippies, really do look like enormous pixie toadstool houses. They were formed over many millennia by erosion that washed away the soft, lower layers of compacted ash (called tuff) to leave the hard upper layers of pumice as teetering grey caps. The *kaleler*, or "castles" as they are known to the locals, are widely varying in their forms. Some are Gothic turrets, others more pyramidal, balancing precarious stone eggs, encouraging vaguely zoological associations. Many, their flaring grey caps atop proud pink shafts, are distinctly porno, making the attraction of Cappadocia to ancient fertility cults obvious. Seeing the valley of spiky monoliths from the top of a high ridge, the overwhelming impression was of something fecund and emergent: the first stirrings of life on a distant planet; a spaceship journey over the tastebuds of God's tongue.

In the modern era Cappadocia is mostly a tourist construct. No such province officially exists, the name referring, roughly speaking, to an area of several thousand square kilometres lying almost in the exact centre of the country. At the heart of Cappadocia lies the village of Göreme, the tourist centre of the region. Göreme is an enchanting place, a Smurf village nestled in the valley. Many of the homes and guesthouses are carved into the *kaleler*, and the rest of the buildings, by government order in deference to its status as a UNESCO national park, are quarried of a very fine local stone, their windows and balconies handsomely carved. In the centre of town, chiselled into a *kale,* is a high Roman tomb, illuminated at night.

Göreme is arguably the most beautiful village in the world, yet, despite this, and regardless of its many other charms, I do not much care for it. Exactly why is difficult to pinpoint. Suffice to say that there was in the village more than a hint of the Third World coming into contact with the First with the usual and not entirely happy results. Göreme exuded the feeling of a very small, very poor community that had suddenly become unevenly wealthy, bringing many comforts and advantages but also creating cultural upheaval and endless jealous peasant lamentations, which, in truth, is pretty much what had happened.

Until the mid-eighties Göreme was relatively obscure. But with the Turkish tourism boom the village rapidly became a backpacker fixture, the result being that, for a few, the village had become a gold mine — foreigners were buying property everywhere and a new breed of luxury hotels with Wi-Fi and room rates the price of an acre of land were opening not only in Göreme but all across Cappadocia. The sense of cultural whiplash was palpable. You only had to walk a couple of blocks from the main square with its scooter shops and internet cafés carefully hewn of local stone to find old ladies with man hands and rheumy eyes wearily chopping bundles of firewood. At night, in half-empty reggae bars, local boys who spoke English with Australian accents rained endless compliments on backpacker girls or drove up and down the main street in loud cars, small-town boredom being a universal principle, no matter how pretty the town. Yet, as is so often the case in the developing world, life in Göreme was not a simple case of the rich taking advantage of the poor.

Turkey is Thailand for women — if men went to Bangkok strip clubs to talk about their feelings — and in every tourist centre of the country I found myself bumping into the same revolving cast of starry-eyed debutantes: tandoori-tanned English alcoholics, German divorcees in blue leather jackets and a seemingly never-ending parade of dippy Californians in cheesecloth pants who talked of goddess worship and thought anyone over fifty who couldn't speak English was a shaman. Amazingly, many of these women seemed genuinely blind to the cultural and economic disparities in their relationships with local men and were willing to make astonishing financial and emotional commitments in exchange for what, to any objective observer, seemed the most self-evident bullshit — a few well-timed compliments and suddenly they were trying on headscarves and remortgaging the condo in Santa Cruz.

For whatever reason, Göreme seemed to attract a disproportionately large number of these hopeless romantics. By bonfires in the valley handsome Mehmets and Murats told them they couldn't wait to get married … just as soon as they got the fifty grand they needed to start that *pansiyon*. According to Hüseyin half the town's hotels had been built with the help of duped women. An exaggeration, no doubt, but the lothario phenomenon had been deemed sufficiently serious for the Turkish government to consider introducing laws designed specifically to combat it, spurred on, in part, by bad publicity surrounding a spate of high-profile incidents involving underage girls. Most notorious of these was the case of Sarah Cook, a chubby twelve year old from a particularly unglamorous part of Essex, who caused an international incident after "marrying" an unemployed waiter she'd met while on holiday with her obviously liberal-minded parents. The incident ignited a tabloid storm in the UK and Turkey, especially after she moved to her in-laws' home near Gaziantep, adopted Islam and became pregnant.

For several months photos of Sarah in a floral headscarf became a staple of the English press, igniting a public campaign for her return. In Turkey, meanwhile, she became a folk hero — sympathetic members of the public showered her with gifts of chocolate and lace and the mayor of her adopted town publicly praised her decision to change her religion and adopt a Turkish way of life. ("I've been to England," he thundered, "and I know about the orgies, the drug parties where people do what this couple chose to do honestly and in keeping with Islam.") Unfortunately, not even these shows of support could save the doomed romance; the marriage was declared illegal and the groom arrested to be charged with statutory rape. Sarah returned to the UK with her child soon after, although only, allegedly, because her husband was too jealous and possessive.

As it happened, the case was a minor obsession of Lady Penelope's. "Do you know what she said when they asked her why she did it?" she asked. "'Because in Turkey I am beautiful.' In Turkey I am beautiful!" her laughter echoed across the Göreme Valley. "I still don't know if that's the funniest or the saddest thing I ever heard." Her tone changed. "But, then again, I suppose it's really the only reason people travel — to feel more beautiful and exciting than they really are."

"And maybe get to meet a carpet dealer, or a paragliding instructor or a Sherpa or something."

"Brendychops."

"Yes?"

"Fuck off."

* * *

Despite my misgivings about Göreme, we would end up staying there — in mid-winter it was one of the few places where things were still open and, besides, it really was quite lovely. During my last trip to Cappadocia the sky had been an immovable grey slab, generating an occasional fall of sleet or light snow that left thin white skullcaps on the *kaleler* each morning. The weather had not detracted from the region's beauty and, indeed, had often added to it. But now, under the blue winter sky, the village a bowl of stony meringues, Göreme took on a new and joyous atmosphere, like Munchkin Land come to life after the death of the witch.

It's easy to get carried away by the beauty of the Göreme Valley: its charms are so many and obvious that even the most jaded traveller is suddenly transformed into a babbling slideshow bore. If I am guilty of skipping too quickly over our first day and the attractions of Göreme, therefore, it should be taken only as a testament to the endless riches of the Cappadocia region, which are so many and varied that you can afford to be blasé about the things within plain view.

The morning was spent at Göreme's main attraction, a complex of cave churches and monasteries known by the deceptively prosaic title of the Göreme Open Air Museum. Reached by a one kilometre walk out of town on a path past a valley so beautiful it hurts your head to think about it, the Open Air Museum is a rabbit warren of rock-cut structures, many of them adorned with some of the world's best-preserved Byzantine frescoes.

Cappadocia was a haven for Christian refugees from the Roman Empire, and later became one of the most important centres of the early church. The entire region is scattered with hundreds of rock-carved monasteries and chapels as well as innumerable fortresses and hide-outs. Some structures served both purposes; a monstrous nunnery a short drive out of town features sheer tunnels soaring 40 and 50 metres into the rock up which sprightly nuns would retreat, using only the power of their obviously sturdy limbs, to pour boiling oil onto invaders below. The thought occurred to me that if the Sisters of Saint Joseph had spent a little more time practising their ninja skills and burning the skin off Arab horsemen, and a little less slapping me with rulers, I'd probably have paid more attention in religious education classes.

The rest of the day was spent exploring the valley and the nearby hills, clambering among the *kaleler* and the caves using a sulky local dog as a guide, the dogs of Cappadocia being famous for their knowledge of the local terrain. (Before she retired to a life of irritable snoozing, Zizou had been especially renowned for her talents in this department and I had heard numerous *Lassie*-like stories involving incredulous drunken backpackers being led through pitch-black wilderness to the safety of town, one nursing a broken arm after a horse riding accident.) The next morning it was decided to move further afield, so we hired a car. By "we", however, I mean Lady

Penelope hired the car while I sat by smiling pathetically as the Hertz man looked at me and said, "What do you mean you can't drive?"

There are many of life's more practical tasks at which I do not excel. I cannot catch a ball, do my tax, fix a fuse or see a magic-eye picture. Yet of all the basic skills that have passed me by, one of the most embarrassing and frustrating, for both myself and those around me, is my inability to drive. I am not proud of the fact I cannot drive; it is not a calculated act of inverted snobbery or an ecological protest. My not learning to drive was merely a conspiracy of economics and laziness and the older I get the more impractical and humiliating the situation has become. This state of affairs is given vivid emphasis in a country like Turkey, a nation which, for all its recent social progress, is still not the kind of place where a man would voluntarily allow himself to be driven by a woman, short of being in a full-body cast.

Doing her best to accentuate my disgrace, Lady Penelope signed the insurance papers with a dramatic, Elizabethan flourish. "I hereby declare you a gaylord of the realm, Sir Brendychops."

As it happens, the car rental guy was friends with Hüseyin from his old days in Cappadocia. "Ah, yes," he said. "I know Hüseyin. Everybody love him very much. Piç Hüseyin we call him. It mean 'bastard'."

"You heard about his mother?" I asked.

"Oh yes, when his mother die we were very sad. They make an announcement over the mosque, 'The mother of Piç Hüseyin has died, please pray for her.' Well," he said, pausing for thought, "they didn't say 'Piç Hüseyin'." He asked us where we were going. I said we didn't have any particular plans.

"If you want to see somewhere really amazing," he said, "go to Soğanlı." He pointed it out on the map. "It is a bit far but no one goes here and it is a very special place." Without thinking he gave the keys to me then watched with exaggerated pity as I handed them on to Lady Penelope.

Once you climb out of the valleys, the landscape of Cappadocia can be deceptively similar to much of central Turkey. For the most, the hills are gentle and brittle-looking, the irrigated fields very flat. Then, without warning, the land becomes stark and bleached, rising up into Death Valley ridges or opening into deep, soft-serve rifts scattered with *kaleler* and villages of boxy houses painted white, pink and yellow. With each turn, the white volcanic peaks of Erciyes and Hasan appear and disappear over the horizon, as if they were spying on you. Following the recommendation of Hüseyin's friend we made our way towards the Soğanlı Valley. First, however, I insisted that we make a stop at the town of Kaymaklı, site of one of Cappadocia's best underground cities.

Cappadocia has dozens of underground cities, a network of tunnels and chambers dug deep into its soft volcanic rock. Many were initially built by the Hittites, mostly as storage facilities, and a number of the towns in the region still utilise the naturally constant temperature within these caves to store their fruit and vegetable crops. Over time these underground caverns were adopted and expanded by succeeding civilisations, most notably the early Christians who escaped Roman persecution by fleeing to Cappadocia. Later, long after Christianity became the official religion of the empire, they provided shelter from Arab raiders. By this stage the cities were immense, hundreds of kilometres of tunnels, some sinking more than twenty storeys below ground and featuring complicated hydraulic and ventilation systems, as well as dispersal systems for smoke and mechanical fortifications. It's estimated that at full capacity they could hold up to thirty thousand people. The scale of these fortresses is almost beyond comprehension, and a mere fraction of the total number have been excavated — the city at Kaymaklı was only discovered in the 1950s and each year more are opened. It seems unlikely that all of them could ever be fully uncovered.

Kaymaklı is the second underground city I have visited. During my previous trip to Cappadocia I had taken a tour of the site at Derinkuyu, the town 10 kilometres to the south (there is evidence to suggest that the two may have been connected by a massive tunnel). Derinkuyu's underground city is, arguably, the better of the two as it features larger, more elaborate chambers, including a chapel big enough to hold thirty chanting Korean Christian fundamentalists who had confused everybody with their presence and caused our guide to storm off noting loudly for their benefit and ours, "Turkey is a secular country!" Today in Kaymaklı there were no Korean fundamentalists, tour buses, guides, or anyone else. We had the whole place to ourselves and as we clambered bent-backed through the tunnels we might have been the only people left in the world, the sole survivors of the apocalypse. I suggested this possibility to Lady Penelope. "Well," she said, "our efforts to repopulate the world should be interesting for a number of reasons."

The underground cities were probably not inhabited outside of times of siege, although the upper levels were used throughout the year for storage. When they were needed, however, they formed not merely a shelter but a functioning town equipped with all the necessities of daily life, except for sunlight or privacy. Each city is decked out with a large variety of grain stores, oil barrels, fermentation vats for wine and stables.

The infrastructure is mind-boggling. Connecting different levels is a network of communications tubes allowing for co-ordination in times of attack. Chimneys travel more than a kilometre to allow smoke to escape and throw people off the track of the city's true location. Air vents are hidden on the surface among the rocks but are so efficient you can feel the breeze tickle the back of your neck in every corner of the cave six storeys below ground. Blocking strategic sections are huge stone wheels that could be rolled across from the inside, making them impossible to move and trapping enemies within twisting passageways, allowing the communications tubes to double as channels for hot oil. The underground cities of Cappadocia are the culmination of every *Fighting Fantasy* daydream ever entertained by a teenage boy anywhere. In a world often regarded as having been drained of mystery and wonder they are a reminder that disenchantment is a kind of arrogance.

Outside, we blinked into the crystal sky, the comparative banality of Kaymaklı a disappointment after our subterranean time travel. Back on the road the land was hilly and the furrowed fields black. The peak of Mount Erciyes stirred memories of Ararat. As we drove to Soğanlı the roads became empty and the landscape barren. Crumbling golden cliffs curved like bobsled tracks into the distance. Following the signs we arrived on a winding country lane shaded by a few ragged trees until, once again, the earth opened and we descended into a deep rift.

The Soğanlı Valley is unlike many others in Cappadocia. Where the Göreme and Devrent valleys are huge undulating fields of stone formations, Soğanlı is a series of narrow chasms with small clumps of *kaleler* rising up the steep, stepped walls. As we drove we noted the thousands of "pigeon houses" carved into the cliffs, little arched niches and caves that can be seen all over Cappadocia where farmers went — and sometimes still do — to collect the rich fertiliser of pigeon shit, perfect for the region's vineyards. The valley enfolded us as we drove deeper. High up on the ridge, a rock-cut church sat at the top of a precarious flight of stairs, like a stone escalator to nowhere. Arriving at the village all was quiet. Here the gorge opened into a Y-shaped rift, our road continuing into the distance and another branching off to our left. In the distance, over a small gully, the village rose up the hill, shadowed by the junction of sheer cliffs. Turning into the tributary gorge we parked by a shabby tea garden, closed for the winter.

As we emerged from the car, a small militia of stout women in flowery bloomers could be seen descending from the hills, converging on the gravel road into a pincer formation that soon had us surrounded. "*Poupee, poupee!*" they cried, each hand clasping a doll in colourful costume, dancing inches from our faces. These dolls were supposed to be a local tradition in Soğanlı, although they struck me as a rather dubious one. A big sign by the tea garden featured a faded rendering with the simple heading "Soğanlı Doll" and nothing more.

The poverty of the village was immediately apparent, not just in the desperation of the villagers but in their weathered faces, dirty clothes and the shabbiness of the homes beyond. Soğanlı was clearly not the kind of place where anyone worried whether local stone had been used to construct the new scooter shop. Slightly unnerved by this barrage — quite unlike anything I had encountered anywhere in Turkey, even the poorest parts of the east — we glanced at one another hesitantly before Lady Penelope turned and announced very firmly, "*Je ne parle pas français. Je suis anglaise. Une femme anglaise.*" Pausing for a moment the sellers looked at one another before thrusting the dolls back in our faces, barking, "*Poupee, poupee!*" Other than the word for doll they, clearly, did not speak French either.

"Brendan," said Lady Penelope after several minutes of futile protests that we weren't in the market for toys, "will you just buy a fucking doll?"

"I don't have any money," I said, truthfully.

"Oh, Christ!" Reaching into her handbag, she produced five lira and thrust it at the first and most insistent doll-bearer, a short excitable man who spoke a smattering of English. "Thank you," he said, handing the doll to Lady Penelope who punted it immediately to me. The others, knowing they were licked, rolled their eyes and plodded slowly back to their homes on the hill. "Come, please," he beckoned. "Come my home."

"Not just now," said Lady Penelope. "We want to go for a walk first."

"OK, OK," he said. "My home." He pointed to a concrete box in the village, begging us to visit once we had finished our sightseeing.

We gave a non-committal response and began to head off deeper into the valley, towards the churches on the hill. "Brendychops," said Lady Penelope as we began to walk, "you might want to consider putting your dolly in the car before we go any further."

As we made our way through the valley the full extent of Soğanlı's beauty was revealed. The gorge was narrow and v-shaped, rising at the very top into a sheer red cliff, punctured with pigeon niches and a few black caves so inaccessible their method of construction could only be a source of speculation. The road was bordered on one side by a creek, feeding the market gardens of the village, and on the other by a gentler slope where goats grazed about a smattering of concrete farm houses. In teetering regiments up the hill, the stony peaks of the *kaleler* congregated in huddles like Klansmen's hats. Most had been carved into, probably as store houses, their thick wooden doors locked and bolted with haunted castle keyholes. The sense of peace and well-being was palpable, the silence of the valley absolute, broken only by the breeze in the trees by the river, the bleating of goats and the occasional, optimistic cry of "*Poupee!*" from a distant concrete hut.

The church up the hill was carved into a *kaleler* complex. Inside, some of the more recent paintings were visible but most had been blackened beyond recognition, probably by the camp fires of squatters. Here and there the eyes stared out, white and spooky from behind the grime. The view from the courtyard allowed a full vantage of the gorges, the cold blue sky contrasting sharply against the geometric cliffs in yellow and red ochre; the leafless cypress trees in the valley were white feathers in the pale winter light.

Back down the hill we walked along the gravel road, moving further from the village and deeper into the gorge. After inspecting another church and many more *kaleler* we began to head back. For our return we decided to follow the creek, necessitating the negotiation of a steep embankment, more perilous than appearances suggested.

"Oh my God," said Lady Penelope as she climbed down in her heel boots, "are those evil goats looking at my arse?"

Once down in the fields, neglected in winter, we tiptoed through the furrows to arrive at the water. The sun had disappeared behind the ridge now, plunging the whole gorge into shadow, and though the sky was still blue, the temperature drop was considerable. We were surprised to find the banks covered in a thin layer of ice, crackling under our feet like the top of a crème caramel. Where branches reached out over the stream, silver shadow-trees jiggled in the current. Cautiously we followed the river, the crispy mud slipping beneath our feet. As we walked we blew air into our stinging hands.

Nearer to the village the banks of the river grew high and steep, crossed by a small, rickety bridge. We noted with disappointment that the rural Turkish habit of throwing household garbage straight into the nearest waterway was practised even in this heavenly place but, compared to other villages I had seen, there was relatively little. Climbing the banks we found ourselves almost within the village. "So," said Lady Penelope, "do you want to go to this bloke's place or not?"

As it was we didn't get the chance to make a decision. Spying us from the village, the doll seller began to run down the hill, calling out and waving as if he were a shipwreck survivor. Deciding that to deny him one cup of tea would be too cruel, we met him at the bottom of the hill where he grabbed my hand and led us towards his home.

The village was as I imagine Göreme must have been fifty years earlier. Other than the telephone wires, ubiquitous satellite dishes and a single rusted motorbike, there was little evidence that we were in the modern world. There were fewer *kaleler* here than in Göreme, although unlike the more famous village, where they were generally used only as storage, the majority of people having built more spacious extensions, many of those in Soğanlı still appeared to be inhabited. One, like a wilting witch's hat, featured a crooked black chimney snaking out from one side and rows of potted geraniums by the step. Most houses were, however, of the standard concrete box variety, their Spartan quality, unlike so many other villages I had seen in Turkey, not detracting from the beauty of the place but adding instead to the general aura of neatness and tranquillity. "My home," he said, leading us up to one of the concrete boxes.

Our host's name was Hüseyin. He was short and stocky and wore a very loud red and green jumper, like a Christmas elf in a department store. With his bald head and brown, creased face he looked a very tired forty, though I was not shocked to discover he was twenty-nine. His enthusiasm for our visit was intense and, as we took off our shoes by the door, he ran around the room aimlessly in his socks, flapping his hands like a flustered courtier. When Lady Penelope struggled to pull off her heel boots he gave a nervous laugh, unsure of whether to help her or not.

The house seemed to consist of only one small room adjoined by a kitchen. In a corner under the window a lanky old man in a woollen beanie and socks lounged against a bolster, stirring tea on the floor. "My uncle," said Hüseyin. The man smiled faintly before returning to his stirring. There was no furniture in the room apart from a handsome black stove, a box for wood and a table stacked with clothes, iron pots, crockery and half-made dolls, made slightly sinister for being stuck all over with pins. The whitewashed walls were completely spare but the floor was covered in thick layers of patterned, machine-made carpets and embroidered pillows. The view from the window was of the golden gorge against the pale sky, a scene made even more beautiful by the blue-painted sill and pots of geraniums on the floor, stretching their tendrils to the sunlight. Despite the sense of wear, all was clean, scrubbed and ordered, and, as we settled cross-legged into the cushions to accept tea poured from the hissing stove-top urn, I thought to myself that I could live in a room like this for the rest of my life.

Pulling a silver pot from under the table Hüseyin offered us food, which we made a show of refusing. But being, by now, ravenous, the farce did not last long. Into our bowls he spooned big scoops of red pilaf flecked with tiny shreds of meat. "This is delicious," said Lady Penelope. "What do you put in it?"

He paused and frowned, trying to form the words. "Do you know 'ketchup'?"

As we ate, he began to work on one of the dolls, sewing the costume while keeping up a steady stream of queries: where were we from? What did we do? Were we married? He understood many people from Europe were not married, but why was this? What was Austria like? All the while the uncle lay on the bolster, smoking and drinking tea as if he were somewhere very far away. We answered these questions as best we could but it was soon apparent that they were all just preliminaries to the question I had been half-expecting. Putting down his doll he looked at me with pleading eyes and said, "How can I go your country?"

I have been asked this question, or variations on it, in many parts of the world and bitter experience has taught me to be cautious, to avoid making promises that cannot be kept. We tried to explain that it was very difficult, that it would cost money and take a lot of time. But how to explain the technicalities of immigration law with no common language to a man who thinks you can catch a bus to Australia?

"What do you do?" I asked finally.

He held up the doll.

Yes, but surely there must be something else, something he did when there were no tourists?

"Goats." He gestured back in the direction of the church.

And a family?

"Three *bebek*. My wife, she make." He held up the doll, but whether he was referring to it or the children I could not tell.

He sensed our apprehension.

"You eat kebap in Australia?" he asked excitedly.

"Yes."

He turned to the old man and made a gesture of triumph, as if to say, Do you see? I told you so! "I can make kebap," he said, turning back to us, miming the making of kebabs. "Very good kebap. I make."

For the first time the old man showed some expression. Looking off into the distance he gave a slight roll of his eyes, and I knew exactly what he was thinking: "Oh God, here we go again. Just accept it, kid. You're gonna die in Soğanlı." And with that I felt very sad at the cruelty of the world, that a man should be born into a place as beautiful as this and wish his whole life only to leave.

With the meal done we decided to make a hasty retreat before we could be the source of any more false hopes. Hüseyin was distraught, insisting that he guide us through Soğanlı and take us up the mountain. After much persistence we finally agreed. Piling into the car we first drove to the end of the shorter gorge. Here was the most impressive church in Soğanlı, dedicated to Saint Barbara and reached by crossing a rickety bridge slung across the river. The frescoes in this church were much better preserved, although many of the chips in the faces looked disappointingly fresh.

"Christian?" asked Hüseyin. Taking our affirmations as his cue he began to point to the different figures painted about the chapel. "Christian," he said, authoritatively. "Christian, Christian."

Near the church, the valley turned to become a very narrow gorge, one half drenched in the last of the weak winter sun, bouncing off the yellow cliffs and dipping the pointed tips of the *kaleler* in gold. After a little hike we made our way back to the car and began the ascent to the top of the gorge. The road was comically dangerous, the wheels slipping beneath us on small landslides of scree that sheered away with every acceleration, the stones bouncing off our undercarriage before flying into the abyss with something close to joyful abandon. While I gripped the safety handle above the door, confident that it should protect me in the event of a one-hundred-metre drop into a bed of stone, Lady Penelope swore loudly and shifted gears as if she were repeatedly punching a very small person in the face. In the back, Hüseyin sat holding the doll on his lap as if it were a child, grinning mutely, though whether from fear or excitement I could not tell.

With our arrival at the top of the final ramp, the tension of the treacherous journey was immediately cancelled out by the beauty of the scene. The plateau was flat and stony, the tough grassy wastes stretching in all directions, sheltered by a vast, Australian sky. The only sign of civilisation was an endless parade of electricity towers, like heroic torsos, shrinking as they multiplied into the horizon, their wires singing lowly. To the northeast, Mount Erciyes was white as egg shell against the blue.

"You know," said Lady Penelope, "Erciyes is the name of a kebab shop near my house."

"Kebap?" said Hüseyin, excitedly. "I make kebap!"

A short walk towards the edge of the cliff and the golden ridges of the gorges appeared before us, their tops segmented into gentle undulations like dinner rolls. Closer still and we could see Soğanlı on its hillside being rapidly swallowed by the shadow of the gorge. Hüseyin beckoned us to the very brink of the cliff. Lady Penelope shot me a dubious look. "Is this where he pushes off, takes the car and buries us in the church with the rest of the tourists?"

For some time we stood and stared at the view, awe-struck. Hüseyin pointed out some distant conical structures rising from the plain which, after some considerable pantomime, we established were burial mounds, Hittite or Phrygian perhaps, and similar to those I had seen in the regions near Troy. Such enormous structures would have been a feat with modern earth-moving equipment and it was astonishing to think that, in the twenty-first century in a relatively modern and accessible part of the world, vast stores of ancient wonder remained completely undisturbed. When people said there was no beauty or romance left in the world I could only assume they weren't looking hard enough.

At Hüseyin's request I took a photo of him with Lady Penelope, their backs to the cliff, then posed for the same shot myself. While we stood with our arms about one another, I couldn't help but notice that his hand had landed gently on my backside. "It's too bright," called Lady Penelope. "You'll have to move to the left." This we did, shuffling about in our pose like mismatched folk dancers. While we waited for her to fiddle with the camera, Hüseyin began to squeeze and knead my buttocks with a firmness and boldness I couldn't help but feel stepped beyond the usual tactility I associated with masculine Turkish friendships. I looked down at him and he looked up at me with a smiling face and blameless eyes, squeezing my arse all the while. To the men of rural Turkey I was, it seemed, some sort of latter-day Helen of Troy.

With the sun getting low we decided, with some reluctance, to leave Soğanlı. Lady Penelope wanted to be on the road before nightfall as she didn't much fancy driving in the dark in a country where safety precautions such as headlights and staying in your own lane were considered the domain only of the hopelessly square. After a terrifying surf down the river of gravel we arrived back in the village, all its buildings completely lost now to shadow, the towering ridge above glowing like a beacon. The final awkward encounter I had been dreading began now to hurry towards its inexorable conclusion. Hüseyin begged us to return to his home for a final glass of tea, but we would not be swayed. Realising the futility of his pleas he asked for a pen and wrote his address for me. "You go Australia," he said. "I come, I come. I make kebap." He had the face of a pound puppy not cute enough for adoption.

"Look, Hüseyin," I found myself saying, "maybe when I get back ..."

"Brendychops, this is really only going to make things worse. I think we should just thank him and go."

Seeing that we intended to leave he gave a pained smile and shook our hands, a gesture I thought he had learned to use with tourists. As we drove off, I turned to see whether he was still behind us. On the back seat the doll was sitting up in the middle, legs bent outwards, arms folded on its lap, just like a little person.

Chapter 26

The next day I turned thirty. "Happy birthday," said Lady Penelope, handing me a jar of cherry jam and a folded piece of note paper with the words "Happy Birthday, Loser" scrawled on it in biro. "I hope you like your present. It's just something I picked out at the last minute. To be honest, I didn't put a lot of thought into it."

Early in the morning we decided to take our chances and head to Konya. Hüseyin told us that he'd spoken with travel agent friends who'd assured him there was not a single vacant room in the whole city, but it seemed silly not to make an attempt — if we couldn't find accommodation, we reasoned, then we could probably get the overnight bus back to Istanbul. Whether we would be able to find tickets to the dervish performance was another matter. But futile or not I was too enamoured of the, admittedly feeble, cosmic coincidence that had seen my birthday fall on the same day as Turkey's biggest religious festival not to at least try.

The word "dervish" conjures certain images to most in the West. There would be few who do not have at least a passing familiarity with the parachute-skirted men in domed hats who seem to make a mandatory annual appearance at the local ethnic food fair. "Whirling Dervish" is not, however, a wholly accurate title, not merely because this is not their real name but because they are only one small part of the dervish tradition. Strictly, and historically speaking, a dervish was a Sufi ascetic who had taken a vow of poverty, sometimes travelling from town to town and relying on charity for his livelihood (this might almost be a description of my life, except that my poverty was less a vow than a resentfully tolerated imposition). A dervish might be said to be analogous to a Hindu sadhu or even certain types of ascetic Christian orders, such as the Franciscans. The word "dervish" is of Persian origin but the more common Arabic term *fakir*, meaning poverty, used often in the Middle East and subcontinent, refers to much the same thing.

The "Whirling Dervishes" of the Western imagination are more properly called the Mevlevi, derived from "Mevlana", the honorific title of their founder, the thirteenth-century poet and theologian Jalal ad-Din Muhammad Rumi, whose full name is often shortened to his nickname, Rumi (the word derives from "Rum", a name for the Byzantine Empire or "Rome", which was associated with Anatolia in the time of Mevlana). Originally from modern-day Afghanistan, Rumi was a Persian, probably a Tajik, who fled his homeland with his family after a Mongol invasion. After numerous adventures and study in various parts of the Middle East, he ended up settling in Konya, ruled in that period by the Anatolian Seljuks. There he became the head of a *madrassa* (religious school) and wrote many poems, including the six-volume masterpiece the Masnavi, for which he is most famous. It was also in Konya, where, according to legend, he was walking through the gold workers district and, upon hearing the sound of their hammers, was suddenly overcome by a deep and ecstatic sense of oneness with God. With each strike he took a step, and with each step chanted the name of Allah until the hammers themselves were repeating "Allah, Allah" and he held out his arms and began to whirl in the middle of the street.

Apocryphal or not, the legend of the origin of Mevlana's whirling meditation technique is of less importance than its subsequent enormous popularity. The whirling was quickly formalised, accompanied by music and chanting, the ritual known as a *sema*. With the coming of the Ottomans to Turkey, and the subsequent expansion of the empire, the Mevlevi spread into the Middle East, Balkans and Egypt, where they are still active. For hundreds of years they were highly influential in Turkish public life until, like all other religious orders, they were banned by the republic and their practices suppressed. A few decades later, whirling rituals were revived in a limited form and allowed to be performed on the anniversary of Rumi's death, his *Urs* or "marriage" with Allah.

The ceremonies, performed nightly in Istanbul and other places in Turkey as a tourist attraction are, for the most, a kind of New Age dinner theatre, although the fact that they are watched mostly for entertainment is not necessarily an indication of the seriousness with which they are performed. And with the increasing laxity of the rules on *tarikatlar* and religious expression in general, the Mevlevi have experienced a considerable resurgence, not merely in Turkey but in the West where they have been seized upon as a gentle and humanistic form of Islam with familiar echoes of other Oriental spiritual crazes. When Madonna announced she was recording an album of Rumi's poetry I'm sure the groans could be heard across the breadth of Turkey.

By the time we reached the Konya *otogar* the sky was a grey sheet raked with silver. The pink monoliths by the bus terminus belched wood smoke from thin, black-coned chimneys, draping the buildings in a hazy veil. The trip had been efficient and unremarkable, save for the presence of the first female conductor I had encountered in Turkey. Sporting her man's uniform and a sculpted frown she cut a ferocious figure, but when I asked for a cup of tea in Turkish she suddenly melted, smiling broadly and clapping her hands in delight. "You realise, don't you," said Lady Penelope, "that you just asked her to marry you."

Leaving our bags at the bus stop in case we couldn't find accommodation, we took the tram into town. It was obvious Konya had grown in the two years since I had last seen it. The traffic was heavier and sections of new overpasses sat in blocks by the side of the road, like future ruins. A multi-storey luxury hotel, still under construction during my last visit, was now complete, its façade a blue blade reflecting the fading light. The tram took much longer than I recalled and by the time we arrived at Alaettin Tepesi (Aladdin's Hill), the heart of the old city, dusk was tracing faint pink furrows through the sky.

On my last visit to Konya I had stayed in a dive hotel in the shoe section of the bazaar. Now, with only memory to guide me and Lady Penelope in my wake making sarcastic remarks about my notorious sense of direction, we made our way towards it. With the smog settling in and the approach of dusk, a spell was cast over the drab back alleys of the city. The internet cafés were cacophonous dens of gunfire and squealing teenagers. In the store windows the unnervingly life-like mannequins were frozen in an awkward breakdance.

Arriving at the hotel I was astonished to discover that not only did they have vacancies but were, indeed, almost empty. "I take it all back," said Lady Penelope as we took our bags to our room. "Next time I need to find a hotel room that stinks of piss during a major religious festival I'll call you."

After checking in — reception clearly perplexed by our demand for single beds — we went out onto the rapidly dimming streets of Konya and made our way to the shrine of Mevlana. Konya is one of the world's most ancient, continually inhabited cities. Just outside town is the Neolithic site of Çatalhöyük which, at 9500 years old, is one of the earliest, large-scale human settlements ever discovered. Since that time the city has been a crossroads and trading post for a roster of civilisations that reads like a Greatest Hits of the ancient world. Unfortunately, comparatively little of Konya's vast history survives, the monuments of the past confined for the most part to a handful of exceptional Seljuk buildings, almost all converted now into a series of jewel-like museums. Most famous of these is, of course, the Mevlana Museum, the tomb of the great man that lies at the end of the street bearing his name.

Our plan was to see the tomb and anything else that might be happening, then sniff out the possibility of finding tickets for a dervish show. Every year the biggest performance of the festival is reserved for the final night and takes place at a purpose-built arena on the other side of the graveyard from the Mevlana shrine. The Prime Minister traditionally attends and the place is often packed with the Turkish political elite. Despite the very remote chance of someone like me gaining admission to such an event I had not entirely dismissed the possibility and, as we walked towards the shrine, I began to rehearse my patented Influential Foreign Journalist speech.

As the museum complex came into view, its fluted turquoise dome like a bundle of fat green pencils, I braced myself for the crowds. It was soon apparent, however, that, far from my visions of heaving throngs of ecstatic worshippers, the shrine was relatively uncrowded — not empty but not much busier than my last visit, which was not during any special occasion. "Maybe everything happened earlier in the week," I said.

"Or maybe it's just dying," said Lady Penelope. While considering the implications of this statement I registered the presence of a familiar figure in the distance. It was Adalet, Tevfik's hippy friend I had met in the shop.

Following the dreadlocked silhouette, we ran into the complex, straight past the ticket collector. "Adalet!" I called.

She turned and, taking a moment to recognise me, said, "Oh, hello. And happy birthday."

"You remembered," I said.

"He's thirty," said Lady Penelope. "One more year and he's officially a failure."

"What will you do tonight?" asked Adalet in her calm, quiet voice.

"I don't know," I said.

"Get pissed, I hope," said Lady Penelope.

"We were looking to find a dervish performance," I said. "But I think it might be very difficult."

"Oh, you will not be able to go to the big one," said Adalet. "You should come with us instead. We will have a *sema*. Go to this shop." She took a pen from me and wrote an address in my journal. "There will be dancing and music. Maybe wine. You should come after about seven o'clock." Nodding goodbye, she pulled her shawl over her head, bundled it about her shoulders and, like some midnight messenger in an eighteenth-century spy novel, disappeared inside to join her friends.

By the door we slipped plastic bags onto our feet, a variation on the usual procedure of shoe removal, and shuffled into the complex. Within the niches where the bodies of the saints lay the light was soft and golden. Overhead, glass chandeliers the width of cartwheels supported radiant tulips on snaking arms. Gilded Ottoman calligraphy tattooed the walls, dissolving the solidity of masonry with the sequinned shimmer of gold leaf. Behind an ornate barrier were the smaller tombs of Mevlana's followers, each sloping coffin draped in a shroud embroidered with extravagant golden tulips and crowned by a tall domed *sikke*, a felt hat shaped like a pencil eraser, worn by the dervish to symbolise a tombstone, commemorating the subjugation or "death" of the ego. In the centre of the final chamber, beneath a high arch, the crowds jostled by the sarcophagus of Mevlana, conspicuous for both its size and the pair of *sikke,* like fat antenna, nestled in turbans at its highest point.

In front of the tomb the worshippers stood praying with the backs of their hands held outwards, as though carrying large invisible bundles, some with tears streaming down their faces. In quiet corners others sat on the floor, headscarves or skullcaps pulled down, reading the Koran, the writings of Rumi or just staring off into space in meditative trances. Initially, this atmosphere of heightened religiosity made me uneasy — as if I were crashing a stranger's funeral. This was countered, however, by a strong sense of occasion, an almost festive quality as people meandered about the complex, chatting freely, pointing out details to their friends or moving from hall to hall staring into the screens of their video phones, as if in the thrall of some electronic idol.

I was impressed by the conviviality of the occasion, by the reverence tempered with joy and the overwhelming sense of peace. There was nothing self-conscious or dogmatic about the scene, no danger of the curious tourist being buttonholed by some smiling fanatic keen to expound upon the Zionist conspiracy in Iraq. This was religion as it ought to be — simple and human, natural and sincere. If this was what indigenous Turkish Islam could be then it gave cause for much optimism.

A peal of laughter brought heads turning. An old woman in a thick coat held her camera out imploringly to the crowds, giggling uncontrollably as if it were a jack-in-the-box. Thrusting it towards me she made it clear through fits of laughter that the thing was broken and I was to repair it. Hesitantly, I took it from her and did my best to rewind the film. Finally, with obvious exasperation, Lady Penelope snatched it from me. "Give it here," she hissed, but her confidence was soon proved reckless. Flicking a catch the door fell open, exposing the film. "Brendychops," she said a little anxiously, "I think I've just destroyed all her photographs."

Seeing this, the old woman began to wildly laugh, this time in a way of one resigned to disaster and the absurd. "Iran!" she said, referring, I suspect, not merely to her camera and herself but a lifetime of technological frustration. "Iran!" She giggled and slapped herself in the head.

For longer than expected we toured the complex which, apart from a resting place of great saints, is also one of the finest museums in Turkey, full of sacred relics and treasures. All around us families cooed at the million-knot carpets and bent over the cabinets, inspecting the gilded Korans, some miniaturised to the size of postage stamps. Others said prayers in front of Rumi's relics, meditating on his coarse tunic and reed flute. The old lady with the broken camera posed for a picture by the case containing the beard of Mohammed and laughed uproariously when it didn't go off. In a quiet corner Adalet sat crossed-legged with a shawl over her head, reading prayers and rocking gently back and forth.

Outside, the last vestiges of dusk had given way to a profound blackness. The mist was growing heavier now, creeping down our coats as if it were alive. The tang of wood smoke had grown sharper and stung our eyes. "Brendychops," announced Lady Penelope, "we need a drink. If you have a sober thirtieth I'll never forgive myself."

Contrary to the Koranic injunctions on wine, Mevlana was a great drinker. His poetry is littered with references to wine and drunkenness, both metaphorical and literal. Despite his party animal reputation, Mevlana's spiritual home was not, it seemed, the kind of town where I might reasonably expect to find a vodka martini to mourn the loss of my twenties. After several dispiriting intrusions into the lobbies of a series of increasingly dire and uniformly booze-less hotels, desperation saw us sniff out a liquor store tucked discreetly into the back of a dark corridor arcade. The owner, a sympathetic fellow dipsomaniac, regretfully confirmed our worst fears: the only bars in the city were at the university, safely quarantined almost an hour from the centre of town. Thanking him and taking as a compensatory gesture a bottle of Soviet surplus industrial cleaning fluid masquerading as vodka, its exotic glyphs evoking snowy shacks in Vladivostok full of dead sailors, we made our way back onto the main street.

Clutching Adalet's address we made our way through the smoky streets of Konya. After some confusion we eventually found the felt shop down an alley not far from the museum. In the window were mannequins draped in dramatic felt cloaks standing among piles of brightly coloured *sikke*, stacked like inverted bowls. Inside, the atmosphere was homely and welcoming. On the wooden floors a pair of teenage hippy girls were making felt pictures. By the door a middle-aged man sat drinking tea with a cat in his lap, like a Bond villain. As we entered he made no effort to acknowledge us, just sipped loudly and stroked the cat, its tail snaking with pleasure.

Music floated down from upstairs. Climbing the wooden staircase we emerged into a broad loft, the rafters hung with nomadic weavings and talismanic mobiles strung with seashells. At the far end of the room a dwarf in a vest sat cross-legged plucking a type of *saz*. The sound was high and vaguely Mongol, like wind on the plains. To one side of him a young man tapped a large set of tablas; to the other a woman in glasses sang a low mournful song with great passion, shaking her head as she hit long notes. In the middle of the room four people, men and women both, twirled in their stockinged feet, arms outstretched, heads cocked to their shoulders like drugged scarecrows. With a disappointing indifference to theatricality, none wore any part of the costume I associated with the dervishes, although a couple had special leather slippers that made a sound like brushed drums on the wooden floor. Around the edge of the room people sat cross-legged or kneeling, gently swaying, joining in with the rhythmic choruses. Against the wall, Adalet was sitting with her legs bundled up, her dreadlocks swaying like seaweed in the tide. As we took off our shoes and sat down she turned and smiled, her eyes glazed. For a moment, I thought she was high, but as she turned back and resumed her swaying I could see she was in a kind of trance.

For a while we watched, a little uncertain of our purpose. I felt out of place but more than that, too. There was a familiar, not entirely comfortable, atmosphere: the whiff of tedious hippy parties, of bongos, firesticks and smug beanbag revolutionaries. One woman in her sixties, the spitting image of Diane Keaton and wearing raw cotton robes and dangly lapis earrings — the Masonic uniform of the white woman in Asia — held her arms in a vaguely teapot posture, shuffling in slow clumsy circles, as though having dropped something while very drunk. I couldn't help but feel disappointed by the realisation that the Mevlevi, like Zen, yoga or swimming with dolphins, had been subsumed into the late-life spiritual quests of American divorcees.

Lady Penelope leaned in. "Is that Diane Keaton?"

Soon the music ended, the dervishes coming to a gradual halt, bringing their hands to their chests, one folded over the other. Walking off, they resumed their seats without any apparent dizziness. The man with *saz*, obviously in some position of power, gave an instruction to the musicians and, as he shifted the instrument in his lap, I realised he was a hunchback. The singer adjusted her glasses and began a new song. The musicians followed. From the edges of the room a fresh crop of dervishes, including Adalet, rose up and began to turn in the centre.

The dervishes grew slowly faster until our friend's clothes fanned out and her hair grew branches from her head. Slowly, my attention grew fixed on the colourful cones of her skirts and the sound of brushed drums. Soon, in defiance of my earlier doubts, I found myself growing docile and hypnotised. Relaxing, I nestled into the pile of coats at my back, feeling my discomfort and sense of estrangement drain away. When the hunchback's phone rang and he carried on a conversation over the music, I barely noticed.

After one more song and another change of dervishes — Diane Keaton, back again — the music stopped for the last time. The hunchback began to address the group in Turkish in a soft, slightly disdainful manner while a German woman translated into English. Everyone was thanked for their support over the last month and some administrative announcements were made. Breakfast and morning buses were mentioned. "So now we all go to the hotel," said the German, "to meet the others. It's important that we are quiet and discreet because people are watching." And with that, the atmosphere of hushed reverence was broken. The room fractured into conversational huddles and some began to ready themselves to leave. I pulled Adalet to one side. She was not visibly drained by her exertions but her eyes still had a sparkly, drugged quality. "Adalet, what is happening? Can we come with you?"

She made a doubtful face. "You must ask him," she said, nodding towards the hunchback.

"Does he speak English?"

"Yes. Tell him you are from Australia. That you are interested in Mevlana. But you must be very…" She made a gesture of abasement.

With a geisha shuffle I made my way to the back of the room where the hunchback was seated on a flat square cushion, idly examining his text messages. From the moment I had arrived on this scene I had taken a dislike to this autocratic dwarf. I bristled at the way he presided over the room, his aloofness, the way he spoke to the congregation with his head turned as though he were communicating from some neighbouring, higher dimension. He had the air of a cult leader, of a man with a grudge or, if you'll pardon the expression, a chip on his shoulder. This encounter only hardened my opinion.

Getting down on my knees I interrupted his telephonic meditations and introduced myself. I said all the things Adalet had told me to say then submitted myself to his examination. He rocked his head like an Indian official. "It is not for me to say," he said. "If you go and they say 'no', I can do nothing." He lit a cigarette. "You must ask their permission, but" — he trailed off and turned his attention back to his bleating phone — "I do not like your chances."

Back on the street the temperature had dipped sharply. The traffic had all but ceased and the carpet shops had closed for the night. The fog and wood smoke were now so thick that the end of the alley had completely disappeared, the distance defined only by the diaphanous silver spheres of the street lights. In a loose zig-zag we made our way back to the main avenue. Diane Keaton led the pack in whispered conference with the German interpreter, the pair wrapped in matching purple shawls. The hunchback dwarf, oblivious to the cold, loped through the mist with twisted but surprisingly determined steps, his vest hanging loosely from his deformed shoulders, an instrument case half the size of his body at his side. Behind me, Adalet, in her layers of ponchos and scarves, her hair a coil of snakes, was a survivor of some future apocalypse.

Lady Penelope leaned in. "Two questions: where are we going and why do I feel like the next person I'm going to meet will be a Transylvanian transvestite?"

Crossing the avenue we continued through the smoky back streets of Konya. The puddles in the gutters were pools of black oil, alive with electric eels in blue, orange and silver. The alleys became narrower and I grew increasingly disoriented: had the museum been this way or that? The hunchback turned a corner. We followed and the alley was suddenly diffused with light. Outside the doors of a brightly-lit hotel, a very old woman, dressed all in red, sat in a wheelchair, a cigarette dangling from her lips. On her head was a crimson headscarf, tightly bound and embroidered with shining metallic discs. Surrounding her were a half dozen younger disciples, all wearing the same style of headscarf, each similarly decorated but in a range of different colours. As they moved the discs caught the light, flashing and changing like reef creatures.

As the hunchback crabbed his way towards the old lady she gave up a cry of recognition. Leaning into her chair he stood on his toes and kissed her, very forcefully, on either cheek, avoiding the smouldering tip of her cigarette. Seeing this, the younger women giggled.

One by one we filed inside. A smiling receptionist gave little bows. Following the crowd we climbed down a deep set of stairs to a large, brightly lit basement. The room was plain; chairs and tables piled into precarious stacks by the door formed a partition to the main area. At a long table to the front sprouting a microphone in its centre, the hunchback was seated beside an old *dede* (grandfather) in a three-piece suit and black skullcap. Unsure of what to do, I scanned the room, wondering who best to approach for permission to attend the meeting. As I fretted, considering whether I should rope in Adalet to act as interpreter, people continued to file in, nodding and smiling at us before seating themselves on the floor, the older women taking the chairs by the walls. Once again, it was left to Lady Penelope to be the voice of reason.

"Brendychops, I don't think anybody gives a shit."

Taking a place on the floor with the others we sat and waited — for what, I didn't know. The atmosphere was churchy and convivial. Nearly all the congregation were women and, it seemed, Turkish, with only a scattering of foreigners, mostly from the felt shop. Occasionally, I caught a snippet of conversation in a language I didn't recognise and I wondered if some were Iranians.

As they arrived, the women bent down to kiss one another. Most of the older women wore plain scarves, tied under their chin, but many of the younger ones wore the brightly coloured fortune teller headscarves, covered with metal discs and knotted in a way I had not seen before in Turkey: tucked into a bun at the back, and rolled along the brow like a headband. If there was some significance to this then I was never to discover what it was.

All at once the woman in the wheelchair arrived, carried into the room by two older men who lifted her, as on a royal litter, over the heads of those on the floor. As she rose up her eyes widened in delight and her still-smouldering cigarette left an arc of smoke in her wake. Depositing her in the centre, the men took their place at the head table. The glittering head of the crippled queen acknowledged the room with stiff bows, her cigarette sending up an occasional volcanic puff.

With the arrival of an enormously tall, wild-looking man there was a mild commotion. With his long frizzy hair, motorcycle boots and studded denim jacket he possessed an aura of unfamiliar celebrity, like a retired German rock star. Stretched across his head was the white skullcap of a haji, fanning his hair out like a nun's veil. Seeing the woman in the wheelchair he smiled broadly, revealing the blackened crenellations of his missing back teeth and, in a manner I found faintly repellent, grabbed her by both hands, kissing her heavily three times on the mouth.

With a few whispered words into the microphone from the *dede* in the suit the room was called to order. With a minimum of ceremony he leaned over and pressed the "play" button on a tape recorder. An unaccompanied song-poem filled the room. The voice was male and high and the recording fairly short. With its end the recorder clicked off. The *dede* took a sharp breath and broke into, what I assumed to be, prayers. The crowd responded, chanting the name of Mevlana. The chanting continued for some minutes; the women closed their eyes and bent their heads back as they responded.

Silence followed the prayers. The hunchback produced his instrument from its case and gave some scattered preliminary notes. The girl who had been singing at the felt shop held up a large drum, wide and shallow like a pie case. Beside her a young man rested a set of tablas on his lap. The hunchback began to play as the girl kept time, tapping the drum with her fingertips and palm, pushing her glasses up the bridge of her nose between beats. Her song was low and very powerful, alternating between verses that were almost spoken to operatic choruses accented by a deep whooping noise. Putting the drum to one side she began a series of hand gestures, her left hand pressed against her heart, right palm held in front of her face, as though staring into a mirror that wasn't there, bringing the two together in slow beats. As she sang, some of the women closed their eyes and began to rock back and forth in imitation of the singer's gestures.

The room grew hotter and hotter. I had stripped to my T-shirt by now, conscious of the sweat trickling down my back and arms. Lady Penelope's face was a dewy tomato staring longingly at the muted air conditioner on the wall. Under their headscarves and bundles of coats, the older women seemed completely immune to the tropical atmosphere. With a serenity I envied they sat with their hands neatly folded, legs tucked under, eyes closed, heads nodding to the beat.

The music was atonal and hypnotic; the singing filled every corner. The crowd responded with chants and soft, spontaneous cries of encouragement to the singer. Behind us, Adalet was rocking back and forth, head lolling insensibly. Little puffs of smoke began to rise from the woman in the wheelchair. The songs came and went and I found myself transfixed by the slow karate chop of the singer's hands, the soft drums and the high, windy sound of the strings. For an hour the performance continued. The heat was almost unbearable. Nevertheless, I felt I couldn't leave. Not merely out of politeness but because, despite my discomfort, I was unable to tear myself away, as if in the thrall of some blissful hypnosis.

Finally the music stopped. The women in the glittering headscarfs ceased their swaying. Around the room many were softly crying and the singer's face glistened with sweat and tears. From behind I watched as the woman in the wheelchair stamped out a cigarette on a little ashtray taped to the arm of her vehicle, then lit another. The *dede* cleared his throat and made an announcement. Taking the opportunity, people who had been waiting by the door began to file into the room. One young American girl began hugging the old women, one-by-one, in a manner I found exhibitionist and vaguely annoying. The spell was broken. Grabbing Lady Penelope by the hand, I rose up and gestured to several women stumbling awkwardly through the crowd. Under the guise of self-sacrifice and chivalry, we stepped over the paving of limbs and disappeared behind the partition of chairs.

For a moment we stood in the relative cool, catching our breath. A group of latecomers crowded the passage. A woman behind a breakfast bar was peeling and segmenting fruit. Seeing us she grabbed two handfuls of orange crescents and thrust them into our hands. Gratefully we took them and ate. They were unlike any orange I had ever tasted: closer to a mandarin, perhaps, but with a different perfume and a sharp tang that fizzled on the back of your tongue. Seeing our appreciation she gave us more. Thanking her, we pushed past the crowds to the stairs.

In the foyer we climbed back into our coats, still clutching the orange pieces in our fists. The receptionist bowed and smiled while two old men on blue velvet couches tinkled the spoons in their tea glasses held by their chests. Outside, the cold was a balm on our skin. Leaving our coats open we ran our fingers through our sodden hair, feeling the sharpness on our scalps and breathing in the mist and smoke. The lights on the hotels and shops were off now, turning Konya into an expressionist shadow play, a Fritz Lang with minarets. In the cold I felt light-headed, partly from relief but from something else too, as if I had just woken from an ecstatically happy dream. From her handbag Lady Penelope produced the vodka. "Happy birthday, Brendychops," she said, taking a swig then handing me the bottle. As we walked we swigged it straight, washing the taste from our mouths with juicy bites of sweet orange.

Chapter 27

On New Year's Eve in Istanbul blood ran in the streets. The festival of Eid-ul-Adha had fallen — coincidentally — on the last day of the year and everywhere across the Islamic world livestock were nervous. Kurban Bayramı (literally: Sacrifice Holiday), as it's known in Turkey, commemorates Abraham's willingness to sacrifice Isaac and the subsequent substitution of a sheep in the place of his son. To mark the annual event, determined by a changing lunar calendar, animals are slaughtered in an especially dramatic and grisly fashion, sprays of arterial blood like horror-movie fire hydrants soaking the streets.

In a concession to both public hygiene and affronted secularists, the public slaughter of animals had, in theory, been banned this year from the streets of Istanbul. In practice, however, many people flouted the law and in an alley in the suburb of Çurkurcuma, only a few blocks from Istiklal Caddesi, with its burger chains, Benneton boutique and Marxist intellectuals in antiquarian book stores, I watched a goat having its throat slit, blood running down the gutters while children watched with curious but solemn faces. (A couple of days before my birthday a scandal rocked the country when Turkish airlines employees sacrificed a camel on the tarmac at Istanbul's international airport to celebrate the return of eleven faulty planes to their manufacturer. "We were going to do a camel for each plane," announced their boss. "But we thought one camel was cheaper and easier." The incident inspired snickers around the world and left many in Turkey utterly mortified, prompting some of the most unintentionally funny newspaper editorials ever written.)

Kurban Bayramı represented a hazard not merely to the squeamish or freshly laundered. On the same day I narrowly avoided being trampled by a cow the width of an alley that bolted from the back of its truck and chased me down the street in a one-man Pamplona that ended only when it slipped on the cobblestones, its keepers dragging it back to the sinister steel doors that shielded its grisly fate.

The pensive, apocalyptic tone of mass slaughter was given added potency by the previous day's execution of Saddam Hussein. In images that shocked the world, video phone footage had been released of the dictator being taunted by his gaolers moments before his body was dropped through the trapdoor. The timing of the execution, and the details of the act, were viewed by many in the Sunni world, including Turkey, as a deliberate and symbolic act of provocation by the Shia majority of Iraq and, by implication, America — a none too subtle attempt to make a mockery of the sacred Sunni holiday. The effect was to turn overnight one of history's most ruthless despots, a dedicated secularist with nothing but an appetite for blood, power and expensive brandy, into a "martyr".

Tevfik, as usual, had much to say on the subject. "This is bad, man," he said, dropping the newspaper back down on the coffee table. "This is some serious shit. These idiots are playing dangerous games."

"Who's playing dangerous games?" I asked.

"All of them — the Americans, the Shias, us. We are all dangerous idiots, man."

It was the first time I had seen Tevfik for a while. After leaving Konya I had returned to Istanbul and, soon after, gone with Lady Penelope to, of all places, Hungary, where she had managed to score some last-minute freelance work from a well-paying English magazine. A deal was struck: I agreed to accompany her to Hungary and stay for Christmas if she would return to Turkey with me and spend New Year's in Istanbul. "Oh, it's so glamorous," she said. "The Orient Express. Christmas in Budapest. New Year's in Istanbul. I feel like Grace Kelly."

The timing of the side-trip turned out to be a happy coincidence. My Turkish visa was dangerously close to expiration and I needed to leave the country to renew it. Furthermore, a trip to Budapest, which had been ruled by the Ottomans for almost 150 years, was not totally out of the bounds of inquiry in a book devoted to Turkey. Lending greater strength to the Turkish theme, Christmas Day had been spent with the family of a friend I had met in the shop during my previous trip to Istanbul (he and his friends had gotten off the train then spent the next week on Hüseyin's couch). Together the three of us had gone walking the streets of Budapest, noting the traces of the Ottoman Empire in that grand and far-off city: the *hamamlar*, the niches facing Mecca in the churches and the tomb of Gül Baba (Rose Father) — dervish warrior poet — revered in his native Istanbul for his mystical poetry and for granting, indirectly, by way of his floral symbol, the red-and-yellow colours to the Galatasaray football team.

I had enjoyed my time in Hungary but by the time we returned to Istanbul a few days before New Year's, pickled with alcohol and stuffed with pork of every conceivable variety, I felt intensely grateful to be back. Europe had much to recommend it: I could sit next to a woman on the bus, old buildings were not considered merely something in the way of a pink apartment block, and nobody could care less what you thought about their country. Then again, nobody seemed to care if you were lost on the subway either, or, for that matter — and here I admit Budapest may not be the most representative example — lying face down in the gutter in a pool of your own vomit. Only now did I realise how much I had taken for granted the tribal friendliness of the Turks, their intense enthusiasm for their country, their constant need to be reassured that you were having a good time. What I had seen before as insecurity and nationalism ("*Turkey güzel?*" etc) I now regarded as unaffected pride, a gentle sincerity and artlessness that Europeans didn't have or, perhaps, had long since lost. In the endless debate about whether or not Turkey was part of Europe, not enough people seemed to be asking why anyone would want to be European.

Back in the shop, something of its old atmosphere had returned. Hüseyin still seemed a little preoccupied but the visit of his Danish friend, Heinrich, accompanied by his Kurdish wife and their two children, seemed to cheer him up. Heinrich was one of Hüseyin's best customers and closest friends. The two had studied Spanish together in Seville and Hüseyin was godfather to his son, an adorable blond-haired scamp who spent much of his time playing outside in the unseasonably warm weather, enduring cheek-pinches from passing strangers. The shop had undergone another change in my absence — Hüseyin had a new employee. Ahmed was a dealer who had previously worked in a big shop in the Grand Bazaar. He was middle-aged with a smooth manner and a native's command of English, French and Italian. "I need Ahmed for Europeans," said Hüseyin, and I could see that he was right, that he needed someone who could be ruthless, someone who was not like Tevfik, and I wondered for how much longer my friend would be tolerated at the shop.

Meeting us in the days before New Year's was Lady Penelope's friend, Izabella, a lovable but utterly infuriating Lebanese–Australian who had come to Istanbul from Beirut for a holiday with her family. Izabella asked constant, meaningless questions, fretted endlessly about trivial details and compared everything in Turkey, unfavourably, to Lebanon — nothing, be it fashion, food or monuments, could ever hope to reach the dizzying heights achieved in all areas of human endeavour by the Switzerland of the Middle East. Izabella's neuroses were immediately explained by a meeting with her parents — Iraqi–Armenians for whom the recent war in their adopted Lebanese homeland was merely the latest chapter in a life spent fleeing certain death and who, as a consequence, seemed to live in a state of constant alert, as though they might have to make a run for it at any minute. When I had asked the day before New Year's Eve if they would like to join us for dinner at a restaurant in the old Armenian district of Kumkapı, her mother had fixed me with a very powerful stare and said, "Is it *clean?*" I assured them it was but the night was a disaster anyway. Halfway through the evening a Gypsy band surrounded them and — clearly confused by their ambiguous ethnicity — began to play the Israeli national anthem. Izabella's father, already certain that the Turks were a race of barbarians, saw this as a deliberate affront. His wife, meanwhile, grew increasingly hysterical. "Make them stop! Make them stop!" she sobbed as the music came to a disharmonious halt.

For our New Year's party we had booked a table for dinner in Taksim where we would meet Izabella, but, other than that, had no plans. In the afternoon, with Hüseyin and Heinrich, we drank champagne on the footpath, in deference to Hüseyin's alcohol ban in the shop, enforced out of respect to the souls in the graveyard. After closing early we went to a bar in Sultanahmet where Hüseyin had booked a table. It was his first time drinking since his mother's death and, despite the urging of Lady Penelope and myself, he had already declared that he had no intention of going anywhere else. "Everything will be packed tonight," he said, but I could see that this was a convenient excuse and that he still wasn't in a party mood.

The atmosphere at the bar was high-spirited and familial. Hüseyin busied himself playing the host, while we sat drinking and chatting, taking turns holding Heinrich's baby. "Oh my God," said Lady Penelope, bouncing her on her knee. "You are so adorable."

"You want one of your own, I think," said Heinrich's wife.

"Certainly not," said Lady Penelope. "I want this one."

Soon, Tevfik arrived, accompanied by a glamorous mystery blonde. He and Hüseyin kissed and we all made room for the pair.

"Everyone," said Tevfik. "This is Julie."

"Hello," said everyone.

"Allo," said Julie with an accent that I took to be French but later proved to be Quebecois. When she got up to buy some drinks I took him aside. "Tevfik, is that the same Julie you were screaming at on the telephone that day?"

"Yes."

"Why is she here?"

He sighed. "She is crazy. She wants to have my baby."

He gave no specific reason as to why he thought this crazy, but with so many to choose from it seemed futile to pick just one. The mystery was compounded by the fact that Julie was clearly not the kind of woman who wouldn't have had other, arguably better, offers for the father of her child. Not only was she — without exaggeration — stunningly beautiful but also owned her own catering company, clearly profitable enough to allow her to take a month off to pursue a man on the other side of the world whose last words to her were something along the lines of "Stop calling me, you crazy bitch." I'd heard of *amour fou*, but this was *amour ridiculous*.

"Are you sleeping with her?" I asked.

"No," he said, and I believed him. But I knew she was paying for him regardless.

At once his tone changed, his eyes grew moist and pleading. "Brendan, I need a favour from you, man."

"What is it?"

"Brendan, please ask Hüseyin not to fire me."

Technically, for someone to be fired implies they were employed in the first place, but I understood his meaning. I looked over at

Hüseyin, nursing Heinrich's baby, laughing and drilling her in the ribs. It was not a decision I could hold against him. Tevfik was a business liability and Hüseyin had done more for his friend than anyone could expect. Like a child watching their parents get a slow and horrible divorce I entertained fantasies that it would all end well, that Tevfik would get it together and everything would be as it was. Who knew, maybe Julie would be good for him?

"I don't know if it will make much difference," I said. "But I'll see what I can do."

★ ★ ★

The rest of the night was a controlled fiasco. Dinner with Lady Penelope and Izabella was an Italian operetta of incompetent waiters, cold meals and furious patrons. Near midnight they began to hand out paper hats and party whistles, but when it became apparent midnight had been missed by more than a minute, the maitre d' ran out and announced the New Year by cutting a net of balloons that dribbled along an empty section of floor and down a flight of stairs. At the sight of this Lady Penelope became insensible with laughter. Izabella, however, was furious. "They've missed midnight!" she screamed over the uproar. "Have they missed midnight? This would never happen in Lebanon!"

Hearing this, Lady Penelope's laughter doubled, then tripled and tears began to roll down her cheeks.

After dinner we went to a bar and I did the lambada with Izabella in front of a pack of panting boys who couldn't have been more than fifteen. After fuelling up on shots of tequila and crème de menthe, we wandered out into the criminal back alleys of Taksim. Near the street where the transvestites plied their trade we met a gang of Nigerian homeboys in gold chains and Air Jordans.

"Hey," said Lady Penelope. "Two questions: can I have a cigarette and where do we hear some good music around here?"

"Come with us," said their leader.

At the club, for reasons that were unclear, we were immediately shunted to the front of the queue, past the rows of shivering black girls in hair braids and mini-skirts. Walking up four flights of stairs, we checked our coats then followed the music past the big double doors. Inside, every African in Istanbul was dancing shoulder-to-shoulder, the black faces punctuated by a small smattering of Turkish women and a group of tiny little Filipino girls dancing in a shy circle. The music was wildly eclectic — from hip-hop to the plinking rhythms of the kalimba. The mix of fashions hinted at all parts of the African continent. There were tarty girls on spiked stilettos, their mini-skirts fanning out over soccer-ball backsides to reveal shiny slivers of underwear. Others were more sporty in white gym boots that laced up over their calves and hair extensions that slapped their skin-tight hot pants. More modest were the group in the centre of the dancefloor in floral dresses with Caribbean ruffles about their shoulders and breasts, swaying like a gospel choir. When the African music came on they broke into chorus lines of co-ordinated backing-dancer moves. Having endured almost four months of mournful Turkish ululations I was overcome. For the briefest moment I thought of the east — of the unbearable sadness of Urfa and Van — and laughed at the absurdity that this was still the same country.

After an hour of dancing, I reluctantly agreed to walk Izabella to the cab rank. "In Lebanon you never have to look for a taxi," she announced, before running off into the dark, presumably in the direction of her much-missed spiritual homeland. Arriving back I discovered Lady Penelope dancing with probably the only Turkish man in the whole club. For the next few hours we lost track of time. Was it one or two hours before she started kissing him? "Brendychops," she shouted. "I'm just going upstairs. I'll be fifteen minutes." I gave a thumbs-up and slipped back into my dancing frenzy.

How long was it before I'd realised she hadn't come back? Half an hour? An hour? More? Looking about me the atmosphere had begun to shift. Fights began to break out. In the toilet queue a Turkish girl fell on her rival, squishing her face into the piss-soaked floor, screaming, "Stay away from my man, you fucking black bitch!" At the door a group of three enormous men in white suits and matching fedoras rushed the door security. Questions began to present themselves: upstairs? What upstairs? Who was that guy? Oh dear God, what have I done?

Forcing my way past the door security I climbed another floor and found a big man standing in front of a bolted steel door. Not even bothering to try my Turkish I began to bang on the door, yelling Lady Penelope's name. The bouncer took me by the shoulder and began to reprimand me in an unexpectedly understanding way. In Australia he'd have thrown me down the stairs. In Turkey, the land of small mercies, he made sympathetic faces and tried to reason with me. Ignoring him, I continued to pound on the door. Suddenly, a short young Turkish man appeared from the stairs behind me. "Can I help you?" he asked in English-school English.

"Yes," I said, growing increasingly frantic. "My friend is inside. I want to see if she is OK. Please, can you see if she is in there?" He paused, taking me in, then smiled gently and said, "I'm sorry, I can do nothing for you." The bouncer opened the door and the little man disappeared inside. Through the closing gap I began to call out for Lady Penelope. The door slammed shut and my desperation turned to fury — they thought she was my girlfriend, that she'd been seduced by a virile Turkish interloper and I was here to avenge my honour. Curse this country, I thought, curse it and its macho bullshit and its tribal crap. In one final eruption of frustration and outrage I began, once more, to bang on the door.

"I am a homosexual," I screamed, "and I demand to see my friend!"

As if in response to a magic incantation, the door opened. Lady Penelope, tousle-haired and red-cheeked, stood before me. "Was that you calling for me?"

"What do you think!"

"Oh, Brendychops, I'm sorry. Do you mind if we get the hell out of here?"

Downstairs we grabbed our coats and ran the gauntlet of the fights that were starting to crackle out of control. The men in white suits were still pressed up against the security and a girl was crying hysterically behind them. Fleeing onto the streets, the purple dawn was haloing the buildings while people crossed the roads with glazed eyes and zombie steps. Jumping into a cab we drove back to our hotel, noting with interest the police riot car that had been turned over in the middle of the road. "Oh, Brendychops. My knight. Were you terribly worried about me?"

"Let me put it this way," I said. "Have you ever seen that Jodie Foster film, *The Accused*?"

"No, what's it about?"

"Never mind. What happened in there anyway?"

"Nothing more than tongues. I think he was famous. People kept offering him cheese platters. But it was difficult to tell — he couldn't speak a word of English." Just then she received a text, obviously from her paramour and obviously written by somebody else. It read: "I love you. You are so beautiful woman." Laughter gripped and shook her violently. "Oh, you see, in Turkey I am beautiful!"

Chapter 28

The realisation that my time in Turkey was over was mostly subconscious. On New Year's Day Hüseyin announced that he would soon be going to America to try and recoup the losses he had suffered on his last visit.

"When are you leaving?" I asked.

"In a week."

"Do you have to leave so soon?"

"Yes. I go broke otherwise."

The idea of me staying on to work in the shop — or even coming with him to America — was vaguely discussed but, with Ahmed firmly ensconced and Hüseyin's father making regular visits, having recently arrived from Kayseri, I didn't feel my presence would serve much purpose.

The situation with Tevfik, meanwhile, was looking increasingly hopeless. Although he still hung around the shop and had even made a couple of token efforts to bring in some business, it was obvious that his presence was being merely tolerated. Despite this, I still maintained the futile hope that he would prove himself enough to Hüseyin to be kept on or, at least, get another job elsewhere — on one occasion he had mentioned going to work with his friend Yavuz at Grand Bazaar, on another he said something about his brother getting him a position at a hotel. Absurd as I knew them to be, I still clung to these scraps of hope because to do otherwise would be to admit the uncomfortable possibility that Tevfik was a lost cause.

Lady Penelope had left two days after New Year's, though not before one last implausibly picaresque escapade in which she was kidnapped by a taxi driver. "It was terrible!" she said, bursting into tears on a packed tram when I went to find her. She dabbed at her eyes. "I'd just finished lunch with Izabella's parents. I got into the cab and he locked the doors and started screaming, saying he was going to kill me. Then he drove me into this little alley and demanded I give him thirty lira."

"That's a very odd sum to rob someone for."

She blew her nose. "I thought so too. And he refused to give me change for the fifty." (The story acquired a final bizarre twist when she rang me later from London and revealed that Izabella's parents had been robbed only half an hour later after being picked up from the same corner by a man answering the description of her kidnapper. "He also demanded thirty lira *and* called her dad a filthy Arab," she said. "I don't think we managed to change their minds about Turkey.")

The final act in the relationship between Hüseyin and Tevfik was played out the night before Hüseyin was due to leave for America. I arrived at the shop in the evening after having spent the day at the Dolmabahçe Palace, the last residence of the Ottoman sultans and the site of Atatürk's death. Built in the mid-nineteenth century in a futile attempt to fool the world into thinking the finances of the Ottoman Empire were in great shape, Dolmabahçe Palace is widely regarded as one of the most remorselessly vulgar buildings of the era. This proved to be no exaggeration: the tiniest shred of taste or individuality had been stripped away to leave nothing but a luxury as oppressive and deadening as anything imagined by Stalin or Ceauşescu.

Dolmabahçe Palace can only be viewed on a tour and my guide was an unusually tall, rigid man with a face as forbidding and expressionless as a Victorian undertaker. His tour consisted of nothing more than a list of various building materials, their weights and country of origin, with an emphasis on crystal that was almost fetishistic. The inherently tedious nature of this information was only given added emphasis by his peculiar, halting diction: "This — is — Water — ford — crys — tal. It — weighs — two — tonnes. *Two* — tonnes.*" From room to room I wandered with a Singaporean tour group, watching them coo over the Baccarat lamps and bearskin rugs, stopping only to hear our guide announce, "This — is — Bo — hemia — crys — tal. It — weighs — three — tonnes. *Three* — tonnes.*" At the end of the tour, after barraging us for almost two hours with a litany of technical detail, completely free of the tiniest hint of historical colour or anecdote, he turned and said, "Any ques — chuns?" One of the Singaporeans put up his hand and, without a trace of irony, said, "What kind of crystal is this chandelier again?"

At the shop, Akil was sitting downstairs with Zizou by the door, his nose buried in a tiny little book, one of a stack that sat on the table beside him. I looked closely. They were all pocket-sized self-help books with titles like *Be the Best You* and *50 Things a Girl Wants to Hear*. "Akil, what are you reading?" I asked.

He held up the little book, dwarfed even further by his giant hands. It was called *Love Yourself to Weight Loss*. "I buy in market, for practise English," he said, his brow furrowing. "But I don't think is good book."

Upstairs, in the antique room, I discovered Tevfik and Ahmed entertaining two customers, a man and a woman, of indeterminate European origin and obvious means. They were, as it happens, Italians who lived in Stockholm and spoke English with an ABBA accent. "I want a pink carpet," she announced, very firmly, "for my apartment at Lake Como. Do you know Lake Como?" she asked, turning to me, almost accusingly.

"Not personally," I said.

For the next half hour she sat in her chair with a pen and notebook, asking prices then jotting them down in a very intense, anxious manner. Her husband, mostly silent, scanned the room with a detached smirk that spoke of having seen all this before, boding poorly, I felt, for the possibility of a sale.

For almost an hour I sat, watching the sales pitch. Ahmed was friendly and eager. Too eager perhaps, tearing out carpet after carpet and rolling them before the woman with grand gestures and rehearsed, impassioned spiels peppered with forced jokes. Tevfik, meanwhile, reclined in the corner, looking slightly disgusted, even behind his shades, moving only to examine a price tag or wave a hand and say, "Just buy this one." I could see how much he despised them and understood why: you can't buy a carpet as if it were a car. It's a process, like falling in love.

Just as we seemed to have nothing more to show them, the sound of heavy breaths signalled Hüseyin's entry to the room. He had a startled, frantic look of one who has just missed something very important, which he had. Immediately he began to play the role of the perfect host, but it was doomed. With his appearance there were now three dealers in the room, plus me, and I could feel the couple draw into themselves like anemones poked with a stick. The notebook was nothing more than a prop now, a dissociative technique. Hüseyin, obviously aware of the farce this had become, sat on the floor and began to quote prices with robotic indifference, his silent fury like a gas leak in the room.

Soon the husband made intimations that it was time to leave. No encouragement or incentive could convince them to stay. With a snap his wife closed her book. Hüseyin and I followed the pair downstairs, smiling and waving farewell as they walked out the door, never to be seen again. Shattered, Hüseyin collapsed onto the couch, his limbs spread yieldingly. Finally he broke his silence. "It's all about timing," he said, shaking his head, speaking to himself more than anything.

"Without the right timing, without making them trust you, there will never be a sale." He looked up, his anger more emphatic now. "I gave them to him. I said, 'Tevfik, make sure they come here for lunch.' I rang him twenty times. 'Where are you?' I could have made fifty thousand dollars from those people. But I didn't. I didn't make anything because that … *asshole* didn't bring them when I asked him to." He exhaled and stared at the ground. "I don't know. You try and give a guy a break but he just keeps throwing it back at you."

Akil brought tea. For a while we sat sipping, saying nothing. When Ahmed left for the day no acknowledgement was made.

Finally I broke the silence. "Hüseyin, are you still going to kick him out?"

He said nothing, just shrugged a little and rubbed his eyes.

"Please, man. I love the guy."

Hüseyin raised his eyebrows, as though slightly offended. "We all love him. I wouldn't be angry if I didn't love him. But he don't love himself and there's nothing I can do about that."

After a while I ventured back upstairs alone. Tevfik lay stretched out in his corner, his head propped on a stack of carpets, a glass of tea untouched beside him. For a while there was silence. He pulled his shades onto his head. "Hüseyin is angry with me?"

"Yes."

"OK, that's fair." He sighed. "But I want you to know that it wasn't my fault. It was that fucking neurotic bitch. She wouldn't come to the shop, man. I wanted to kill her." For a moment I wondered why he didn't try to explain this to Hüseyin. Why he didn't see how important it was to patch things up with him. But then I saw that, despite what he said to the contrary, he didn't want to reconcile, that this was all part of his slow campaign of withdrawal from the world, and I wondered where it all might end.

"Don't worry about it," I said.

A low cough at the door signalled an unexpected visitor.

"Hello, Julie," said Tevfik, with barely concealed weariness.

"Tevfik, would you like to go to Burger King now?"

He sighed. "Not now, Julie. Maybe come back some time tonight." With only a stare of intense disappointment, she turned and disappeared. Tevfik pinched the bridge of his nose. "Brendan, I am having a panic attack. A big one. Do you have anything?"

"No, sorry."

"It's OK." He pulled down his shades and drew his arms into a vampiric X across his chest.

While Tevfik lay snoozing I began to file through the antiques, something I had done many times over the previous months. There were pieces I coveted and as I rifled through them I could feel the inevitable gaining momentum: I was selling to myself. Carefully I laid out the two I liked the most, deciding which one I could not do without. I imagined how I would feel if somebody else bought them, some woman with an apartment at Lake Como and a smirking rich husband, for instance.

"Those are beautiful carpets, man," said Tevfik from the corner. "I'm impressed. They're the best he has. Buy them both, but bargain hard."

Hüseyin joined us. Seeing the carpets he nodded towards them. "You like these?" he asked. I tried to appear disinterested. It seemed a bad time to be buying. I was worried it would appear a compensatory gesture, but he would be gone the next day so it was now or never.

Downstairs we rolled them out under the lights. One was a Konya piece, dominated by a happy canary-yellow field, set with distinctive medallions radiating like comic-book punches. The other was a *Yahyalı*, a style from Cappadocia found in their thousands in every shop in Istanbul, but this one was special. Small but exquisite, its proportions and colours were perfect; the borders full of archaic symbols unlike anything I had seen. It was obvious that, despite my protests, I would have them both. "And this one?" said Hüseyin pointing to a large *cicim* on the wall, a piece he instinctively knew I had been eyeing. "Oh no, that's too expensive," I said.

"I will name a crazy price for you."

"No, no, no … I couldn't."

I did, of course.

Ignoring Tevfik's advice there was no bargaining. Hüseyin named prices on the three and I agreed. This broke the cardinal rule of buying from any carpet dealer, but I couldn't see Hüseyin as a dealer, only a friend. Besides, I knew that some of the prices were wholesale. Akil took the carpets away and wrapped them up. By the end of it I'd spent nearly all my savings. Carpet madness can do that to you.

Looking up from the couch, Tevfik pulled his shades up onto his head. "What will you do now? He has bought all your good stuff."

"Excuse me?" said Hüseyin, with mock civility.

"You have nothing left."

"You shut up!" he exploded. "You just cost me the sale of the year."

Tevfik *tsk*ed. "You exaggerate."

"Excuse me?" said Hüseyin, cocking his head.

"I said, you exaggerate. The prices you asked were too high."

"If you say one more word …"

Tevfik made a gesture of exasperation. "Your prices are too high."

"Oh my God … if you say one more word."

For a moment I was worried they would come to blows. But after a tense pause, Hüseyin suddenly issued a loud, resigned laugh while Tevfik, in both submission and protest, closed his eyes and pulled down his shades.

Hüseyin called out an instruction in Turkish. In response, Akil began to haul a big pile of carpets across the room, new stock that needed to be catalogued before he left. Sitting cross-legged on the floor, his tea glass and ashtray by his side, Hüseyin began to examine each one, calling out prices which Akil then wrote down in code on paper tags.

"How do you remember all those wholesale prices?" I asked.

"I don't."

"So ... is your wholesale price *really* your wholesale price?"

He gave one of his jungle bird laughs and smoke curled off his tongue. Without warning, the door opened, bringing Zizou to attention and sending a breeze through the shop, setting Tevfik's hair on end. "Tevfik," said Julie from the doorway, "would you like to come to Burger King now?"

Tevfik sighed heavily.

Chapter 29

On my final day in Turkey, almost as if it had been arranged to commemorate it, there was a bomb scare outside the shop. A suspicious bag had been spotted by the tram tracks and, within a few minutes, the area had been cordoned off behind ribbons of yellow tape. Tevfik, ignoring the admonitions of the security staff, wandered into the forbidden area and leaned over the barrier by the tracks. The station manager, abandoning any attempts to force a retreat, was soon sharing cigarettes with him while the crowds surrounding the halted trams craned their necks for a better view.

Watching the unfolding drama from the vantage point of the shop I was impressed by the pragmatic handling of the affair. In Australia a bomb scare would warrant a state of national hysteria — the closing of public transport networks, the marshalling of helicopters and sniffer dogs, panicky news bulletins and hundreds of column inches in newspapers across the country devoted to agonised editorials mourning the death of our nation's innocence. In Turkey two cops in bullet-proof vests and welder's helmets turned up, walked over to the bag, opened it, tipped the forgetful businessman's papers on the ground, put them back in the bag, wandered back to their car with the offending satchel, and left. As they drove off down the tram tracks Tevfik waved goodbye like a kid at a parade. Returning to the shop, he lit a cigarette and said, "Not even a bomb. Man, this country can't even blow itself up anymore."

After Hüseyin left for America my days tapered off into a round of waiting in the shop, tea with Tevfik and aimless wanderings through the city. I had already decided to leave Turkey but there seemed no rush and with no dramatic developments the journey had reached a frustrating impasse — fate's infinite corridors had led me to no neat or logical conclusion.

To occupy myself I took long walks along the Golden Horn where street dogs and homeless men slept in bald flower beds. Other days I rode the ferries back-and-forth without purpose, watching dolphins skip through the water, gold in the winter sun. One evening I returned to the shop from one of these excursions. It was a foggy Sunday night and the streets were deserted. Passing the graveyard, I saw a man praying at the gates, his palms upturned by his shoulders, like a figure on an ancient Egyptian temple frieze. As I walked past I looked straight at him but he made no acknowledgement of my presence, just continued staring at the graves, chanting lowly. I had seen people praying at the graveyard before. But now, in the fog, on the empty street, with the low hooting sounds of the cranes in the trees, the scene seemed eerie and unfamiliar and I was suddenly filled with a sense of my foreignness and an attendant overwhelming desire for home. The next morning I booked my return ticket.

The last few days with Tevfik were mostly quite pleasant. He was still miserable, of course, and, now that Julie had returned to Canada ("We broke up," he said, as if they'd ever been together), I was paying again, but didn't mind. One night we ate spicy liver kebabs then went to a bar and spoke about religion. I asked him if he believed in God. He sighed and said, "Put it this way: if God exists, what the hell am I gonna do about it?" a philosophy that seemed to sum up Tevfik's life, for good or bad.

Not everyone still regarded him with the affection I did. Hüseyin's father clearly despised his freeloading, especially his habit of showing up every day in time for lunch. One afternoon he stormed off upstairs to cook, making it quite clear that Tevfik was not invited. Tevfik, like a puppy that's pissed on the rug, skulked off and sat on the couch with his arms crossed and his eyes downcast, doing his best to look pathetic. Akil, delighted with this scandal, approached me in the tea room, his eyes shining and his face set in one of his rare gleeful grins. "Hüseyin father hate Tevfik. He don't want to give him food!"

It was a similar story when we went to visit Spike for the last time. After getting a slightly cold reception we sat on the couches for a while drinking tea, but it was soon obvious that nothing more was forthcoming. As we left the shop I pulled Spike aside. "Tell me, did you really get guys to beat up Hüseyin with baseball bats?"

"Ha, is that what he thinks?"

"Yes."

"Don't listen to anything that guy says."

But he didn't say "no".

A few days later I was standing in the shop with my bags, ready to head to the airport. After the bomb scare, the morning had been spent with Tevfik trying to retrieve some money a leather shop owed a friend of mine for a faulty jacket she'd had made. When they said they didn't have any money and were on the verge of closing down, Tevfik assured me they were telling the truth. "Everyone on this street is on the edge, man," he said, a statement that might easily have been true for the whole country, though it was easy to forget sometimes. As we left, Tevfik promised me to keep asking them for the money.

After my attempts at debt collection I went and farewelled some of the dealers. "Ah, Mr Brendy," said Bull Ant. "You go now. I hear you buy many excellent pieces from the Hüseyin. Maybe you like to have one quick look at my collection?"

Back at the shop, I made my round of goodbyes. From his now customary corner Ahmed smiled tightly and waved. Hüseyin's father exclaimed, put down his paper and shook my hand, then recrossed his legs and stiffened the paper before his face. Zizou looked up with the commotion then went back to snoozing in her patch of sun. On his stool by the door, Akil was reading out loud from one of his books, sounding each word. "Try ... to ... have ... a ... think ... thin ... be ... thin ... day."

"Goodbye, Akil."

"Oh, Brayn-dan. You are going," he said with swami-like simplicity, before beaming one of his open flower smiles and crushing my hand within his.

"I will miss you, man," said Tevfik. "I haven't got any present to give you."

"Don't worry about it," I said.

"No, I must give you something. Wait here," he said. "I'm just going to go home." With more dynamism than I had ever seen him display, he bolted out the door and ran down the street. A minute later he returned, panting and clutching a cardboard tube. "It's a painting," he said, opening the package and producing a rolled-up sheet of cardboard. "It used to be on the wall at my old shop. It's the last thing I have from those days. I want you to have it, man."

I unrolled the cardboard. It was a gouache of an Ottoman tile pattern, stylised tulips and arabesques. "My friend did it," he said. "It was her artwork at university." He pointed to some patchy paint splatters about the border. "Sorry about those bits," he said, gritting his teeth in fury. "Some Spanish ... *motherfucker* did that."

"Don't worry, man. It's beautiful, thanks."

Picking up my bags and tucking the painting under my arm, we walked to the tram station. On the platform we waited in silence, dramatic goodbyes not being my forte. When the tram came Tevfik hugged me tight. "See ya, *bebek*," he said, kissing me wetly on both cheeks. "It's been great to have you. Your friendship means a lot to me, man."

I'd been so eager for his approval I hadn't even noticed how much he craved mine.

"Promise me you'll take care."

"I will, *abi*."

Gathering my bags I squished my way into the crowds on the tram, turning to wave goodbye through the glass. As the doors closed, the passengers turned and stared in silent alarm as Tevfik broke into a round of high-stepping chorus-line kicks on the platform.

Epilogue

My carpets beat me home. I'd shipped them off before I left and when I walked through the door they were waiting for me in the hallway in a package the size of a UN food drop. In defiance of my exhaustion I immediately grabbed a knife and sliced carefully through the top, the thick pile of my Konya piece spilling out like a bright yellow wound. As I pulled them out one-by-one, like a magician doing a scarf trick, I began to realise the full scale of my purchases. Along with the three I'd bought from Hüseyin there was also the *sofra* from Van and, of course, the two I'd bought from Tevfik which, in the confines of my small home, suddenly seemed much bigger than I remembered. Including the three I had bought on my last trip to Turkey, I now had more rugs than floor.

A few days later, tragedy engulfed Turkey. Hrant Dink, a Turkish–Armenian journalist and editor of a small Armenian community newspaper in Istanbul, was shot in the head at point-blank range while leaving his office near Taksim Square. The killer was a seventeen-year-old boy from Trabzon, identified by his own father from security video. Six others in the city, all connected to extremist nationalist groups, were quickly arrested for conspiracy. Later, many more would be implicated and video footage would be released of a group of smiling policemen posing proudly next to the murderer holding a Turkish flag.

The murder hit a nerve in Turkey because Dink had been widely regarded as a sane and reasoned voice in a debate characterised almost solely by hysteria. When questioned, the boy said, "I said my prayers and shot him. I feel no remorse. He said Turkish blood was dirty blood." This quote, widely attributed to an editorial written by Dink, was complete nonsense. What he had, in fact, written was that Armenians should not allow a hatred of Turks to poison their blood, a statement that, incomprehensibly, was used as evidence by nationalists to prosecute Dink under Article 301 because he had implied that Turkish blood was poisonous. And if you think that's ridiculous then wait until you hear the one about how they still kept prosecuting him, on a fresh charge, three weeks after he was killed.

Despite all this madness, some small good might be said to have come of Dink's death. A couple of days after the event, mass rallies moved through the streets of many Turkish cities, marchers waving placards that read "We are all Armenians. We are all Hrant Dink". The very real feeling expressed across Turkey was palpable and when the nationalists staged rallies in response, chanting, "We are all Turks!" they only managed to muster a few hundred supporters.

A few days after Dink's murder I rang Tevfik. The whole incident had upset him greatly and he had taken part in the march in Istanbul. "Man, I tell you, this country is run by crazy people. Everyone says I am crazy but really I am just a sane person in a country run by lunatics."

"How's life?" I asked.

"Well," he said, sheepishly, "I've got some good news and some bad news. The good news is I got your friend's money back from the leather shop. The bad news is I spent it."

"That's OK," I said. "I knew you would." In a happy coincidence the sum matched the original price of his carpets.

In the months to come I watched with interest as Turkey faced a series of political crises. The conservative Islamic government was returned with an increased majority and, in defiance of mass public rallies, lifted the ban on headscarves at universities. Opposition elements countered by launching an appeal to the Supreme Court to have the government dismissed, and universities ignored the edict anyway. Meanwhile, with unprecedented boldness, the PKK stepped up their attacks, unleashing a series of deadly bombings in various parts of the country, including Istanbul and, of course, Diyarbakır. In response the Turkish army moved into northern Iraq, attacking alleged PKK strongholds and opening a new front in the Iraq war.

In the wake of these actions a tide of nationalism swept Turkey, resulting in some incidents that, even by the standards of a nation where the slaughtering of a camel on the tarmac of a major international airport was not unknown, were truly bizarre. At an anti-PKK rally in Bodrum, for instance, a fashion designer who, like many in the crowd, was wearing a T-shirt emblazoned with the word "Turk", was arrested for putting the same shirt on his poodle. Complainants charged that by doing so he had implied Turks were dogs and he was duly charged under Article 301 with "insulting Turkishness". Some months later, a children's choir from Diyarbakır sparked an investigation after they reportedly sang the "national anthem" of the northern Iraqi regional government at a music festival in San Francisco. Local prosecutors demanded the details of the children and their choir masters and began investigations. Meanwhile, a group of high school students stirred national controversy when they presented the head of the armed forces with a letter stating their willingness to be "martyred" for their country and a framed Turkish flag painted, over a period of some months, with their own blood. In a public speech the general praised the fervour of the children, pointing to their patriotism as an example for the nation.

Possibly the craziest, and certainly the most entertaining, development was the discovery of a secretive ultra-nationalist gang called "Ergenekon". Taking its name from an epic creation myth of the ancient Turkish nomads, Ergenekon counted among its members respected lawyers and journalists, as well as retired high-ranking military officials, including a general. In the first round of arrests thirty-three people were taken in as investigations were made into a plot to overthrow the government, as well as assassination plans for Orhan Pamuk and other high-profile "anti-Turkish" figures, including Hrant Dink, shedding new light on the case. Investigations also began into the organisation's connection to various bombings previously blamed on the PKK, in addition to other terror incidents, such as the murder of the Italian priest in Trabzon and the missionaries in Malatya.

Tellingly, many of the Ergenekon plotters had connections to the "Susurluk scandal" — the infamous car crash that revealed the possible existence of the illegal government hit squad, the Deep State — including Sami Hoştan, a.k.a. "Sami the Albanian", right-hand man to the late Abdullah Çatlı. Another star player was the lawyer Kemal Kerinçsiz, head of the "Union of Jurists", the group that had prosecuted both Pamuk and Dink under Article 301. (In a twist that had me vowing to never again make fun of Turkish conspiracy theorists, it was later revealed that, as part of their plan to incite chaos and till fertile ground for a coup, the group had plans to kill *him* and blame it on external enemies of the Turkish state.)

Of all the suspects perhaps the most curious was Sevgi Erenerol, a woman described only as "Public Relations Officer of the Turkish Orthodox Patriarchate". Established in the early years of the Turkish Republic, the Turkish Orthodox Patriarchate is a breakaway of the legitimate Orthodox Patriarchate, and was encouraged by Atatürk as a state-friendly, Turkified alternative to the existing institution. The church, which is almost unknown in Turkey or anywhere else, has only a handful of parishioners (all of whom have been ex-communicated by the legitimate church and are mostly related) yet has vast land-holdings in Istanbul, including churches commandeered from the real Patriarchate, one of which may have been used as the group's headquarters.

Imagine *The Da Vinci Code* as written by George Orwell and you might get close to the spirit of Turkish politics.

Throughout this eventful year I kept in touch with everyone in the shop: Hüseyin and Mehmet because they were friends and I would have done so anyway, and Tevfik because he was a friend, but mostly because I worried about him. After his mother's death Hüseyin had much recovered, though I sensed a change in him. When we spoke he was still extravagantly cheerful but his conversation seemed strained and was peppered with complaints. He even spoke of giving up on being a full-time carpet dealer. "People are not buying, man. Where did all these goddamn cheap tourists come from?" The wall, he bitterly informed me, remained firmly in place. There was talk of him becoming a wholesaler in America or even of turning the shop into a hotel, but this seemed unlikely: the trade ran in his veins and, besides, in what other profession could he ever hope to receive the amount of attention needed to feed his ego? When I asked if he had any plans to marry he said, "Do you know anyone? I'm on the market, baby!" and gave his trademark laugh.

On the subject of Tevfik he was generally conciliatory, but it seemed that the rift between the two, at least in business terms, was final. Not long after I left, there had been some dark conspiracy involving a dodgy Iranian donkey bag and Hazım had declared a life ban. "Hazım doesn't like me," said Tevfik when I rang him a while later. "We had some problems, but it's OK. I'm not angry at him. I'm not angry at anybody." As he spoke I could picture the little flat above the pub, its curtains drawn to keep in the heat, the little Stonehenge of medication by the sink. "I am living a terrible life, man," he said in his soft, croaky voice. "I don't work. I don't leave my flat. I just sit around all day writing suicide letters to my friends."

"Oh come on! Don't say things like that. You make me really upset."

"I'm sorry. You have a right to be angry with me. But don't worry, I don't send them."

After a few more months, Tevfik dropped out of sight. I rang a couple of times but he didn't answer his phone. Hüseyin said that he had seen him on occasion and given him food but suspected he was in dire straits, that even his family had deserted him. "We hope everything will be OK for him," he said, ominously. The more time passed the more I found myself unable to call Tevfik, afraid of what I might discover. Towards the end of the northern summer, I sent Mehmet round to his flat to check up on him. "He's OK," said Mehmet. "A bit sad, but he said maybe his son will come soon from Japan." Like many of the other plans I had heard Tevfik mention — a trip to China with his brother, the job at a hotel — I had my doubts that this one would eventuate.

Imagine my pleasant surprise, therefore, when Tevfik's son really did come to visit him and the two spent several weeks together in Istanbul. During this time I finally spoke to him and he sounded much improved. Even the recent re-election of the pro-Islamic government was not a source of concern. "At least they will make some progress," he said, echoing, I suspect, the sentiments of many Turkish voters. "And anyone is better than the MHP." The MHP being the extreme nationalist party who count among their most senior representatives a convicted murderer who narrowly escaped the death penalty, a woman who once kicked down a locked door during party negotiations, and a former Minister of Health who tried to get Turkish blood samples returned from an American leukaemia research facility because "foreigners can obtain our genetic codes".

For a while we spoke about his hopes for the future, about the Alevi community he was looking to join, about the Mevlevi ceremonies he had been attending: "I just sit and listen, man, nothing more." He sounded optimistic, if not cheerful, and I allowed myself to entertain some notions that it was not too late for him; that he would, perhaps, find a spiritual path through his morass.

As we spoke it occurred to me that I had never asked him why he had become a carpet dealer in the first place. In the atmosphere of spiralling madness within the shop, such simple inquiries seemed redundant. He brightened up. "Ah, I will tell you the whole story. When I was young my father kicked me out and made me find work. So I went to Sultanahmet, met Spike and started selling carpets for commission. At first I didn't care at all about carpets, I just did it for the girls and for the money. I mean, Spike was ripping us all off but we were still making crazy money and those Japanese girls … man, they loved me.

'But then, one day, Spike takes me to see a carpet someone had for sale, a very special carpet. We stood there, looking at the carpet and Spike just says one sentence: 'This is a fucking beautiful carpet.' And I look and realise that this carpet was kind of … inside me, like I was in love with it or something. It's hard to describe. After that day, I spent all my time in Spike's shop, looking at carpets and *kilims*, learning as much as I could." He paused. "Carpets are like a meditation for me. I didn't think of them like that at the time, but they are. They fly in my mind. I see them and they live for me. The colours and symbols are like poems in my heart. Carpets are everything to me and I will always love them."

Soon after our conversation, with a modest optimism for Tevfik's future, I began to prepare for sleep. One of the carpets I'd bought from him had, by now, made its way to my bedroom — the red one with the goat's hair weft, strong as wire but with crooked edges and three symbols shaped like wonky Prussian crosses. Where once I had regarded it as crude and rough I now saw it as dramatic and bold — the red was bright and natural and I loved the way the goat hair fringe had been worn away in the middle, the spot where people had stepped on it constantly or picked it up to fold it away and take it on their travels to the next patch of desert. Many times I had examined it closely and soon found that if I put my nose right up to the pile I got a potpourri of familiar earthy smells: cigarettes, sesame seeds, coffee, burnt fat and dirty dog. It was the smell of the shop and of Turkey, and as I slipped that night into an unburdened sleep — free now of all those petty fears, of career, of achievement, of *making something of myself* — images from that funny, in-between country began to visit me and I offered a small and silent prayer, thanking heaven for small mercies.